Orby Shipley

Annus Sanctus

Hymns of the Church for the Ecclesiastical Year

Orby Shipley

Annus Sanctus
Hymns of the Church for the Ecclesiastical Year

ISBN/EAN: 9783744771924

Printed in Europe, USA, Canada, Australia, Japan

Cover: Foto ©Lupo / pixelio.de

More available books at **www.hansebooks.com**

ANNUS SANCTUS.

PUBLISHED BY
BURNS AND OATES

LONDON	NEW YORK
GRANVILLE MANSIONS,	CATHOLIC PUBLICATION
28 ORCHARD STREET,	SOCIETY CO.
PORTMAN SQUARE, W.	9 BARCLAY STREET.

PRINTED BY
BALLANTYNE, HANSON AND CO.

EDINBURGH	LONDON
PAULS WORK.	CHANDOS STREET, W.C.

Annus Sanctus

HYMNS OF THE CHURCH FOR THE ECCLESIASTICAL YEAR

Translated from the Sacred Offices by various Authors, with Modern, Original and other Hymns, and an Appendix of Earlier Versions.

SELECTED AND ARRANGED

BY

ORBY SHIPLEY, M.A.

VOL. I.

SEASONS OF THE CHURCH: CANONICAL HOURS: AND HYMNS OF OUR LORD.

London and New York:
BURNS AND OATES.
MDCCCLXXXIV.

NIHIL OBSTAT.

   EDUARDUS S. KEOGH, CONGR : ORAT :
     CENSOR DEPUTATUS.

IMPRIMATUR.

   HENRICUS EDUARDUS,
     CARD : ARCHIEP : WESTMONAST.

DIE 25 APRILIS, 1884.

Preface.

Two main objects, one being devotional and one literary, are proposed by the publication of this volume of hymns.

Annus Sanctus is intended, in the first place, to be used as a book for spiritual reading, the contents of which have been compiled from the Sacred Offices or other authorised sources, and arranged according to the sequence of the seasons of the Church. It is meant, secondly, to be made a store-house for the in-gathering and preservation of much valuable hymnological labour, which, from the lapse of time, is in actual danger of being forgotten, and from the decay of books is in danger of being entirely lost.

In addition to these main objects, the compiler of *Annus Sanctus* had other ends in view. He ventured to hope that the book might be accepted as a contribution, chiefly in the way of selection, towards the study of comparative English hymnody. He thought from its being almost, though not altogether, an exhaustive collection of the efforts of English Catholics in this direction—within certain limits and up to the present time — that the book might become the treasury, whence could be drawn the component parts of a Catholic Hymn-book of the future. And by a Catholic Hymn-book is meant a book for public use in

Preface.

church, a book for singing : for, though some admirable collections exist, yet it may be said (without detraction) that all of them admit of certain improvements. In any case, he believed, it would direct attention to an amount of honest work done in this field of literature by the hands of Catholics, which was previously unknown to, as well as furnish specimens of a character and value which were previously unexpected by, this generation of readers. And it would show to all who were interested in the topic, that the love of Catholics for their own hymns is no recent, much less no modern fancy; that the idea of their translation and employment in the vernacular is no imitation of outside influences; and that the results achieved are not less wide in extent, not less worthy in merit than attempts in the same direction of Protestant translators however distinguished. These facts have been somewhat hidden or overlooked by Protestant and Catholic writers alike, and even by Catholic translators : and it is not amiss to recall the attention of the student of hymns to these facts. As an element in the discussion, it may be observed that the contents of this volume are purely Catholic, not only, of course— so far as they are ancient—in their original form, but also in the modern dress in which they are now presented to the English reader. The translations of the hymns of the Church, for certain times and days and hours, here collected, chiefly for devotional purposes, have been made by Catholics alone. It is true that some versions were made, previously to conversion, by their respective authors who were not born-Catholics : but no translations have been admitted by those who either are not living, or who have not lived and died, within the bounds of the one true Fold.

Preface.

Twenty years ago and amongst his first efforts in literature, the compiler of this volume, by the kindness of many friends which is gratefully remembered, was enabled to publish three volumes of religious poetry under a common title of *Lyra—Eucharistica, Messianica,* and *Mystica,* respectively. After a varied amount of success, these three collections of hymns and verses have long been forgotten and will not be reprinted. The *Lyræ* were compiled on no other principle than that of producing, or printing for the first time, the best translations of ancient and mediæval hymns, or the best original specimens of sacred verse, which at that date were attainable. Nor was the principle a bad one from a literary stand-point: and Catholic contributions, by the liberality of their authors, in those days freely accorded to Protestant editors, stood side by side with those that came from non-Catholic sources. But this literary principle, if so it may be called, becomes no principle at all, or rather becomes a false principle, when a similar compilation is made on behalf of children of the Church. Intellectual gratification is not to be secured at the cost of spiritual edification. For the use of faithful Catholics one requires, in a book for devotional purposes, in the first and foremost place, unity of belief in writer and reader. This condition is essential. But, whether or not, in such a book as this, poetical talent be superadded to the gift of faith, is a point of secondary moment; a question of taste indeed, in which none would be consciously and wilfully deficient, but one which may safely be decided between the editor, his critics and his readers.

In the case, however, of Catholic contributions towards English hymnody there is little fear of the ab-

Preface.

sence of poetical talent as an accidental adjunct to dogmatic exactitude. English hymnology has, as a fact, been enriched by Catholic authors to a wider extent and to a greater degree than by the efforts of Protestant translators. The representative Protestant collection, entitled *Hymns, Ancient and Modern*—in substance a compromise between the various sections of conflicting religious thought in the Establishment—is a typical instance. That collection is indebted to Catholic writers for a large fractional part of its contents. If the hymns be estimated which are taken from Catholic sources, directly or imitatively, the greater and more valuable part of its contents owes its origin to the Church. That the obligation is not as generally acknowledged as the circulation permits may be regretted. But it is a matter for congratulation that so many million copies of Catholic hymns are dispersed broad-cast, even in an imperfect and mutilated form, in a Protestant country. Under any conditions, however, the only or chief difficulty which arises to a Catholic editor who will be at the pains to exhaust his materials, is caused by the superfluity of resources and the perplexities of choice. But the present book must in no sense be considered as a reproduction of the *Lyræ*, if only on the grounds that the design aimed at is diverse, and that but very few of the hymns are common to the two compilations. Yet, there is a deeper difference between the earlier and the later collections. *Annus Sanctus* has been compiled on a definite principle : and that principle, whether or not it be critically accepted as sound, consists in this, viz., using for devotional reading the sacred poetry provided by authority in each suc-

Preface.

ceeding season of the Church, and reading such poetry in the language of Catholics.

Such being the principle on which this volume was conceived, the manner of its compilation may now be indicated. It is in brief as follows. Not unnaturally, the efforts of translators of Catholic hymnody have been directed chiefly and in the first instance to the Breviary and Missal hymns of the Church. This attraction has resulted in the creation of a large body of English hymns from a comparatively few common sources. For instance, as regards the Office hymns, in many seasons a single Latin hymn does duty for the whole course of the season. But, inasmuch as most of the greater seasons of the Church, e.g., Advent, Lent and Easter-tide, extend beyond the limits of one week; and as the Latin hymns for any given season have been rendered into English by different hands and at different times, a variety of vernacular hymns may be obtained for each week of the season in succession by a system of judicious selection. In this way, English hymns by various authors have been arranged in *Annus Sanctus,* for the different weeks of each recurring season of the Church. This arrangement is productive of a double effect : for there exists in general a sufficient diversity of treatment in the several hymns to prevent sameness, and there is a sufficient oneness in a common source to keep each selected hymn in harmony with the mind of the Church. The plan is not unlike to that of a common musical composition repeated in different keys, set to different harmonies, performed by different instruments —there is organised unity accompanied by diversity in details and modes of treatment. This effort after variety in conjunction with identity has been still

Preface.

further sought by the addition of modern, original and other hymns, which have been placed in a part by themselves. These non-liturgical hymns enhance the value of the collection by their contrast in character and contents to the English versions of ancient hymns ; and from the more subjective and personal view which they take of facts, dogmas and mysteries in the teaching of the seasons of the Church.

The hymns in this volume are confined to general hymns for the seasons of the Church and their subdivisions, to a selection of hymns for the Canonical Hours, and to hymns specially addressed to our Lord. They are arranged, with one exception, according to the order of the seasons and the sequence of holy-days in the Breviary. The position of the hymns for the Hours forms the exception. As they will presumably be used more frequently, all the year round, than the hymns for any given season or day, they have been placed mid-way in both parts of the book. In this arrangement, the example set in some editions of the Missal has been followed, in which, for convenience sake in the use of the volume, the Ordinary and Canon of the Mass is printed after the season of Lent and before that of Easter.

The contributions towards the compilation of *Annus Sanctus* admit of a three-fold classification ; 1. Hymns that are already well known and highly prized, household words amongst Catholics; 2. Comparatively recent hymns, that are either little known or altogether unknown at the present day, many of which have not hitherto emerged from the privacy of MS.; and 3. Earlier hymns that, once popular and widely used, have been at last utterly forgotten and stand a fair

Preface.

chance of being permanently lost to the Church. A few words on each class may not be considered out of place ; and the earlier and less well-known hymns may take the precedence.

I. It is not without reason the statement is made, that a whole class of Catholic English hymns stands in danger of being lost. No estimate is here made of the critical value of this class of hymns; the reader will be able to judge of some of them and frame his own verdict of their worth. But, of their historical and literary and what may be called their sentimental value, too high an estimate in the eyes of Catholics can hardly be made. Yet, the fact remains that not many persons are conscious of the existence of these hymns ; none, with but one exception of those who have been consulted, proved otherwise than vague in their knowledge of them ; and none, without an exception, knew the extent of the class. At the present moment there exist but very few copies of the books which contain them, whether in a collected form, or as individual specimens.

These books are generally hidden away in public libraries, in the libraries of religious houses of England, in private libraries of old Catholic families. They are usually over-looked by their present owners or guardians ; and the class for whom they were originally compiled, religious or secular, have been provided with newer and not always better manuals of devotion. Hence it has come to pass, that these books have almost died out of existence and out of memory ; and it has been thought by the compiler a work of piety to make an effort to preserve for the future these versions which though not all of value in themselves,

Preface.

are all of interest as evidence of spiritual vitality in times of persecution and disability, and of importance as being links with the noble past history of English Catholicism.

To say all or much that can be said on this topic in this place is impossible. It must suffice to place on record these points. First, that, so far as it is yet known, there are extant four distinct families of English versions of the Breviary hymns which were made prior to the eighteenth century. Next, that the last of these four families became the pattern or type which more or less exactly was preserved and repeated in the English hymns which obtained in the Church for upwards of a century; and that these, the few that survived, were gradually displaced by more modern translations. Thirdly, that the latest version of the Breviary hymns—a comparatively modern and greatly superior one to the three earlier renderings, was first printed in the year 1706, though its contents, or some of them, were of prior date by at least six years. In all probability these hymns, or the major part of them, owe their origin to the great English poet, Dryden, who was converted to the faith in the year 1685, and made an edifying death in 1700. It appears to be certain that some of these versions are from his pen; and these are inseparably connected with others to which they bear strong internal and external resemblance. Lastly, the whole of these versions—so far as they enter into the plan of the present work—have been reprinted here. The authorship of the three earlier sets of translations is unknown, and probably can never be even hypothetically recovered. They appeared in a series of editions of the one popular book of English private devotion of the times in ques-

Preface.

tion, viz. *the Primer, or Office of the Blessed Virgin Mary in English*—a book which it is much to be wished might again become popular, and which was valuable from the presence of features, both devotional and poetic, which have now been omitted from similar books of piety. The dates at which the *Primers* referred to were printed are 1604, 1619, 1685 and 1706. For facility of comparison and in order not to increase too largely the bulk of the volume, the hymns of the four heads of families have been reprinted in a smaller type in parallel pages as an Appendix.

On two of these points, the authorship of the translations which bear the dates of 1706 and 1619, a few remarks of an historical nature may be excused. They will be of a positive and negative character respectively; and will be designed to show that one author, who has failed to claim his work, ought to be credited with the honour; and that another, on whose behalf a claim has been posthumously made, ought to have such credit withdrawn.

1. An outline of the claims of Dryden, and how such claims forced themselves on the compiler of this book, can here be indicated only. Popular Catholic tradition assigns to Dryden the authorship of several versions of the Hymns of the Church. In the case of certain hymns, tradition is as clearly at fault as it is almost demonstrably true in others. In the case of more than one hymn, tradition—written or handed down in religious houses—asserts that the version was made in fulfilment of an imposed penance : and this, under the circumstances of the author and his life and works, is no improbability. Indeed, it is not improbable that two other elements in the argument were self-inflicted by the popular poet and dramatist,

Preface.

as he drew towards his end and devoted his later efforts to the service of the Church—viz. the anonymity with which the hymns were printed, and their non-publication during the author's life-time. Under any conditions, however, three hymns are definitely ascribed to Dryden's pen by the last great biographer of the poet, Sir Walter Scott. These, as every one knows, are *Te Deum*, a paraphrase of the *Veni Creator*, and the Hymn for St. John's Eve. The other hymns, rightly or wrongly ascribed to the same origin, of late or formerly, need not be particularised; nor need the authorities be named. But, it may be remarked, as singular in one so familiar with certain aspects of the Church, and so sympathetic with the romantic side of Catholicism, that Scott's attention seems to have been called to these hymns—though then actually existing in print for a century past—only as his edition of Dryden's works was passing through the press; and that he supposed the hymns had been "preserved" in MS. up to his date by "the English Catholics," to one of whom (apparently) he was indebted for this addition to his editorial labours.

It was with this scanty amount of information and suggestion that the compiler was placed on the track of Dryden's translations. More than this he was unable to learn from very wide-spread inquiries amongst English Catholics and some Protestants who were hymnological students. At last he came upon the only two copies of the *Primer* of 1706 which, in its original edition, he could find in England; though he has since heard of another; and a fourth has recently been recovered in a curious way, from the library of an exiled religious house in France, and lies before him as he writes. In this edition may be found, not

Preface.

only some of the translations traditionally and rightly held to be Dryden's, and the three hymns printed by Sir Walter Scott; but also the whole of the Breviary Hymns, for Vespers, Matins, Lauds, and other Canonical hours, with other hymns—notably the *Dies Iræ*, in all probability wrongly attributed to Lord Roscommon—commonly used in England at the date of translation. This was a most valuable discovery: and a comparison of the renderings of the Vespers hymns with those of earlier date proved them to be practically fresh versions, and critically to be of indisputable value. Of course the Matins and Lauds hymns—so far as present knowledge can decide—were entirely new.

Who was the author of these translations? was the question which then arose. Much incidental and direct evidence, which cannot here be given, combined to point to Dryden as the author. A fact, which is critically conclusive in regard to one set of hymns, may be mentioned as an argumentative specimen of the rest. The translation called by Scott a "hymn for St. John's Eve," in reality, is the Vespers hymn for the festival of the patron-saint of the poet. Such a rendering from such a source might well have been preserved in the author's handwriting, by friends and fellow-religionists, for the period of a century and a quarter. But in the *Primer* of 1706, this hymn stands first of three hymns, "On the feast of the Nativity, of St. John Baptist, June 24th," at Even-song, Matins, and Lauds, respectively. These hymns in their English dress are clearly by one and the same hand. A common doxology appears for two of them. And all three are rendered in a metre, singular in itself, unknown to the translators of the day or previously, and

Preface.

not hymnological in form. Evidence of authorship on the score of language, ideas, style, manner, and the poet's idiosyncrasies and history, cannot be dwelt upon here. But one of the points in indirect confirmation of this theory of authorship may be stated. Another student of the same question, from a totally different point of view, and entirely independently of the present writer, has arrived at a like conclusion in regard to Dryden's claims on the *Primer* in question. Indeed, the two inquirers were ignorant of each other's researches and were mutually unknown until both had formulated their own opinion. It is much to be hoped that the new and valuable edition of Dryden's works, which is now in course of publication, may do justice to the poet in relation to his literary work on hymns. In the meantime, and whilst awaiting the decision of competent critical authority on the whole question, it may be stated in conclusion, that though all the hymns in the *Primer* of 1706 are not here credited to Dryden's handiwork; yet it is highly probable that a large, perhaps the largest portion of them are his: and though this book has the honour of first re-introducing the hymns to public notice in this century, it has been thought judicious not to add Dryden's name in the text at the foot of each hymn conditionally assigned to him in the table of contents, but only to indicate in that place the undoubted source whence it has been taken.

2. A circumstance in relation to the version of the Vespers hymns, which appeared in the *Primer* of the year 1619, deserves notice; but it can only be here noticed briefly. The edition of 1619, was published at St. Omer by the printer whose name is so well known in the imprint of Catholic books of that date,

Preface.

John Heigham. About a score of the hymns from this edition appear, and as a rule appear word for word, under the heading of 'Divine Poems' in the posthumous poetical works of William Drummond of Hawthornden. Of these twenty hymns—one being a fragment only, and suspiciously altered dogmatically—some are for the days of the week, and some for holydays and seasons of the Church. The versions for Advent, Christmas, Lent, Ascension, Whit-Sunday and Trinity Sunday, are printed in the Appendix of this book. The fact of identity was, in the first instance, noticed by a friend who has a wide acquaintance with hymns, and possesses, perhaps, the largest collection of hymn-books hitherto made.

This identity being admitted, two theories have arisen in explanation of it. On the one hand, the idea is warmly entertained that Drummond was the author of the translations in question. On the other, this idea is held to be utterly untenable under the admitted circumstances. That John Heigham, the Catholic publisher, living in the Low Countries early in the seventeenth century, should have applied to a Scotch Protestant, Drummond of Hawthornden, or have obtained from him a translation of the Vespers hymns of the Church, is *primâ facie* highly improbable. Other matters connected with the case, which need not be here stated, tend to confirm this improbability. But there is nothing intrinsically improbable in the opinion that, as a cultured and travelled man; as a man whose library contained ascetical and other Catholic books; as a poet, translator and writer of devotional verse—Drummond should have copied the versions of the hymns in question. He copied them, if at all, for his own private edification. And the

Preface.

additional circumstance that he failed to publish them himself is, to some minds, additional evidence that, as an honest man, he did not, because he could not, publish the hymns as his own literary work.

If space allowed, much collateral evidence might be adduced in support of this opinion—both as to the character of the miscellaneous MSS. left behind him by Drummond; and also as to his intercourse with Ben Jonson in the year in question, 1619—who, although he is said to have previously apostatised, yet probably was acquainted with the new edition of the *Primer* and might have directed the attention of Drummond to the book. Circumstantial evidence, therefore, seems to point to the conclusion, that Drummond by some means obtained a copy of the *Primer* of 1619, that he copied some of its contents for devotional or other purposes, but that he did not include them in his own works because they came from the pen of another.

II. As a contribution towards a collection of English hymns which are little known, or altogether unknown to Catholics of the present day a valuable offering has been made. The MS. poetical remains of two able translators of Latin hymns have, by the kindness of the respective representatives of the authors, been placed at the disposal of the compiler. These MSS. in the order in which they were happily met with are as follows. The first was the work of the late Robert Campbell, Esq., of Skerrington, a Scottish advocate, who shortly after making a translation of a series of hymns from the Breviary, the Paris Breviary and the Missal in 1850—versions which were accounted by no mean authority as the very best which had then

Preface.

appeared amongst Protestants—submitted himself to the Catholic Church. The residue of his life was spent in good works as a thank-offering for the blessing of conversion; and he died a devoted son of the Church in 1868. The second collection of MSS. came from the pen of the late Very Rev. Father Aylward, of the Order of Preachers, a cultured and talented priest of varied powers and gifts, whose memory is held dear by all who knew and were influenced by him. He went to his reward in the year 1872, after nearly forty years profession as a Dominican; and was buried in the picturesque cloistral-cemetery of Woodchester, of which model and peaceful religious house he was the first Prior.

The MSS. of both priest and layman were entrusted to the editor. They were both in a condition which ensured weeks and even months of work to decide on the form in which each integral portion should be reproduced in print. Both were beautifully written originally, but both had been so altered, re-altered and sometimes altered back again—specially in the case of Father Aylward's MSS.—often in half-erased pencil-marks, that the task, though a labour of love, was one of extreme difficulty, to decide on the reading to be adopted for publication. Abstract criticism, personal taste, and probability as to the author's meaning and wishes had to be balanced. A decision, or rather endless decisions had to be made by one outside the lives of both poets. If errors of judgment, therefore, are discovered, the blame must not fall on the original translators. It is only necessary to add that some of the hymns of Father Aylward and many of the hymns which bear Mr. Campbell's name have already appeared in print at dates varying from thirty

Preface.

to forty years ago. But the versions in both cases, as they appear in the present volume, are printed from the MSS. of the respective translators ; and by reason of the changes to which they have been subjected, may be considered as practically new, at least to this generation of readers.

III. Of the hymns in this selection, whether they be original or translated, which already have left their mark upon the hymnody of the present day, there is only need to refer to those whose authors, though dead, still speak to us through their hymns as if living. It might be impertinent for the editor to estimate the hymns of those who are still fighting with us in the battle of life. And there are hymnodists, who are perhaps equally favourites and are even more widely known outside the pale of the Church than within. Amongst these stand in the first place, both for their talent and the extent to which they employed it in this direction, two sons of St. Philip Neri in England. The vigorous dogmatic hymns of Father Caswall in the first part of this volume are well supplemented in the second portion by the more subjective, emotional and personal hymns from the large heart of Father Faber. But these two great names in modern hymnology by no means exhaust the list of deceased Catholic translators, or authors, who are acknowledged as masters in their art. Doubtless there are more. Indeed, from no fault of the compiler, one successful translator of hymns finds no place in the following pages. And from the inexorable exigencies of space others—and this applies to the living also—are but indifferently represented in point of quantity. Still, there is a band of men of whose talents in this direc-

Preface.

tion we may well be proud ; and at the number of whose names, even apart from their living co-adjutors, some may feel surprised. The list includes the following : 1. The Venerable Provost Husenbeth, one of the very earliest translators (he dates from 1831) if not the first Catholic poet who again rendered the Breviary Vespers and Missal hymns into the vernacular. 2. The Rev. Professor Potter, perhaps best and most widely known in his spirited hymn—mutilated and un-allotted to him though it be in Protestant Hymn-books— "Brightly gleams our banner :" though he also has done into English most of the Vespers hymns of the Church. 3. Another Irishman, the Spanish critic and translator of Calderon, the sweet and powerful versifier, D. F. MacCarthy. And 4. yet another, the poet "Shamrock" of the National movement in 1848, who could write devotional poetry for Sisters of Charity as well as patriotic songs for his countrymen, R. D. Williams. 5. The scholar, divine, controversialist and missionary priest, Canon Oakeley. 6. An Anglo-Saxon student and professor, a man of varied gifts as antiquary, astronomer and civil-engineer, the Rev. A. D. Wackerbarth. 7 and 8. Two noteworthy lay converts ; the very early one in the history of the Oxford Tractarian movement, who was a great benefactor to the Church, Ambrose L. Phillipps ; and the death-bed convert, R. S. Hawker, who was remarkable both for the deep thought of his original poetry and for his successful imitations. And last, not least, 9, 10 and 11, three women poets : Lady Catherine Petre, whose thoughtful and devotional verses will, it is hoped, shortly be collected and published ; the popular English writer of verse, Adelaide A. Procter ; and the graceful Irish teller of "Tales for

Preface.

the Young," Miss Caddell, who is only less popular in England because she is less widely known. Since the above was in type, a twelfth name must be added to this list of deceased writers of Catholic hymns. Mr. Robert Monteith of Carstairs, Lanark, who has been well described as " one of the foremost and most devoted sons of the Church in Scotland," after a long life of doing good, has passed to his reward. *Requiescant in pace.*

Annus Sanctus, though it represents the work of some years, and though complete in itself so far as it goes, forms only a portion of a wider plan which proposes to include all the best English hymns of the Church. It professes to embrace and was designed to exhaust certain divisions only of Catholic hymnody. A glance at the title-page will show the limits aimed at: and the results attained in the text will suggest the wealth of the field of Catholic literature which in this volume has been gleaned. If the book secures the reception which its compiler believes that the value of its contents demands, he hopes to be enabled in the future to produce another volume which will supply some deficiencies of the present one. But, under any circumstances, certain portions of hymnody have been intentionally neglected in this collection. The wide range of hymns to our Blessed Lady would almost fill a volume by itself; it would obviously be treated imperfectly as a fraction of a book which aimed at supplying hymns for the Seasons of the Church. Holy Communion is another fruitful source of hymns which, saving in its aspect as a rite of the Church commemorated at certain seasons, is not treated in *Annus Sanctus.* The Four Last-Things is

Preface.

another class of topics which space did not permit any dealing with in this book, save in the season of Advent. Miscellaneous hymns, of a more subjective character, have also been omitted, except under each heading of the second part. And a class of hymns which from its nature, variety and extent would also form a collection by itself, viz., hymns to the Saints and Angels, has not for the present been undertaken. Indeed, when one considers the amount of hymnological wealth which has been neglected, an apology is due, even at the beginning of this somewhat bulky volume, for its many and serious deficiencies. Such an apology is due not only for classes of subjects which have been deliberately ignored, but also for the paucity of specimens which have been reproduced from the works of some of the writers. Perhaps in the future some of the last-named faults of omission may be rectified: and perhaps, also, fresh sources of hymns may be opened to the compiler in the compositions in MS., or otherwise, of some writers to whom he has not had the benefit of access for this volume.

To these details of editorial work, one point of minor importance may be added. The compiler has endeavoured, however unsuccessfully, to adopt a uniform plan of printing in regard to capital letters and punctuation. With so numerous a list of contributors, a definite system was required, if only to avoid endless inconsistencies. These may still exist; but an effort has been made to secure uniformity, and the compiler is responsible for the result.

In conclusion, the editor's grateful thanks are due to many friends who have co-operated with him in the

Preface.

production of this book, and without whose varied aid the book could not have been produced. First and foremost must be placed the literary executors and representatives, whether clergy or laymen, as well as the publishers of the works of deceased contributors, most of whom indeed, it may be added, accorded to the editor full permission for the use of their hymns during their lifetime. Amongst others may be mentioned Messrs. Burns and Oates, Toovey, Pickering and Co., and Gill and Son of Dublin. Next, to the authors who have themselves, recently, or again placed their contributions to hymnody at the disposal of the compiler, and still more to those who have given time and labour to the task of translation for the present book, are acknowledgments offered. Then, to editors of periodicals, specially of the *Month*, the *Messenger* and the *Irish Monthly*, which contributed largely to the compilation—*Annus Sanctus* is proportionately beholden. And lastly, the compiler is deeply indebted to the Reverend censor of the book, to a Dominican father and to a lay friend, for aiding him in the drudgery of editing by carefully reading, annotating and correcting the proof-sheets as they passed through the press, and also, to another friend who afforded valuable information on the source of the hymns. It seems unnecessary, however, to mention the names of any friends excepting those to whom, being publishers, the book is under what may be called copy-right obligations. Should there be any whose copy-right has been unwittingly infringed, they are begged to forgive the accident and to accept an apology before-hand. For the rest, all who have in any way co-operated in this work, and one who has generously helped it in a manner which he would not like to see particularised

Preface.

—with two others also who have generously afforded aid—are asked not to consider that the thanks here returned, individually or in combination, are the less hearty because they are the more brief.

Finally, it may be convenient and will be curious to collect into a focus the names of all who have assisted in this work, at least, of all who may be mentioned. Amongst the contributors some desire to be anonymous—the translators of the hymns from St. Alphonsus, and of the hymns in the *Roman Breviary* and *Order of Compline.* Some are unknown. Some have affixed to their contributions their initial, or other letters only: e.g., W. M. A.: T. E. B.: F. A. J.: S. J.: F. J. P.: S.: and Σ. Of the rest the following names are arranged in alphabetical order:

Prior Aylward: Rev. G. F. L. Bampfield: J. R. Beste: W. K. Blount: Miss Bowles: Alfred, Lord Braye: Matthew Bridges: Miss Caddell: Robert Campbell, of Skerrington: Father Caswall: Father H. Collins: John Dryden: J. C. Earle: Father Faber: Lady Georgiana Fullerton: R. S. Hawker: Provost Husenbeth: Charles Kent: Mrs. F. G. Lee: Howel W. Lloyd: D. Florence MacCarthy: Robert Monteith: Miss Mulholland: Cardinal Newman: Canon Oakeley: Justice O'Hagan: Rev. H. N. Oxenham: Lady Catherine Petre: Ambrose L. Phillipps: Professor Potter: Miss Procter: Father Rawes: Father Russell, S.J.: Father H. I. D. Ryder: Rev. F. Stanfield: Aubrey de Vere: Rev. A. D. Wackerbarth: Dr. Wallace: R. Dalton Williams ("Shamrock"): W. F. Wingfield.

ORBY SHIPLEY.

LONDON, *April 25th,* 1884.

PRELIMINARY NOTE

TO THE

Contents.

IN order to diminish the bulk of the Table of Contents and to prevent needless repetition of the same details under different headings, the following facts are stated at length by way of preface :—

I. The revision from their earlier form of the Office Hymns in the Breviary was made under the authority of Pope Urban VIII. (1631), himself a writer of hymns, by Casimir Sarbriewski, Strado and Petruchio. In the following table, allusions to the original hymns, and the notes of alteration and change, refer to the revision made in the Seventeenth Century. As a rule the revision was slight.

II. The hymns in the present work are numbered in the contents, though not in the text of the volume. In the case of a different translation of the same hymn being annotated, the source and history of the original is not repeated; but the reader is referred back, by the numbers prefixed, to the first occasion on which these details are given of the original hymn.

III. Details of the earlier translations and their sources; of the authors' or translators' names, styles and titles; the titles of their books; and other facts which are given in full in the first instance, are afterwards abbreviated, or omitted.

IV. The dates assigned to both originals and translations are, in general, only approximately stated; and except in

Preliminary Note.

the case of new versions, and in a few other instances, are not repeated after the first reference to the author.

V. The hymns termed Ambrosian are supposed to have been written in the Fourth and Fifth Centuries; and those called Gregorian, in the Sixth and Seventh Centuries. The Benedictine editors do not assign more than twelve hymns to the pen of St. Ambrose, who was Bishop of Milan from A.D. 374 to 397; and not more than eight to Pope St. Gregory the Great, who died A.D. 604.

VI. The hymns in the Paris Breviary, where they are new, were composed by the two de Santeuils, who died at the close of the Seventeenth Century; and by Charles Coffin, Rector of the University of Paris, who died in 1749.

VII. The full titles of the old English books of devotion rom whence quotations are made, are—

1. The Primer, or Office of the Blessed Virgin Mary, with a new and approved version of the Church Hymns. Printed in the year 1706. The last edition was published in 1780.
2. The Evening Office of the Church in English and Latin, containing the Vespers or Even-song for all Sundays and Holydays of Obligation. Collected from the Roman Breviary. Printed in the year 1710. Of this book, and of a similar one with the same title, many editions were issued. A fifth edition of the last was published in 1785.
3. The Divine Office for the Use of the Laity. 4 vols. Printed in the year 1763. 2 vols. 1780.

VIII. As this book does not aspire to critical exactitude, the peculiar nomenclature of the Paris Breviary has not been followed in English; and the Hymns for Nocturns are called Matins Hymns. Nor has the difference been specified between Hymns for the First and Second Vespers of a feast; nor between Hymns for the feast and its octave.

IX. Most of the originals of the Office Hymns can be found —and when revised, both in their earlier and later form— in Daniel's *Thesaurus Hymnologicus*, Leipsic, 1855-1856.

Preliminary Note.

X. As a rule, the Hymns from the Sacred Office—excepting in the "Canonical Hours"—are arranged according to their position in the Breviary, beginning with Vespers.

XI. In order to prevent misapprehension, it may be well to repeat what has been otherwise said in the preface, viz., that, as a rule, all hymns in the Tables of Contents which bear a date earlier than 1883 have been previously printed. These hymns appeared either in periodicals, or in collections of sacred verse, or in the works of their respective authors: and the titles of the author's works have been added at the first reference to the quotations from them. The exceptions to the rule are these: the MS. hymns, in part or wholly, of Father Aylward, Mr. Campbell, Lady Georgiana Fullerton, Mr. Kent, Lady Catherine Petre, and Rev. Francis Stanfield.

ANNUS SANCTUS.

PART I.

Contents.

HYMNS FROM THE SACRED OFFICES.

Advent.

First Week of Advent.

NO.   PAGE

1. CREATOR alme siderum. Revised from *Conditor alme siderum.* Ambrosian Vespers Breviary Hymn. *Bright Maker of the starry poles.* From the Evening Office of the Church, 1710. Based on the Primer of 1685, with alterations after the Primer of 1706, and both revised.
Author unknown.   3

2. Verbum supernum prodiens e Patris. Revised from *Verbum supernum prodiens a Patre.* Gregorian Matins Breviary Hymn. *Supernal Word, proceeding from.* From Verses on Various Occasions, 1868.
John Henry, Cardinal Newman, 1834-1842.   4

3. Instantis adventum Dei. Matins Hymn from the Paris Breviary, by Charles Coffin, Rector of the University of Paris. *The coming of our God.*
Robert Campbell, of Skerrington, 1849-1850.   4

4. Vox clara ecce intonat. Original of *En, clara vox redarguit.* Ambrosian Lauds Hymn from the Salisbury Breviary. *Clear rings a voice; it chides the world. Alfred, Lord Braye,* 1883.   5

5. En, clara vox redarguit. See No. 4. *A heavenly voice and early ray.* From the Primer, 1706.
(Probably) John Dryden, 1685-1700.   6

NO.   PAGE

6. Dies iræ, dies illa. Sequence in Mass for the Dead,
from the Missal. By Thomas of Celano, Order
of Friars Minor, Thirteenth Century, *Day of
wrath, that day whose knelling.*
Justice John O'Hagan, 1874.   6

Second Week of Advent.

7. Conditor alme siderum. Original of *Creator alme
siderum.* From the Salisbury Breviary. See
No. 1. *Thou builder of the starry skies.*
*Very Rev. Prior James A. Dominic Aylward,
Order of Preachers,* 1843-1850.   8

8. Verbum supernum prodiens e Patris. See No. 2.
O thou, who thine own Father's breast. From
Hymns and Poems, 1873.
*Father Edward Caswall, Birmingham
Oratory,* 1848.   9

9. Vox clara terris nos gravi. Lauds Hymn from
the Breviary of Noyon. *A thrilling voice rings
clear and high.*
Father Henry Ignatius D. Ryder, Birmingham Oratory, 1883.   10

10. In noctis umbra desides. Compline Hymn from
the Paris Breviary, by C. Coffin. *When clouds
of darkness veil the sky.*
Robert Campbell.   10

11. Dies iræ, dies illa. See No. 6. *Day of wrath, the
heart dismaying.*   *F. J. P.,* 1860.   11

Third Week of Advent.

12. Creator alme siderum. See No. 1. *Maker of the
starry sphere.*   *Robert Campbell.*   13

13. Verbum supernum prodiens a Patre. See No. 2.
From the Salisbury Breviary. *Supernal Word,
who didst proceed.*   *John Charles Earle,* 1883.   13

14. Jordanis oras prævia. Lauds Hymn from the
Paris Breviary, by C. Coffin. *What sound doth
Jordan's streams appal?*   *W. M. A.* 1883.   14

Contents.

NO.		PAGE
15.	En, clara vox redarguit. See No. 4. *Hark, an awful voice is sounding.* *Father Caswall.*	15
16.	Dies iræ, dies illa. See No. 6. *That day of wrath, that dreadful day.* From Prayers for the Dead. *W. F. Wingfield,* 1845.	15

Fourth Week of Advent.

17.	Conditor alme siderum. See No. 1. *O thou, the maker of each star.* *Lord Braye,* 1883.	17
18.	Statuta decreto Dei. Vespers Hymn from the Paris Breviary, by C. Coffin. *Predestinate of God most high.* *W. M. A.,* 1883.	18
19.	Verbum supernum prodiens e Patris. See No. 2. *The period is come; and lo, to-day.* Primer, 1706. (*Probably*) *John Dryden.*	19
20.	Instantis adventum Dei. See No. 3. *The advent of our God at hand.* *T. C. Earle,* 1883.	20
21.	En, clara vox redarguit. See No. 4. *Hark, a joyful voice is thrilling.* *Cardinal Newman.*	20
22.	Dies iræ, dies illa. See No. 6. *That day of wrath and grief and shame.* *Prior Aylward.*	21

Christmas and Circumcision.

Part One.

23.	Jesu, Redemptor omnium. Revised from *Christe, Redemptor gentium.* Ambrosian Vespers Breviary Hymn. *Jesu, our soul's redeeming Lord.* From the Catholic Psalmist, 1859. *Rev. Professor Thomas J. Potter, All Hallows College, Dublin,* 1857-1858.	24
24.	Jam desinant suspiria. Matins Hymn from the Paris Breviary, by C. Coffin. *Now signs of mourning disappear.* *Lord Braye,* 1883.	25
25.	Felix dies, quam proprio. Matins Hymn from the Paris Breviary, for the Circumcision, by Benault, priest of Sens, 1726. *Blest day, when from the Saviour flowed.* A fragment. *Robert Campbell.*	26

NO.		PAGE
26.	A solis ortus cardine. An alphabetical Hymn. Lauds Breviary Hymn, by Caius Cœlius Sedulius, Fifth Century. *From every part o'er which the sun.* Primer, 1706. (*Probably*) *John Dryden.*	26
27.	Puer natus in Bethlehem. From the Mayence Hymnary. *A Boy is born in Bethlehem.* *Father Ryder*, 1883.	27
28.	Adeste fideles. Sequence, from the Cistercian Gradual, of the Fifteenth-Sixteenth Century. *In triumph, joy and holy fear.* Paraphrase of a longer version than is generally used. Verses 3, 4, 5, and 6, are here for the first time rendered into English. *J. C. Earle,* 1881.	28

Part Two.

29.	Jesu, Redemptor omnium. See No. 23. *Lamb, whose blood for all men streamed.* *Robert Campbell.*	29
30.	Jam desinant suspiria. See No. 24. *Ye people, cease from tears.* *Robert Campbell.*	30
31.	O ter fecundas, O ter jucundas. Sequence by Marburne, Order of St. Benedict, Abbot of Livry, Fifteenth Century. *O night of nights, supreme delights.* *J. C. Earle,* 1883.	31
32.	Salvator mundi Domine. Compline Hymn from the Salisbury Breviary. *O Saviour of the world forlorn.* *Lord Braye,* 1883.	32
33.	Adeste fideles. See No. 28. *Hasten, ye faithful, glad, joyful and holy.* From Church Hymns, 1849. *J. Richard Beste,* 1839.	32

Part Three.

34.	Jesu, Redemptor omnium. See No. 23. *Jesus, Redeemer, ere the light.* From the Vespers Book. Very Rev. Provost F. C. Husenbeth, 1840–1841.	33
35.	Debilis cessent elementa legis. Vespers Hymn, for the Circumcision, from the Paris Breviary. *Now ancient shadows flee.* *Robert Campbell.*	34
36.	Missum Redemptorem polo. Lauds Hymn from the Paris Breviary, by C. Coffin. *Sent from his heavenly throne on high.* *W. M. A.,* 1883.	35

Contents.

NO.		PAGE
37.	Mundi salus qui nasceris. Compline Hymn for the Vigil of Christmas, from the Paris Breviary, by C. Coffin. *Holy Babe, our great salvation.* Robert Campbell.	36
38.	Adeste fideles. See No. 28. *Come, O faithful, with sweet voices.* Charles Kent, 1870–1883.	36

Part Four.

39.	Jesu, Redemptor omnium. See No. 23. Partly a cento from the Primers of 1685 and 1706, revised and altered; and partly original. *Jesu, the Ransomer of man.* Evening Office, 1710. Author unknown.	37
40.	Victis sibi cognomina. Vespers Hymn, for the Circumcision, from the Paris Breviary, by Benault. *To earthly kings fresh names accrue.* Lord Braye, 1883.	38
41.	A solis ortus cardine. See No. 26. *From the far-blazing gate of morn.* Father Caswall.	39
42.	Puer nobis nascitur. Ancient prose. *A Child for us is born this day.* Evening Office, 1748. Author unknown.	40
43.	Adeste fideles. See No. 28. *Oh come, all ye faithful.* Robert Campbell.	40

Epiphany and Season after.

Epiphany and Octave.

44.	Crudelis Herodes, Deum. Revised from *Hostis Herodes impie.* Vespers Breviary Hymn, by Sedulius. *Why, ruthless Herod, why should fear?* Prior Aylward.	42
45.	Quæ stella sole pulchrior? Vespers Hymn from the Paris Breviary, by C. Coffin. *What beauteous sun-surpassing star?* Robert Campbell.	42
46.	Fac, Christe, nostri gratia. Matins Hymn from the Paris Breviary, by Jean-Baptiste de Santeuil, Canon-Regular of St. Victor, 1630–1697. *Thou from the cradle to the grave.* Robert Campbell.	43

NO.		PAGE

47. O sola magnarum urbium. Lauds Hymn from the Breviary, by Aurelius Prudentius Clemens, Fourth Century. *Bethlehem, of noblest cities.* Father Caswall. 44

Second Week after Epiphany.

48, 49, 50. Jesu, dulcis memoria. Jesu, rex admirabilis. Jesu, decus angelicum. Vespers, Matins, and Lauds Hymn, for the Holy Name, from the Breviary. Cento from Hymn of St. Bernard, Abbot of Clairvaux, Twelfth Century. *The memory sweet of Jesus' name. O Jesu, Lord, most mighty king. Crown of the angels, thy sweet name.* Prior Aylward. 45, 46.

51, 52, 53. The same as Nos. 48, 49, 50. *Thy sweet remembrance, Lord, imparts. Jesu, king o'er all adored. Jesu, highest heaven's completeness.* Robert Campbell. 47, 48.

Third Week after Epiphany.

54. Crudelis Herodes, Deum. See No. 44. *What makes thee, cruel Herod, shake?* Based on the Primers of 1685 and 1706, but partly original. Evening Office, 1710. Author unknown. 49

55. Clamantis, ecce, vox sonans. Vespers Hymn from the Paris Breviary, by Nicholas le Tourneux, Seventeenth Century. *Hark in the wilderness.* An imitation. Robert Campbell. 50

56. Linquunt tecta Magi principis orbis. Lauds Hymn from the Paris Breviary, by C. Coffin. *The princely city passing by.* J. C. Earle, 1883. 50

Fourth Week after Epiphany.

57. Crudelis Herodes, Deum. See No. 44. *Why, cruel Herod, dost thou fear?* Provost Husenbeth. 52

58. Verbum quod ante sæcula. Vespers Hymn from the Paris Breviary. *Word of God, eternal Son.* Robert Campbell. 53

Contents.

NO.		PAGE
59.	Qua lapsu tacito stella loquacibus. Matins Hymn from the Parisian Breviary, by C. Coffin. *The beauteous star that beams on high.* *Robert Campbell.*	53

Fifth Week after Epiphany.

60.	Crudelis Herodes, Deum. See No. 44. *Why, cruel Herod, dost thou fear?* *Professor Potter.*	54
61.	Christus tenebris obsitam. Vespers Hymn from the Paris Breviary, by de Santeuil. *The bright and morning star arose.* *Robert Campbell.*	53
62.	Non abluunt lymphæ Deum. Matins Hymn from the Paris Breviary, by le Tourneux. *God needeth not the cleansing wave.* A paraphrase. *Robert Campbell.*	55
63.	O sola magnarum urbium. See No. 47. *Let other cities strive, which most.* Primer, 1706. (*Probably*) *John Dryden.*	56
64.	Alleluia, dulce carmen. Hymn of the Thirteenth Century, for the week before Septuagesima, from the Magdeburg Breviary. *Alleluia, sweetest lay.* *Robert Campbell.*	57

Septuagesima, Sexagesima and Quinquagesima.

Septuagesima.

65.	Aspice, ut Verbum Patris a supernis. Vespers Hymn from the Friburg Breviary. *See the eternal Word descending.* From Hymns of the Church. *Dr. Wilfrid Wallace, Benedictine Priory, Erdington,* 1873-1874.	38
66.	Te læta, mundi conditor. Vespers Hymn from the Paris Breviary, by C. Coffin. *Thou, Creator, art possessed.* *Robert Campbell.*	59
67.	Venit e cœlo Mediator alto. Lauds Hymn from the Friburg Breviary. *Daughter of Sion, cease thy bitter tears.* *Father Caswall.*	59

Contents.

NO.   PAGE

Sexagesima.

68. Mœrentes oculi, spargite lacrymas. Vespers Hymn from the Friburg Breviary. *With sorrow deep oppressed, now let us sadly wail.*   *Professor Potter.*   60

69. Aspice, infami, Deus ipse, ligno. Matins Hymn from the Friburg Breviary. *Behold our God upon the rood.*   *Dr. Wallace.*   61

70. Sævo dolorum turbine. Lauds Hymn from the Friburg Breviary. *O'erwhelmed in depths of woe.*   *Father Caswall.*   62

Quinquagesima.

71. Exite, Sion filiæ. Vespers Breviary Hymn. *Go forth, ye Sion's daughters, now.*   *Dr. Wallace.*   63

72. Rebus creatis nil egens. Matins Hymn from the Paris Breviary. *Thou didst not need creation's aid.*   *Robert Campbell.*   64

73. Legis figuris pingitur. Lauds Breviary Hymn. *Christ's peerless crown is pictured in.*   *Father Caswall.*   64

Lent.

PART I.—SUNDAYS IN LENT.

First Sunday in Lent.

74. Audi, benigne Conditor. Vespers Breviary Hymn by Pope St. Gregory the Great. (Unrevised.) *O gracious Lord, Creator dear.*   *Robert Campbell.*   66

75. Ex more docti mystico. Ambrosian Matins Breviary Hymn. (Two stanzas revised.) *Now with the slow-revolving year.*   *Father Caswall.*   66

76. O Sol salutis, intimis. Lauds Breviary Hymn. *O sovereign Sun, diffuse thy light.* Primer, 1706.   (*Probably*) *John Dryden.*   68

Contents.

Second Sunday in Lent.

77. Audi, benigne Conditor. See No. 74. *O gracious Lord, incline thine ears.* Based on the Primers of 1685 and 1706, with variations from both. Evening Office, 1710 and 1748.
Author unknown. 68

78. Quod lex adumbravit vetus. Revised from *Ex more docti mystico.* Matins Hymn from the Paris Breviary, by C. Coffin. *The fast, that in the ancient law.* The first stanza is Mr. Earle's, and the last is by Mr. Campbell, entirely. *R. Campbell*, 1850, *& J. C. Earle*, 1883. 69

79. Lugete, pacis angeli. Matins Hymn from the Paris Breviary, by C. Coffin. *Angels, look down and weep.* *Robert Campbell.* 70

Third Sunday in Lent.

80. Audi, benigne Conditor. See No. 74. *Creator, bounteous and benign.* *Provost Husenbeth.* 71

81. Fando quis audivit, Dei. Vespers Hymn from the Paris Breviary, by C. Coffin. *Who hath heard what God hath wrought?* *Robert Campbell.* 72

82. Solemne nos jejunii. Lauds Hymn from the Paris Breviary, by C. Coffin. *Again the time appointed see.* *Robert Campbell.* 73

Fourth Sunday in Lent.

83. Audi, benigne Conditor. See No. 74. *O gracious Maker, bend thine ears.* *Professor Potter.* 73

84. Ex more docti mystico. See No. 75. *From heaven's own school's mysterious ways.* Primer, 1710.
(Probably) John Dryden. 74

85. O Sol salutis, intimis. See No. 76. *The darkness fleets, and joyful earth.* *Father Caswall.* 75

Fifth Sunday in Lent.

86. Audi, benigne Conditor. See No. 74. *Benignant Maker, hear at last.* *Charles Kent*, 1883. 76

87. Opprobriis, Jesu, satur. Matins Hymn from the Paris Breviary, by C. Coffin. *Like faithful Abraham's holy child.* *Robert Campbell.* 76

NO.		PAGE
88.	O splendor æterni Patris. Compline Hymn from the Paris Breviary. *O Christ, the true and endless Day.* Robert Campbell.	77

Palm Sunday.

89. Gloria, laus et honor. Processional Hymn (said to have been written in prison) from the Missal, by Theodulphus, Bishop of Orleans, Eighth-Ninth Century. (Six out of eleven stanzas.) *Glory and praise to thee, Redeemer blest.* Father Caswall. 78

90. Gloria, laus et honor. See No. 89. *To thee, O Christ, be glory, praises loud.* Evening Office, 1738. Author unknown. 78

PART II.—WEEK DAYS IN LENT.

First Week in Lent.

91. Quænam lingua tibi, O lancea. Vespers Breviary Hymn. *On Calvary with what a mystery gleams.* From the Roman Breviary, 1879. Anonymous. 79

92. Salvete, clavi et lancea. Matins Breviary Hymn. *Hail, holy nails; hail, blessed spear.* Dr. Wallace. 79

93. Tinctam ergo Christi sanguine. See No. 92 (of which this hymn is a continuation). *Oh, turn those blessed points, all bathed.* Father Caswall. 80

Second Week in Lent.

94. Gloriam sacræ celebremus omnes. Vespers Hymn from the Friburg Breviary. *Jesus, when on thy fatal day.* The Roman Breviary, 1879. Anonymous. 81

95. Mysterium mirabile. Matins Hymn from the Friburg Breviary. *A wondrous mystery this day.* Dr. Wallace. 82

96. Jesu, dulcis amor meus. Lauds Hymn from the Breviary. *Jesu, as though thyself wert here.* Father Caswall. 82

Third Week in Lent.

97. Ecce tempus idoneum. Gregorian Vespers Hymn from the Salisbury Breviary. *Behold the appointed time to win.*   *Robert Campbell.*   83

98. Prome vocem, mens, canoram. Vespers Hymn from the Paris Breviary, by Claude de Santeuil of Saint-Magloire, and brother of Jean-Baptiste. *Slow and mournful be our tone.*
  Robert Campbell.   84

99. Quæ te pro populi criminibus nova. Lauds Hymn from the Paris Breviary, by Claude de Santeuil. *O thou who, though high-priest, art victim made.*
  J. C. Earle, 1883.   84

Fourth Week in Lent.

100. Festivis resonent compita vocibus. Vespers Breviary Hymn. *With glad and joyous strains now let each street resound.*   *Professor Potter.*   85

101. Ira justa conditoris. Matins Breviary Hymn. *He who once, in righteous vengeance.*
  Father Caswall.   86

102. Salvete, Christi vulnera. Lauds Breviary Hymn. *Hail, holy wounds of Jesus, hail.* From the Sentence of Kaïres, and other poems.
  Rev. Henry Nutcombe Oxenham, 1854-1867.   87

Fifth Week in Lent.

103. Stabat Mater dolorosa. Breviary Hymn (divided for Vespers, Matins and Lauds), by the Franciscan, Jacobus de Benedictis, Thirteenth-Fourteenth Century. (Ten out of thirteen stanzas; only verbally and slightly altered.) *By the cross, on which suspended.*
  Denis Florence MacCarthy, 1870.   89

104. Stabat Mater dolorosa. See No. 103. *Weeping sore, the Mother stood.*   *Prior Aylward.*   91

105. Stabat Mater dolorosa. See No. 103. *By the cross of expiation.* From Hymns and Sacred Poems.   *Aubrey de Vere*, 1864.   93

PART III.—PASSION-TIDE.

NO.   PAGE

106. Vexilla regis prodeunt. Originally a Processional, now the Vespers Breviary Hymn, by Venantius Fortunatus, Bishop of Poitiers, Sixth–Seventh Century. (Slightly revised and shortened by one verse.) *Banners of our King are streaming.*
                                            Charles Kent.   94

107, 108 and 109. Pange lingua gloriosi, lauream. (Including 1. Crux fidelis, 2. Pange lingua, and 3. Lustra sex, originally one hymn.) Matins and Lauds Breviary Hymn, by Venantius Fortunatus, Bishop of Poitiers, Sixth–Seventh Century. (Very slightly altered.) 1. *O faithful cross, of trees the fairest;* 2. *O sing my tongue, God's glory sing;* 3. *Already thirty years have shed.*   *Charles Kent.*   95, 96, 97

110. Vexilla regis prodeunt. See No. 106. *Behold the royal ensigns fly.* Partly from the Primer of 1685 and partly from the Primer of 1706, both altered. Evening Office, 1710.
                                     Author unknown.   98

111, 112 and 113. Pange lingua gloriosi, lauream. See No. 107. 1. *O faithful cross, O noblest tree;* 2. *Sing, O my tongue, devoutly sing;* 3. *Full thirty years were freely spent.* Apparently an original version, the translator, however, having before him the Primer of 1706, and occasionally borrowing from its language. From the Divine Office, 1763.   *Author unknown.*   99, 100

114. Vexilla regis prodeunt. See No. 106. *Behold, the royal banners fly.*   *Prior Aylward.*   101

115, 116 and 117. Pange lingua gloriosi, lauream. See No. 107. 1. *O faithful cross, O peerless tree;* 2. *Sing loud the conflict, O my tongue;* 3. *Now, when full thirty annual suns.*
                                           Prior Aylward.   102

118. Vexilla regis prodeunt. See No. 106. *The King of kings his banner rears.*
                                     Robert Campbell.   104

Contents.

NO.		PAGE
119, 120 and 121.	Pange lingua gloriosi, lauream. See No. 107. 1. *Holy cross, blest tree, outvying* (R.C.); 2. *Sing my tongue, with glowing accents* (T. J. P.); 3. *Soon the sweetest blossom wasting* (R. C.) *R. Campbell and Professor Potter.*	105

Canonical Hours.

PART I.—DAYS OF THE WEEK.

Sunday.

122. Primo die, quo Trinitas. Revised slightly and shortened by the penultimate verse, from *Primo dierum omnium*. Matins Breviary Hymn, by Pope St. Gregory the Great. *To-day the blessed Three in One.*   Cardinal Newman.   108

123. Æterne rerum conditor. Lauds Breviary Hymn, by St. Ambrose. (Slightly revised.) *Maker of the earth and sky.* A fragment.   Robert Campbell.   109

124. Lucis creator optime. Vespers Breviary Hymn, by Pope St. Gregory the Great. (Verbal alterations only.) *Blest Maker of the radiant light.* Primer, 1706.   (*Probably*) *John Dryden.*   110

Monday.

125. Somno refectis artubus. Matins Breviary Hymn, by St. Ambrose. (Verbal alterations only.) *Sleep has refreshed our limbs, we spring.*   Cardinal Newman.   110

126. Splendor Paternæ gloriæ. Lauds Breviary Hymn, by St. Ambrose. (Verbally altered only.) *Splendour of the Father's glory.* Robert Campbell.   111

127. Immense cœli conditor. Ambrosian Vespers Hymn. (Verbally altered only.) *Creator, God immense and wise.* Primer, 1706.   (*Probably*) *John Dryden.*   112

Tuesday.

128. Consors Paterni luminis. Matins Breviary Hymn,

by St. Ambrose. *O God from God, and Light from Light.*   Cardinal Newman.   112

129. Ales diei nuntius. Lauds Breviary Hymn, by Prudentius. *The herald of the morn.*
   Robert Campbell.   113

130. Telluris alme conditor. Ambrosian Vespers Breviary Hymn. (Slight verbal alterations.) *O God, who, when at nature's birth.* Primer, 1706.   (*Probably*) *John Dryden.*   113

Wednesday.

131. Rerum creator optime. Ambrosian Matins Breviary Hymn. (Slight verbal alterations.) *Who madest all and dost control.*
   Cardinal Newman.   114

132. Nox et tenebræ et nubila. Lauds Breviary Hymn, by Prudentius. *Swift as shadows of the night.*   Robert Campbell.   115

133. Cœli Deus sanctissime. Ambrosian Vespers Breviary Hymn. (Verbally changed only.) *O source of light, whose glorious ray.* Primer, 1706.   (*Probably*) *John Dryden.*   115

Thursday.

134. Nox atra rerum contegit. Ambrosian Matins Breviary Hymn. *All tender lights, all hues divine.*   Cardinal Newman.   116

135. Lux ecce surgit aurea. Matins Breviary Hymn, by Prudentius. *As at morn's golden ray.*
   Robert Campbell.   117

136. Magnæ Deus potentiæ. Ambrosian Vespers Breviary Hymn. (Slight verbal changes.) *O God, whose watery stores supply.* Primer, 1706.
   (*Probably*) *John Dryden.*   117

Friday.

137. Tu Trinitatis Unitas. Ambrosian Matins Brevi

Contents. xxi

NO.   PAGE

ary Hymn. (Verbally revised.) *May the dread Three in One, who sways. Cardinal Newman.* 118

138. Æterna cœli gloria. Ambrosian Lauds Breviary Hymn. (Verbally revised.) *Christ, the glory of the sky. Robert Campbell.* 119

139. Hominis superne conditor. Revised (slightly) from *Plasmator hominis Deus.* Ambrosian Vespers Breviary Hymn. *Man's sovereign God, to whom we owe.* Primer, 1706.
(*Probably*) *John Dryden.* 119

Saturday.

140. Summæ parens clementiæ. Revised (verbally) from *Summæ Deus clementiæ.* Ambrosian Matins Breviary Hymn. *Father of mercies infinite. Cardinal Newman.* 120

141. Aurora jam spargit polum. Ambrosian Lauds Breviary Hymn. (With slight verbal revision.) *Morning shines with Eastern light.*
Robert Campbell. 121

142. Jam sol recedit igneus. Vespers Breviary Hymn, by St. Ambrose. *The fiery sun now rolls away.* Primer, 1706. (*Probably*) *John Dryden.* 121

PART II.—HOURS OF THE DAY.

143. Nocte surgentes. Matins Breviary Hymn, by Pope St. Gregory the Great. (Slight verbal change.) *Let us arise and watch by night.*
Cardinal Newman. 122

144. Ecce jam noctis. Lauds Breviary Hymn, by Pope St. Gregory the Great (Revised throughout). *Paler have grown the shades of night.*
Cardinal Newman. 122

145. Jam lucis orto sidere. Ambrosian Breviary Hymn for Prime. *The star of morn to night succeeds.*
Cardinal Newman. 123

146. Nunc sancte nobis Spiritus. Ambrosian Breviary

xxii   *Contents.*

NO.   PAGE
Hymn for Terce. *Come, Holy Ghost, who ever One. Cardinal Newman.* 123

147. Rector potens, verax Deus. Ambrosian Breviary Hymn for Sext. (A single verbal alteration.) *O God, who canst not change nor fail.*
                                         Cardinal Newman. 124

148. Rerum Deus tenax vigor. Ambrosian Breviary Hymn for None. (A verbal alteration only.) *O God, unchangeable and true.*
                                         Cardinal Newman. 124

149. Lucis creator optime. Vespers Breviary Hymn, by Pope St. Gregory the Great. (Only verbally altered.) *Father of lights, by whom each day.*
                                         Cardinal Newman. 124

150. Te lucis ante terminum. Ambrosian Compline Breviary Hymn. (Verbal changes only.) *Now that the daylight dies away. Cardinal Newman.* 125

Easter.

First Week.

151. Ad regias Agni dapes. Re-written throughout (saving verse one) from *Ad cænam Agni providi.* Ambrosian Vespers Breviary Hymn. *Sing, for the dark Red Sea is passed.*
                                    Rev. H. N. Oxenham. 126

152. Chorus novæ Hierusalem. Vespers Hymn from the Salisbury Breviary, by Fulbert, Bishop of Chartres, Tenth-Eleventh Century. *Jerusalem, thy song be new.* *Lord Braye*, 1883. 127

153. Rex sempiterne cœlitum. A fragment, and re-written from *O rex æterne Domine.* Ambrosian Matins Breviary Hymn. *O thou, the heaven's eternal King.* *Father Caswall.* 128

154. Aurora cœlum purpurat. Re-written throughout from *Aurora lucis rutilat;* a hymn of which *Sermone blando angelus* forms a portion. Am-

Contents.

NO.		PAGE
	brosian Lauds Breviary Hymn. *Aurora spreads her cheerful rays.* Primer, 1706. (*Probably*) *John Dryden.*	129
155.	O filii et filiæ. Prose of the Twelfth-Thirteenth Century. Also in the Roman Processional of the Sixteenth Century. *O maids and striplings, hear love's story.* *Charles Kent.*	129

Second Week.

156.	Ad regias Agni dapes. See No. 151. *The Red Sea now is passed, and now.* *J. R. Beste.*	131
157.	Rex sempiterne cœlitum. See No. 153. *Eternal King, whose equal reign.* Primer, 1706. (*Probably*) *John Dryden.*	132
158.	Aurora cœlum purpurat. See No. 154. *The dawn was purpling o'er the sky.* *Father Caswall.*	133
159.	Victimæ paschali laudes. Sequence of the Twelfth-Thirteenth Century from the Missal. *The holy paschal work is wrought.* *Robert Campbell.*	133

Third Week.

160.	Ad regias Agni dapes. See No. 151. *Come to the regal feast displayed.* *Provost Husenbeth.*	134
161.	Aurora lucis rutilat. See No. 154. *The ruddy light now newly born.* *Lord Braye*, 1883.	135
162.	Rex sempiterne cœlitum. See No. 153. *High heaven's eternal Lord.* *Robert Campbell.*	136
163.	O filii et filiæ. See No. 155. *Young men and maids, rejoice and sing.* Evening Office, 1748, and Divine Office, 1763. *Author unknown.*	137

Fourth Week.

164.	Ad regias Agni dapes. See No. 151. *At the Lamb's high feast we sing.* *Robert Campbell.*	138
165.	Aurora cœlum purpurat. See No. 154. *The morn had spread her crimson rays.* *Robert Campbell.*	139
166.	Jesu, Redemptor sæculi. Compline Hymn by C. Coffin, from the Paris Breviary. *Jesu, the earth's Redeemer, thou.* *Robert Campbell.*	140

NO.		PAGE
167.	Victimæ paschali laudes. See No. 159. *Bring, all ye dear-bought nations, bring.* From the complete Office of the Holy Week. *W. K. Blount,* 1670.	141

Fifth Week.

168.	Ad regias Agni dapes. See No. 151. *Now to the Lamb's high festival.* *Professor Potter.*	141
169.	Chorus novæ Hierusalem. See No. 152. *Ye choirs of new Jerusalem.* *Robert Campbell.*	142
170.	Sermone blando angelus. See No. 154. *The angel's gracious message came.* *J. C. Earle,* 1883.	143
171.	O filii et filiæ. See No. 155. *Ye sons and daughters of the Lord.* *Father Caswall.*	144

Sixth Week.

172.	Ad regias Agni dapes. See No. 151. *The Red Sea's dangers now are past.* Evening Office, 1710. *Author unknown.*	145
173.	Adeste, cœlitum chori. Matins Hymn by le Tourneux, from the Paris Breviary. *Heavenly choirs with anthems sweet.* *R. Campbell and J. C. Earle.*	146
174.	Sermone blando angelus. See No. 154. *How sweet those words of soothing were.* *Lord Braye,* 1883.	148
175.	Jesu, Redemptor sæculi. See No. 166. *Jesus, who didst redeem mankind.* *J. C. Earle,* 1883.	149
176.	Victimæ paschali laudes. See No. 159. *Christians, your voices raise.* *Anonymous,* 1868.	149

Ascension.

Part One.

177.	Salutis humanæ Sator. Re-written from *Jesu, nostra Redemptio.* Ambrosian Vespers Breviary Hymn. *Saviour of men, who dost impart.* *Provost Husenbeth.*	151

Contents. xxv

NO.		PAGE
178.	Æterne rex altissime. Revised and shortened from older Hymn with the same beginning, of which *Tu, Christe, nostrum gaudium* is a portion. Matins Breviary Hymn, Sixth-Ninth Century. *O thou eternal King most high.* Father Caswall.	151
179.	Tu, Christe, nostrum gaudium. See No. 178. *O Christ, the source of our delight.* J. C. Earle, 1883.	152

Part Two.

180.	Salutis humanæ Sator. See No. 177. *Jesus, who man's Redeemer art.* Evening Office, 1710. Author unknown.	153
181.	Opus peregisti tuum. Vespers Hymn from the Paris Breviary, by C. Coffin. *Thy sacred race, O Lord, is run.* R. Campbell and J. C. Earle.	154
182.	Sensus quis horror percutit? Matins Hymn from the Paris Breviary, by de Santeuil. *Fearful thought of endless doom.* Robert Campbell.	155

Part Three.

183.	Salutis humanæ Sator. See No. 177. *Jesu, slain for earth's release.* Robert Campbell.	156
184.	Jesu, nostra Redemptio. See No. 177. *Jesu, our ransom from above.* Prior Aylward.	157
185.	Æterne rex altissime. See No. 178. *O Saviour Christ, O God most high.* Primer, 1706. (Probably) John Dryden.	158

Part Four.

186.	Salutis humanæ Sator. See No. 177. *Hail thou, who man's Redeemer art.* Professor Potter.	158
187.	Felix dies mortalibus. Vespers Hymn from the Paris Breviary by de Santeuil. *O day, so dear to man once lost.* Robert Campbell.	159
188.	Jesu, nostra Redemptio. See No. 177. *O Jesu, our redemption.* Father Caswall.	160

Whit-Sunday.

Part One.

NO.   PAGE

189. Veni, creator Spiritus. Vespers Breviary Hymn, ascribed to Charlemagne, though it is probably earlier than the Eighth Century. *Creator-Spirit, all-divine.*   *Prior Aylward.*   161

190. Jam Christus astra ascenderat. Revised from an earlier hymn, with the same beginning. Ambrosian Matins Breviary Hymn. *Above the starry spheres.*   *Father Caswall.*   162

191. Beata nobis gaudia. (Slight verbal revision only.) Lauds Breviary Hymn by St. Hilary, Bishop of Poitiers, Fourth Century. *The rolling year pursues its way.* Primer, 1706.
(*Probably*) *John Dryden.*   163

192. Veni, sancte Spiritus. Sequence from the Missal, by King Robert II. of France. *Come, O Spirit, Lord of grace.* Verses 4 and 6, J. C. E.
R. Campbell and J. C. Earle.   164

Part Two.

193. Veni, creator Spiritus. See No. 189. *Creating Spirit, come, possess.* Evening Office, 1710.
Author unknown.   165

194. Beata nobis gaudia. See No. 191. *Hail, this joyful day's return.*   *Robert Campbell.*   166

195. Veni, sancte Spiritus. See No. 192. *Come, Holy Ghost, to us send down.*   *J. R. Beste.*   166

Part Three.

196. Veni, creator Spiritus. See No. 189. *Creator-Spirit, from thy throne.*   *Provost Husenbeth.*   167

197. Jam Christus astra ascenderat. See No. 190. *Now, far above the starry plain.*
Prior Aylward.   168

198. Veni, sancte Spiritus. See No. 192. *Come, Holy Ghost, send down those beams.* Divine Office, 1763.   *Author unknown.*   169

Contents. xxvii

Part Four.

NO.		PAGE
199.	Veni, creator Spiritus. See No. 189. *Creator-Spirit, Lord of grace.* Robert Campbell.	170
200.	Jam Christus astra ascenderat. See No. 190. *Now Christ had pierced the skies to claim.* Primer, 1706. (*Probably*) *John Dryden.*	171
201.	Beata nobis gaudia. See No. 191. *Again the slowly circling year.* Father Caswall.	172
202.	Veni, sancte Spiritus. See No. 192. *Holy Spirit, come and shine.* Prior Aylward.	173

Trinity Sunday.

Part One.

203. Jam sol recedit igneus. Vespers Breviary Hymn, by St. Ambrose. *Behold, the radiant sun departs.* Robert Campbell. 175

204. Summæ parens clementiæ. Revised slightly from *Summæ Deus clementiæ.* Ambrosian Matins Breviary Hymn. *O God, by whose command is swayed.* Primer, 1706.
(*Probably*) *John Dryden.* 175

Part Two.

205. Jam sol recedit igneus. See No. 203. *The fiery sun now rolls away.* Evening Office, 1710.
Author unknown. 176

206. Tu Trinitatis Unitas. (Slight verbal alterations.) Ambrosian Lauds Breviary Hymn. *O thou, who dost all nature sway.* Father Caswall. 176

Part Three.

207. Jam sol recedit igneus. Hours of the Holy Trinity. *Blest Light, eternal Trinity.*
Prior Aylward. 177

Part Four.

208. Jam sol recedit igneus. See No. 203. *While fades the glowing sun away.* Professor Potter. 178
209. Tu Trinitatis Unitas. See No. 206. *Thou great mysterious Three and One.* Primer, 1706. (*Probably*) John Dryden. 178

Part Five.

210. Jam sol recedit igneus. See No. 203. *Behold the fiery sun recede.* Provost Husenbeth. 179
211. Tu Trinitatis Unitas. See No. 206. *Blest Three in One and One in Three.* Robert Campbell. 179

Corpus Christi.

Part One.

212. Pange lingua gloriosi corporis. Vespers Breviary Hymn by St. Thomas Aquinas, Thirteenth Century. *Sing, my joyful tongue, the mystery.*
Prior Aylward. 180
213. Sacris solemniis juncta sint gaudia. Matins Breviary Hymn by St. Thomas Aquinas. *Let old things pass away.* Father Caswall. 181
214. Verbum supernum prodiens, nec. Lauds Breviary Hymn by St. Thomas Aquinas. *The Word supernal from the heavens descending.*
Charles Kent. 182
215. Lauda, Sion, Salvatorem. Sequence from the Missal by St. Thomas Aquinas. *Zion, thy Redeemer praising.* From Lyra Ecclesiastica. Rev. Athanasius Diedrich Wackerbarth, 1842-1843. 183

Part Two.

216. Pange lingua gloriosi corporis. See No. 212. *Hail, the body bright and glorious.*
Robert Campbell. 185

Contents. xxix

NO.   PAGE

217. Verbum supernum prodiens, nec. See No. 214.
The eternal God, by human birth. Primer, 1706.
(Probably) John Dryden. 186

218. Adoro te devote, latens Deitas. Rhyme of St. Thomas Aquinas. *Thee prostrate I adore, the Deity that lies.*   *Prior Aylward.* 187

Part Three.

219. Pange lingua gloriosi corporis. See No. 212.
Sing, my tongue, the body glorious.
Rev. H. N. Oxenham. 188

220. Adoro te devote, latens Deitas. See No. 218.
Hidden God, devoutly I adore thee. From Emmanuel: a Book of Eucharistic Verses, 1878.
Justice John O'Hagan, 1874. 189

221. Verbum supernum prodiens, nec. See No. 214.
Proceeding forth the Word supernal.
Prior Aylward. 190

Part Four.

222. Pange lingua gloriosi corporis. See No. 212. *Of the glorious body bleeding. Rev. A. D. Wackerbarth.* 191

223. Sacris solemniis juncta sint gaudia. See No. 213.
Welcome with jubilee.   *Prior Aylward.* 192

224. Verbum supernum prodiens, nec. See No. 214.
Word of God to earth descending.
Robert Campbell. 193

225. Lauda, Sion, Salvatorem. See No. 215. *Sing forth, O Sion, sweetly sing.*   *Prior Aylward.* 194

Sacred Heart of Jesus.

Part One.

226. Auctor beate sæculi. Vespers Breviary Hymn.
O Christ, the world's creator bright.
Provost Husenbeth. 197

227. En, ut superba criminum. Matins Breviary Hymn. *Lo, how the savage crew.*
Father Caswall. 198

228. Cor, arca legem continens. Lauds Breviary

Contents.

NO.   PAGE

Hymn. *Jesus, behind thy temple's veil.* The Roman Breviary, 1879.   *Anonymous.* 198

Part Two.

229. Quicumque certum quæritis. Vespers Hymn from the Franciscan Breviary. *Haste, all who 'mid life's thorny ways. Professor Potter.* 199

230. Summi Parentis filio. Lauds Hymn from the Franciscan Breviary. *To Christ, the Prince of peace. Father Caswall.* 200

Part Three.

231. Auctor beate sæculi. See No. 226. *Great Maker of the world's wide frame. Professor Potter.* 201

232. En, ut superba criminum. See No. 227. *Of sin and love the Lord had died.* The Roman Breviary, 1879. *Anonymous.* 202

233. Cor, arca legem continens. See No. 228. *O tender Heart, strong ark which doth enshrine. Rosa Mulholland,* 1883. 203

Transfiguration.

Part One.

234. Quicumque Christum quæritis. Vespers Breviary Hymn from the Cathemerinon of Prudentius. *O ye who seek the Lord. Cardinal Newman.* 204

235. Quicumque Christum quæritis. See No. 234. *O ye, the truly wise. Robert Campbell.* 204

236. Lux alma, Jesu, mentium. Lauds Breviary Hymn. *O Christ, when thy chaste light inspires.* Primer, 1706. *(Probably) John Dryden.* 205

Part Two.

237. Quicumque Christum quæritis. See No. 234. *All you who seek the Lord of love. Professor Potter.* 206

Contents. xxxi

NO.		PAGE
238.	Lux alma, Jesu, mentium. See No. 236. *Light of the troubled heart.* *Robert Campbell.*	206

Part Three.

239. Quicumque Christum quæritis. See No. 234. *All that desire with Christ to rise.* A cento, 1706–1763.   *Author unknown.*   207
240. Quicumque Christum quæritis. See No. 234. *O you who truly seek your Lord.*   *Provost Husenbeth.*   208
241. Lux alma, Jesu, mentium. See No. 236. *Light of the anxious heart.*   *Cardinal Newman.*   208

Holy Redeemer.

Part One.

242. Creator alme siderum. See No. 1. *Great Maker of the glittering stars.*   *Professor Potter.*   210
243. Jesu dulcis memoria. See No. 48. *The memory of Jesus blest.*   *Justice John O'Hagan.*   211

Part Two.

244. Creator alme siderum. See No. 1. *Creator of the stars above.*   *Provost Husenbeth.*   212
245. Jesu, dulcis memoria. See No. 48. *Jesus, the only thought of thee.* Primer, 1706.   *(Probably) John Dryden.*   213

Part Three.

246. Creator alme siderum. See No. 1. *Creator of the starry pole.*   *Cardinal Newman.*   215
247. Jesu, dulcis memoria. See No. 48. *Jesu, how sweet the thought of thee.*   *J. R. Beste.*   215 ✓

Holy Cross.

Part One.

248. Vexilla regis prodeunt. See No. 106. *The great King's banner shines above.*   *Provost Husenbeth.*   218

xxxii   *Contents.*

NO.   PAGE

249. Ita suos fortiores. *Thus its votaries it assureth.*
                            Rev. A. D. Wackerbarth. 219
250. Patris sapientiæ, veritas divina. Little Hours of the Holy Cross. *'Twas at the solemn Matins-hour, when by the traitor's sign.*
                                  Prior Aylward. 219

Part Two.

251. Laudes crucis attollamus. Rythmical Hymn in praise of the Holy Cross. *Come, let us with glad music.* From Horst's Paradise of the Christian Soul.   *Howel W. Lloyd,* 1850. 222

Part Three.

252. Vexilla regis prodeunt. See No. 106. *See, see the royal banners fly.*   *J. R. Beste.* 225
253. Salva crux sancta. *All hail, O cross divine.*
                                  Prior Aylward. 226
254. Patris sapientiæ, veritas divina. Little Hours of the Holy Cross. *As night departing brings the day.* Primer, 1706. *(Probably) John Dryden.* 227

PART I.
HYMNS FROM THE SACRED OFFICES.

Annus Sanctus

HYMNS OF THE CHURCH

Advent.

First Week of Advent.

Creator alme siderum.

BRIGHT Maker of the starry poles,
Eternal light of faithful souls,
Christ, man's deliverer, espouse
Our cause and hear our humble vows.
　Who, lest the frauds of hell's black king
Should mankind to destruction bring,
Didst, by an act of generous love,
The fainting world's physician prove.
　Who, that thou mightst our ransom pay
And wash the stains of sin away,
Wouldst from a Virgin's womb proceed,
And on the cross a victim bleed.
　Whose glorious power, whose saving name
No sooner any voice can frame,
But heaven and earth and hell agree
To honour them with trembling knee.
　Thee, of the last accounting day
The sovereign judge, we humbly pray,
Of heavenly grace such plenty send,
As may thy Church from foes defend.
　Let endless times aloud proclaim
The glory, power, praise and name
Of God, the Father and the Son
And Holy Spirit, Three in One.

Evening Office, 1710.

Verbum supernum prodiens.

Supernal Word, proceeding from
   The eternal Father's breast,
And in the end of ages come
   To aid a world distrest;

Enlighten, Lord, and set on fire
   Our spirits with thy love,
That, dead to earth, they may aspire
   And live to joys above.

That, when the judgment-seat on high
   Shall fix the sinner's doom,
And to the just a glad voice cry,
   Come to your destined home;

Safe from the black and yawning lake
   Of restless, endless pain,
We may the face of God partake,
   The bliss of heaven attain.

To God the Father, God the Son
   And Holy Ghost, to thee,
As heretofore, when time is done,
   Unending glory be.
Cardinal Newman.

Instantis adventum Dei.

The coming of our God
   Our thoughts must now employ;
Then let us meet him on the road
   With songs of holy joy.

The co-eternal Son,
   A Maiden's offspring see;
A servant's form Christ putteth on,
   His people to make free.

Mother of saints, arise
   To greet thine infant king,

Advent: First Week.

And do not thanklessly despise
  The pardon he doth bring.

In glory from his throne
  Again will Christ descend,
And summon all that are his own
  To joys that never end.

Let deeds of darkness fly
  Before the approaching morn,
For unto sin 'tis ours to die,
  And serve the Virgin-born.

Our joyful praises sing
  To Christ, that set us free;
Like tribute to the Father bring,
  And Holy Ghost to thee.

R. Campbell.

Vox clara ecce intonat.

Clear rings a voice; it chides the world
In clouds of nightly dimness furled;
Darkness away, begone, vain dreams,
'Tis Christ from highest heaven gleams.

Awake, ye souls, benumbed and chill,
Stained, wounded, by your sinful will;
Lift up your eyes and see the star
Whose rays are balm for every scar.

Sent from above, the Lamb is nigh,
To pay our debts he deigns to die;
Therefore forgiveness brought so near
Make we our own by prayer and tear:

So that hereafter, when he come
To strike the world with judgment dumb,
Our guilt may not provoke his arm,
But mercy keep us from the harm.

Praise, honour, power, glorious praise
To Father and to Son upraise;
To Paraclete like tribute be,
A triple praise eternally.

Lord Braye.

En, clara vox redarguit.

A heavenly voice and early ray
Now chide the lazy night away;
With watchful hearts and waking eyes,
Behold the sun of justice rise.

O rising Sun, attract our mind,
Like morning dew from earth refined,
That we may learn with thee to rise,
And pay our morning sacrifice.

Behold, the Lamb is sent to pay
The debt our nature can't defray;
May all, at least, compound the arrears
With humbled hearts and grateful tears.

That when he late returns in ire,
To judge the trembling world by fire,
We may escape the judge, and find
A God, a father and a friend.

May each succeeding age proclaim
Thy glory and eternal fame,
And sing with the celestial host,
The Father, Son and Holy Ghost.

Primer, 1706.

Dies iræ, dies illa.

Day of wrath, that day whose knelling
Gives to flame this earthly dwelling;
Psalm and Sibyl thus foretelling.

Oh, what agony of trembling,
When the judge mankind assembling,
Probeth all beyond dissembling.

Advent: First Week.

Pealing wondrous through the regions,
Shall the trumpet force obedience,
And the graves yield up their legions.

Startled death and nature sicken,
Thus to see the creature quicken,
Waiting judgment terror-stricken.

Open, then, with all recorded,
Stands the book from whence awarded
Doom shall pass with deed accorded.

When the judge is throned in session,
All things hid shall find confession,
Unavenged be no transgression.

Wretch, what then shall be my pleading?
Who my patron interceding?
Scarce the just securely speeding.

Thou, O king of awful splendour,
Saving grace dost freely render;
Save me, fount of pity tender.

Think, 'twas I, my lost condition,
Caused, O pitying Lord, thy mission;
Spare my soul that day's perdition.

Seeking me, thy footstep hasted;
Me to save, the cross was tasted;
Be not toil so mighty wasted.

Righteous judge of retribution,
Grant the gift of absolution
Ere the day of restitution.

Me my culprit heart accuses;
Inmost guilt my face suffuses;
Heal, O Lord, thy suppliant's bruises.

Thou who Mary's sin hast shriven,
Thou who broughtst the thief to heaven,
Hope to me hast also given.

Nothing worth is mine endeavour,
Yet, in ruth, my soul deliver
·From the flame that burns for ever.

With thy sheep, thy chosen, place me,
Severed from the goats embrace me;
On thy right-hand, ransomed, place me.

When the reprobate confounded
Lie with wrathful fire surrounded,
May my call to bliss be sounded.

Crushed to dust and prostrate bending,
All my heart contrition rending;
I implore thee, gua'rd my ending.

Oh, that awful day of mourning,
When, from earthly dust returning,

Guilty man shall bide his sentence;
Spare him, God, for his repentance.

Jesus, Lord, thy mercy lending,
Grant them rest, thy rest unending.

J. O'Hagan.

Second Week of Advent.

Conditor alme siderum.

Thou builder of the starry skies,
   Thou light of every faithful breast,
Thou, our redeeming sacrifice,
   Oh, hear the vows to thee addressed:
Who, lest the fraudful demon-foe
Should work the world too deep a woe,
Thyself, for very love, wouldst be
Its healing balm and remedy.

Pure from thy Maiden-mother's womb
   The toilsome pathway thou wouldst trace
E'en to the cross, to change the doom
   And cleanse the guilt of all our race:

Advent: Second Week.

To sing thy glories heavenly bright,
Thy name, thy power, let all unite;
And things above and things below
To thee in trembling reverence bow.

Dread judge and righteous, grant that we,
  When thou shalt come to judge our race,
Safe from our foe may guarded be
  With the bright panoply of grace :
Be honour, praise and glory shown
To God the Father, God the Son
And to the Paraclete divine,
While heaven's eternal glories shine.
J. D. Aylward.

Verbum supernum prodiens.

O thou, who thine own Father's breast
  Forsaking, Word sublime,
Didst come to aid a world distressed
  In thy appointed time ;
Our hearts enlighten with thy ray,
  And kindle with thy love ;
That, dead to earthly things, we may
  Live but to things above.
So when before the judgment-seat
  The sinner hears his doom,
And when a voice divinely sweet
  Shall call the righteous home ;
Safe from the black and fiery flood
  That sweeps the dread abyss,
May we behold the face of God
  In everlasting bliss.
To God the Father, with the Son
  And Spirit evermore,
Be glory while the ages run,
  As in all time before.
E. Caswall.

Vox clara terris nos gravi.

A thrilling voice rings clear and high,
  To rouse from sleep the slumber-bound;
Sink night, and all her shadows fly—
  Salvation is for mortals found.

The expected time at length is here;
  Rain down, ye heavens, and give us God,
Ye clouds; and let the just appear,
  Birth of the germinating sod.

The world's health thou; the Father's Word,
  To thee afflicted Sion prays;
Oh, let the mourner's prayer be heard,
  And from the ground the sinner raise.

Come, O Redeemer, and at last
  Relieve thy people from their sin;
Heaven's-gates thy Father's wrath shut fast
  Open, and let the suppliants in.

To thee be glory uttermost,
  Whom we the world's Redeemer know,
With Father and with Holy Ghost,
  While ages everlasting flow.
                              H. I. D. Ryder.

In noctis umbra desides.

When clouds of darkness veil the sky,
And wrapt in sleep our bodies lie,
The faithful soul more freely may
Herself arouse to watch and pray.
  Desired of all, thou Lord of grace,
Redeemer of our ruined race,
Oh, hear the cries of them that groan,
The prayers of those by sin o'erthrown,
  Lord Jesus, come, our debt forgive,
And bid thy ransomed children live;

Advent: Second Week.

If death our doom in Adam be,
Eternal life we claim in thee.
To Christ, who comes our bonds to break,
In praises let our souls awake;
The Father equally adore,
And Holy Spirit evermore.

R. Campbell.

Dies iræ, dies illa.

Day of wrath, the heart dismaying—
Hear the king and Sibyl saying—
Earth shall melt in flames decaying.

Oh, what fear and bitter crying
Shall there be when, all things trying,
Comes the judge, the All-descrying.

Through the tombs of nations swelling
Thrills the trump, of judgment telling,
All before the throne compelling.

Death and time in consternation
Then shall stand, while all creation
Rises at that dread citation.

Lo, the open book is giving
Witness sure to dead and living,
And the world its doom receiving.

Then the judge shall sit, revealing
Every hidden thought and feeling,
Unto each requital dealing.

Who will aid me, interceding,
For a wretched sinner pleading,
When the just thy grace are needing?

Heavenly king of dreadful splendour,
Fount of love and pity tender,
Be my Saviour and defender.

Thou didst bear for my salvation
Toil and anguish and privation;
Leave me not to condemnation.

Weary didst thou seek me straying,
On the cross my ransom paying;
By thy passion hear my praying.

God of justice, my petition
Hear, and grant me full remission,
Ere that awful day's decision.

Shame and grief my soul oppressing,
I bewail my life's transgressing;
Spare me, Lord, my sins confessing.

Thou didst spare the sinner grieving,
Thou didst save the thief believing,
Me, too, hope of pardon leaving.

Worthless are my prayers and mourning,
Yet, good Lord, in pity yearning,
Save me from the endless burning.

With the sheep assign my station
On thy right-hand of salvation,
At that fearful separation.

When the sentence dread is given,
And the lost to hell are driven,
Call me with the blest to heaven.

Conscious guilt my spirit lading,
Hear, O God, my self-upbraiding;
Come, in death thy suppliant aiding.

Oh, that day of tears and trembling—
From the wreck of worlds assembling,
Guilty sinners stand before thee;
Spare them, God, we here implore thee:
Lord of mercy, Jesu blest,
Grant them everlasting rest. *F. J. P.*

Third Week of Advent.

Creator alme siderum.

Maker of the starry sphere,
Light to all thy people dear,
Jesu, Saviour, Lord of all,
Hearken to thy people's call.
　When our nature fainting lay,
Crushed by Satan's cruel sway,
Blest physician, 'twas thy love
Brought us healing from above.
　In the blessed Mary's womb
Purest flesh thou didst assume,
That to God above might rise
The all-holy sacrifice.
　Unto heaven exalted now,
At thy sacred name shall bow
All that on the earth do dwell,
All in heaven, and all in hell.
　Thou, who on the judgment-day
Our most secret thoughts shalt weigh,
Shield us now with pitying care,
Guard us from temptation's snare.
　Honour, glory, love and praise,
Be through never-ending days,
To the Father and the Son
And the Spirit, Three in One.
　　　　　　　　　R. Campbell.

Verbum supernum prodiens.

Supernal Word, who didst proceed
　Forth from the Father, conquering aid,
Who, in our time of desperate need,
　A Child of man for men wast made :

Shine in our bosoms, shine ;
Burn up what is not thine ;

And by thy glorious gospel chase
Far hence all spirits foul and base.

So when, as judge, thine eye
Our secrets shall descry,
And nothing shall pass by,
And thou wilt ill for ill
And good for good in measure strict fulfil,

We may not for our wilful sin
The just rewards of evil win,
But at the very fount of joy
Our virgin-hearts in praise employ.

To God the Father and the Son
   Our songs with one accord we raise ;
And to the Holy Spirit, one
   With them, be ever equal praise.

J. C. Earle.

Jordanis oras prævia.

What sound doth Jordan's streams appal?
   The Baptist's voice they hear ;
Before that herald's solemn call
   Let soft sleep disappear.

Ocean and earth and ambient air
   Their maker's advent know ;
Their tremors his approach declare,
   Their joys his presence show.

Make straight the way, cleanse every breast
   For God who draweth nigh ;
Prepare for such a worthy guest
   Due hospitality.

Thou, Jesus, hast our bulwark stood,
   Thou our unfailing aid ;
Deprived of thee—as we of food—
   The race of man doth fade.

Unto the sick thy saving hand
  Grant, nor the prostrate spurn ;
Show forth thy face ; and straight command
  That grace to earth return.

To thee, who camst to set us free,
  O God the Son, be praise ;
To thee, O Father, and to thee
  Blest Spirit, through all days.

W. M. A.

En, clara vox redarguit.
Hark, an awful voice is sounding ;
  ' Christ is nigh,' it seems to say ;
' Cast away the dreams of darkness,
  O ye children of the day.'

Startled at the solemn warning,
  Let the earth-bound soul arise ;
Christ her sun, all sloth dispelling,
  Shines upon the morning skies.

Lo, the Lamb so long expected,
  Comes with pardon down from heaven ;
Let us haste, with tears of sorrow,
  One and all to be forgiven.

So when next he comes with glory,
  Wrapping all the earth in fear,
May he then as our defender
  On the clouds of heaven appear.

Honour, glory, virtue, merit,
  To the Father and the Son,
With the co-eternal Spirit,
  While eternal ages run.

E. Caswall.

Dies iræ, dies illa.
That day of wrath, that dreadful day,
When heaven and earth shall pass away,
Both David and the Sibyl say.

What terror then shall us befal,
When lo, the judge's steps appal,
About to sift the deeds of all.

The mighty trumpet's marvellous tone
Shall pierce through each sepulchral stone,
And summon all before the throne.

Now death and nature in amaze
Behold the Lord his creatures raise,
To meet the judge's awful gaze.

The books are opened, that the dead
May have their doom from what is read,
The record of our conscience dread.

At length the judge his seat hath ta'en,
And nothing hidden may remain,
While each receives its mead of pain.

What then shall I most wretched say?
Or whom to advocate me pray?
When scarce the just is saved that day?

O king, of dread inspiring face,
Who savest freely, fount of grace,
Amongst thy saved ones grant me place.

Remember, Jesu, for my sake
Thou didst thy manhood undertake,
Thou wilt not, Lord, thine own forsake.

In weariness thy sheep was sought;
Upon the cross his life was bought;
Alas, if all in vain were wrought.

Thou righteous judge that dost repay,
Oh, grant me pardon while I may,
Before that dreadful reckoning day.

In sense of guilt I wretched groan;
Mine eyes with conscious shame cast down;
Oh, spare me suppliant at thy throne.

For thou who loosedst Mary's grief,
And heardst upon thy cross the thief,
E'en me hast granted hope's relief.

My feeble prayers can make no claim,
Yet, gracious Lord, for thy great name,
Redeem me from the quenchless flame.

Amongst the sheep, oh, bid me stand,
And severed from the goats' lost band,
Dispose me on thy glad right-hand.

When thou the cursed shalt confound,
In bitter chains for ever bound,
Let me amongst the blest be found.

In suppliant prayer I prostrate bend,
My contrite heart like ashes rend,
Regard, O Lord, my latter end.

Oh, on that day, that tearful day,
When man to judgment wakes from clay,

Be thou the trembling sinner's stay,
And spare him, God, we humbly pray.

Holy Jesu, Lord most high,
Grant them rest for whom we cry.
W. F. Wingfield.

Fourth Week of Advent.

Conditor alme siderum.

O thou, the maker of each star,
True light of all who faithful are,
Redeemer, Christ, bow down thine ear
Our supplicating voice to hear.

Who, moved with grief that earth should lie
Sin's victim destined but to die,
Didst save the weary world and give
An healing means that it might live.

When fell the evening of our race,
And darkling clouds did lower apace,
Forth from a Maiden's purest womb,
As from thy chamber, thou didst come.

Thee, girt with strength, most mighty, thee
Adores on earth each bended knee;
All things in earth, all things in heaven,
Own by thy look their life was given.

Most holy Lord, to thee we pray,
The world's dread judge the world's last day,
Preserve us every passing year,
Safe from our foeman's loathèd spear.

Praise, honour, power, glorious praise
To Father and to Son upraise;
To Paraclete like tribute be,
A triple praise eternally.
Lord Braye.

Statuta decreto Dei.

Predestinate of God most high,
The appointed times are drawing nigh;
Purchased by cost of many a year,
The heavenly day at length shines clear.
   By crime too horrible to say,
The Father's offspring wounded lay;
Beneath the deepest shade of death
The race of Adam drew its breath.
   Victims of heaven's undying ire,
Devoted to eternal fire,
Their souls possest by ceaseless fear
Until the just judge should draw near.
   Ah, of such ruin, who shall dare
The heavy losses to repair?
For wound so terrible, what hand
A healing unction can command?

Thou Christ, thou canst, and thou alone,
Thou, who didst leave thy proper throne;
Thou to thine image canst restore
The loveliness which once it bore.

Drop down, ye heavens, supernal grace;
Let earth the Holy One embrace;
And her rich bosom opening
To a lost world salvation bring.

Honour and praise to thee, O Lord,
Incarnate, consubstantial Word;
To Father and to Spirit be,
Now and through all eternity.
W. M. A.

Verbum supernum prodiens.

The period is come; and lo, to-day
The Son of God begins his way,
To rescue at his wondrous birth
A world enslaved to sin and earth.

Our minds, O God, with light inspire,
And warm our hearts with heavenly fire,
'Till flaming with seraphic love
We relish only things above.

That at the great and dreadful day,
When heaven and hell contend for prey,
And Christ our judge appoints for this
Damnation, and for the other bliss;

Our lot with theirs maynt be the same
Who feed an unconsuming flame;
But rather grant, that we may see
Thy heavenly face eternally.

To God, the Father and the Son
And Holy Spirit, Three in One,
Be endless glory, as before
The world began, so evermore.
Primer, 1706.

Instantis adventum Dei.

The advent of our God at hand,
Let us with ardent prayer demand,
And grasp the gifts of grace sublime,
With psalms and hymns of festal rhyme.

    The eternal offspring doth not scorn
Of Maiden-mother to be born ;
Is made a servant, that our yoke
Of sin and slavery may be broke.

    He comes, he comes, the clement Child ;
Haste, Sion, meet thy Saviour mild,
Nor spurn the gracious terms of peace
He offers for thy soul's release.

    Soon folded in a cloud of light
He will return the world to right,
And through the heaven's triumphal arch
His feet will speed their radiant march.

    Let darkness and her demon spawn
Recede before the hastening dawn ;
Let the old Adam yield to grace,
The Second Adam hold his place.

    O thou who com'st to set us free,
O Son, be highest praise to thee—
The Father and the Spirit, Three
In undivided Unity.

J. C. Earle.

En, clara vox redarguit.

Hark, a joyful voice is thrilling,
  And each dim and winding way
Of the ancient temple filling ;
  Dreams depart, for it is day.
Christ is coming—from thy bed,
  Earth-bound soul, awake and spring—

With the sun new-risen to shed
  Health on human suffering.
Lo, to grant a pardon free,
  Comes a willing Lamb from heaven ;
Sad and tearful, hasten we,
  One and all, to be forgiven.
Once again he comes in light
  Girding earth with fear and woe ;
Lord, be thou our loving might,
  From our guilt and ghostly foe.
To the Father and the Son
  And the Spirit, who in heaven
Ever witness, Three and One,
  Praise on earth be ever given.

Cardinal Newman.

Dies iræ, dies illa.

That day of wrath and grief and shame,
Shall fold the world in sheeted flame,
As psalm and Sibyl songs proclaim.

What terror on each breast shall lie
When, downward from the bending sky,
The judge shall come our souls to try.

The trump, through death's dominions blown,
Shall summon with a dreadful tone
The buried nations round the throne.

Nature and death in dumb surprise
Shall see the ancient dead arise,
To stand before the judge's eyes.

And lo, the written book appears,
Which all that faithful record bears,
From whence the world its sentence hears.

The Lord of judgment sits him down,
And every secret thing makes known ;
No crime escapes his vengeful frown.

Ah, how shall I that day endure?
What patron's friendly voice secure,
When scarce the just themselves are sure?

O king of dreadful majesty,
Who grantest grace and mercy free,
Grant mercy now and grace to me.

Good Lord, 'twas for my sinful sake,
That thou our suffering flesh didst take;
Then do not now my soul forsake.

Thou soughtest me when I had strayed;
Thy blood divine my ransom paid;
Shall all that love be fruitless made?

O just avenging judge, I pray,
For pity take my sins away,
Before the great accounting-day.

I groan beneath the guilt, which thou
Canst read upon my blushing brow;
But spare, O God, thy suppliant now.

Thou, who didst Mary's sins unbind,
And mercy for the robber find,
Dost fill with hope my anxious mind.

Though worthless all my prayers appear,
Still let me not, my Saviour dear,
The everlasting burnings bear.

Give me at thy right hand a place,
Amongst thy sheep, a child of grace,
Far from the goats' accursed race.

Yea, when thy justly kindled ire
Shall bind the lost in chains of fire,
Oh, call me to thy chosen choir.

Lo, here I plead and suppliant bend,
Nor cease my contrite heart to rend,
That so thou spare me in the end.

Oh, on that day, that day of weeping,
When man shall wake from death's dark sleeping,

To stand before his judge divine,
Save, save this trembling soul of mine :

Yea, grant to all, O Saviour blest,
Who die in thee, the saints' sweet rest.

J. D. Aylward.

Christmas and Circumcision.

Part One.
Jesu, Redemptor omnium.

JESU, our soul's redeeming Lord,
The God by loving hearts adored,
Who ere the dawn of primal light
Didst share in all the Father's might;

Glad brightness of thy Father's rays,
The crowning hope of all our days,
Whilst through the world thy children bend,
Oh, to our lowly prayers attend.

Remember, Lord, thou didst assume
Within thy stainless Mother's womb
Our mortal form, that clad in flesh
Thou mightst our sinking souls refresh.

As yearly comes this solemn day,
Glad homage all thy children pay,
Its tidings sweet they all confess,
And thee, their sole Redeemer, bless.

The heavens above, the rolling main
And all that earth's wide realms contain,
With joyous voice now loudly sing
The glory of their new-born king.

And we, too, ransomed by the tide
Which issued from thy sacred side,
On this thy natal-day rejoice,
And homage pay with eager voice.

Jesu, to thee, the Virgin's Son,
Be everlasting homage done;

To God the Father we repeat
The same, and to the Paraclete.

T. J. Potter.

Jam desinant suspiria.

Now signs of mourning disappear,
God from on high doth deign to hear;
Comes through the gates of heaven wide
The promised peace to man supplied.

Lo, breaking in upon the night,
The choir supernal meets our sight;
The tidings of their joyful lay
Tell of the Saviour's birth to-day.

As press the little shepherd throng
To hallowed cave the path along,
Go we with them and kiss the shrine,
The manger-wood they found for sign.

What manner of a sight is this
That opens on us for our bliss—
Poor swaddling-clothes, the crib, the straw,
Mother and Child so poor they saw?

Is this the Christ, the Son of God,
Who in the eternal light abode?
O little Infant, hushed and calm,
Bear'st thou the worlds upon that palm?

E'en so, and faith can move afar
The clouds that round thy being are;
I know thee him whom angels see,
Adoring thy divinity.

Teaching in silence from that chair,
Thou wouldst a doctrine new declare—
All that the flesh desires, to shun;
To all it dreads, to boldly run.

O nourisher of loves most pure,
For human pride the sovereign cure ;
In these our hearts this Christmas-morn
Deign, Child eternal, to be born.
Lord Braye.

Felix dies, quam proprio.
Blest day, when from the Saviour flowed
The precious drops of infant blood ;
Blest day, on which began the doom
That leads him to the cross and tomb.

Behold, he hastens to fulfil
His heavenly Father's holy will ;
The law's own Lord the law obeys,
The sinless blood for sinners pays.

The law that made the Saviour bleed
Must fall, and love's own law succeed ;
O Saviour, in our conscience write
Thy law, and stamp thine image bright.

Jesu, the Virgin-born, thy praise
Be sung through never-ending days ;
The Father and the Spirit be
Adored alike, O Lord, with Thee.
R. Campbell.

A solis ortus cardine.
From every part o'er which the sun
Does in its rolling compass run,
May creatures all conspire to sing
The praises of our new-born king.

The God of nature, for our sake,
Our servile nature chose to take ;
With flesh to lend our flesh his aid,
And save the works his hand had made.

In Mary's womb he takes his place,
And there erects his seat of grace ;
In silence she adored and blest
The sacred mystery in her breast.

Christmas: Part One.

Her virgin-womb, that chaste abode,
Becomes the temple of her God;
And she, of nature's works alone
Above nature's laws, conceives a son.

Thus does the bearing Maid unfold
The mystery Gabriel foretold;
Which John within his mother's womb
Foresaw, and blest the Lamb to come.

Behold him in the manger laid,
A sheaf of straw his royal bed;
And he, whose bounty feeds the rest,
Lies craving at his Mother's breast.

Here angels to their maker sing;
Here heaven's loud choirs with echoes ring;
Whilst shepherds here adore, and know
Their pastor and creator too.

May age to age for ever sing
The Virgin's Son and angels' king;
And praise with the celestial host
The Father, Son and Holy Ghost.

Primer, 1706.

Puer natus in Bethlehem.

A Boy is born in Bethlehem,
Joy bringing to Jerusalem.

He lieth in a manger poor
Whose kingdom shall for aye endure.

The ox and ass knowing adored
The Infant, that was Christ the Lord.

The kings of Saba come and bring
Gold, myrrh and incense to their king.

The offspring he of Virgin bright,
Made Mother only by heaven's might.

One after one the cot forlorn
Entering, they hail their prince new-born.

The serpent's venom knows him not,
Though of our blood his own he got:
Made like to us in human kin,
Unlike us in respect of sin.

That like him he might make us be,
And with himself and God agree.

In this birth's joy let all accord,
And bless for ever Christ the Lord.

Glory and everlasting praise
To thee, O Virgin-born, always.

H. I. D. Ryder.

Adeste fideles.

In triumph, joy and holy fear,
Draw near, ye faithful souls, draw near;
The infant King of heaven is here:
   None treads aright but Bethlehem-ward;
   Come hither and adore the Lord.

A Maiden pure—oh, wondrous sight—
Has borne the very Light of Light:
God is begotten out of night:
   All grace is in this Infant stored;
   Come hither, come, adore the Lord.

By angels called that bliss to taste,
The shepherds leave their flocks and haste
To see him in a manger placed:
   Then need we further be implored
   To hasten and adore the Lord?

The Wise-men too—a star their guide—
By Herod sent, from Salem ride,
With incense, gold and myrrh supplied:
   And with their gifts our hearts be poured
   At those dear feet of Christ the Lord.

The glory of the eternal Sire
Veiled under flesh we shall admire,

Nor quail before his awful fire :
That Infant swathed shall be adored :
Come hither, come, 'tis Christ the Lord.

Such love as this—who would not yearn
To love the lover in return?
Behold, with reverent zeal we burn
   To see the Babe proud kings ignored,
   And kiss the feet of Christ our Lord.

Ye choirs of blissful angels, sing ;
Ye vaults of heaven, responsive ring,
' All glory to our God and king ; '
   Let floods of harmony be poured
   From men below to Christ the Lord.

To thee be glory, who, to-day
In Bethlehem born, dost live alway :
Jesus, let none their steps delay
   To visit thee, the eternal Word
   Made flesh, and worship Christ the Lord.

J. C. Earle.

Part Two.

Jesu, Redemptor omnium.

Lamb, whose blood for all men streamed,
Light, that shone ere morning beamed,
God and God's eternal Son,
Ever with the Father one ;

Splendour of the Father's light,
Star of hope for ever bright,
Hearken to the prayers that flow
From thy servants here below.

Lord, remember that in love
Thou didst leave thy throne above,
Man's frail nature to assume
In the holy Virgin's womb.

Now thy Church, each circling year,
Celebrates that love so dear;
Love that brought thee here alone,
For the guilty to atone.

Let not earth alone rejoice,
Seas and skies unite their voice
In a new song, to the morn
When the Lord of life was born.

Ransomed by the holy tide
Shed from thy most precious side,
Joyful let us hail the morn
When the Lord of life was born.

Virgin-born, to thee be praise,
Now and through eternal days;
Father, equal praise to thee,
With the Spirit, ever be.

R. Campbell.

Jam desinant suspiria.

Ye people, cease from tears,
  Your prayers are heard above;
And from his throne in heaven appears
  The God of peace and love.

O'er Bethlehem's silent plains,
  Hark, heavenly voices sing,
Announcing in triumphant strains
  The birth-day of our king.

The faithful shepherds hear,
  And haste the Babe to greet;
Let us like them with joy draw near,
  And worship at his feet.

But say—oh, strange surprise—
  What spectacle is seen;
An Infant in the manger laid,
  His parents poor and mean?

Say—do we here behold
The Son of God most high,
Who doth within his hand infold
The earth and sea and sky?

Faith penetrates the veil,
And through the cloud drawn o'er,
Sees him whom angels trembling hail,
The God whom they adore.

O Babe, thy birth despised
And lowly manger tell,
To flee from all below that's prized,
And with the meek to dwell.

From sinful shame and pride
Guard us, thou Child divine;
Then wilt thou in our hearts abide,
Thy cradle and thy shrine.

R. Campbell.

O ter fecundas, O ter jucundas.

O night of nights, supreme delights,
Thy watches charm and bless;
And joys of heaven, profusely given,
Refresh earth's wilderness.

The sad, sick world through Eve lies furled
In clouds of death and night;
But God doth rise in human guise
To be its life and light.

Whom angels own as God alone,
Is clothed by mortal hands;
In cattle-stall, the Lord of all
Sleeps clasped in swathing-bands.

In cradle laid, his voice is stayed,
Who is the eternal Word:
The sun grows pale, his forces fail;
What means all we have heard?

O shaft of love, to God above
  A rock-hewn home is given:
Farewell ye stars; hail, crib and bars;
  A manger is my heaven.

J. C. Earle.

Salvator mundi Domine.

O Saviour of the world forlorn,
Who man to save this day wast born,
Our days are sinking to their night,
In darkness save, save us in light.

Let thy most blessèd favour be
Around us as we bend the knee;
Blot out our sin; thy heavenly ray
Dispels the gloom and makes our day.

No sleep shall thus weigh down the mind,
Nor ghostly foe unguarded find;
Nor reason yielding to a dream
Wake less responsive to thy beam.

O thou that makest all things new,
With cravings of the heart we sue,
Our lives may, fresh from thee their source,
Renew the pureness of their course.

To God the Father endless praise,
And to his only Son we raise;
An equal glory as is meet
Be sung to God the Paraclete.

Lord Braye.

Adeste fideles.

Hasten, ye faithful, glad, joyful and holy,
  Speed ye to Bethlem to honour the Word;
See there the King of angels is born lowly—
  Oh, come and kneel before him;
  Oh, come and all adore him;
Oh come, oh come, rejoicing to honour the Lord.

Christmas: Part Three.

God of the Godhead, true Light unabated,
    Mary the Virgin has borne the Adored;
True God eternal, begot, uncreated—
    Oh, come and kneel before him;
    Oh, come and all adore him;
Oh come, oh come, rejoicing to honour the Lord.

Sing, all ye angels, till echoes rebounding
    Swell through your halls, for ever be heard;
'Glory to God,' through all heaven resounding—
    Oh, come and kneel before him;
    Oh, come and all adore him;
Oh come, oh come, rejoicing to honour the Lord.

Praise to the Infant, who this day descended;
    Glory to thee, blessed Jesus adored;
Word, in whom two natures join, yet unblended—
    Oh, come and kneel before him,
    Oh, come and all adore him;
Oh come, oh come, rejoicing to honour the Lord.

J. R. Beste.

Part Three.

Jesu, Redemptor omnium.

Jesus, Redeemer, ere the light,
Born in transcendant glory bright;
Effulgent thou, with equal beam
Proceeding from thy Sire supreme;

Thee the great Father's light we know,
Eternal hope of all below,
Regard our prayer, to thee we fly,
Oh, hear thy suppliant servants' cry.

Redeemer, blest Creator, thou
For our redemption once didst bow;
Assuming, to avert our doom,
Man's nature from the Virgin's womb.

This joyful day returns to prove
That miracle of boundless love,
When by the Father's only Son
The world's salvation was begun.

Him the bright stars, the earth, the sea
And all beneath heaven's canopy,
The author of our birth anew,
Praise with new hymns and glory due.

And we, whom thy atoning blood
Has cleansed with pure redeeming flood,
With hymns on this thy natal-day,
The tribute of our homage pay.

Jesus, of Virgin born, to thee
May praise and glory ever be,
With Father and with Holy Ghost,
By men and heaven's eternal host.
F. C. Husenbeth.

Debilis cessent elementa legis.
  Now ancient shadows flee,
  Now night and terror cease;
Thy God, O earth, begins with thee
  A covenant of peace.

  He who is Light of Light,
  The true unclouded sun,
Bleeds to remove sad nature's blight,
  From wrongs that we have done.

  This day he doth bestow
  The first-fruits of that blood,
Which will hereafter richly flow
  To be our cleansing flood.

  He takes that sacred name
  At which we bend the knee;
Oh, how befitting him who came
  Our sacrifice to be.

The Son who gave his blood,
The Father of our Lord,
The Holy Ghost—one God most good,
For ever be adored.

R. Campbell.

Missum Redemptorem polo.

Sent from his heavenly throne on high,
Let the whole world beneath the sky
Adore the Saviour newly come,
The prince born of the Virgin's womb.

He who created heaven and earth
Is clothed in frame of mortal birth;
That flesh by flesh may be set free,
Nor his own creatures ruined be.

The Word which ere time's course began,
Forth from his Father's bosom ran,
Obedient now to time and death
A helpless Infant draws its breath.

On straw the Almighty lays his head,
Nor spurns the manger for his bed;
And he who all creation feeds
The milk of human Mother needs.

They guide the starry spheres, those hands
That now are wrapped in swathing-bands;
All weak and weeping there he lies,
That he may raise us to the skies.

Hope of the whole wide earth, that Child,
Who calls us to his cradle mild,
How of such love our fitness prove
Save by return of answering love?

All honour, laud and glory be
O Jesus, Mary's Son, to thee;
To Father and to Spirit praise
Now and through endless length of days.

W. M. A.

Mundi salus qui nasceris.

Holy Babe, our great salvation,
    Jesu, born to save the earth,
Let pure hearts with love unfailing
    Celebrate thy wondrous birth.
Loving shepherd, night descending
    Calls us soon to needful sleep;
But thou still, thy flock defending,
    From the wolf wilt guard thy sheep.
From the bosom of thy Mother,
    Thou, like us, didst nurture find;
Be thou then our elder brother,
    And protector ever kind.
Hail, the Day-spring of salvation;
    Virgin-born, to thee be praise;
Father, thine be adoration;
    Spirit, thine through endless days.
                      R. Campbell.

Adeste fideles.

Come, O faithful, with sweet voices
Lift the song that heaven rejoices,
    Song to Bethlehem glory bringing:
Where the swathing-clothes enfold him,
King of angels, there behold him:
    Come, with thoughts to heaven upsoaring;
    Come, with lowly knees adoring;
        Come, angelic anthems singing.

God of God, in him there finding,
Light of Light, with glory blinding,
    These to Virgin sweetly clinging;
Come, in tender Babe beholding
Unbegotten might unfolding:
    Come, with thoughts to heaven upsoaring;
    Come, with lowly knees adoring;
        Come, angelic anthems singing.

Christmas: Part Four.

Hark, angelic pæans sounding
Fill heaven's vault with song astounding,
   Song sweet peace to earth now bringing :
Chant thou, 'Glory in the highest',
To the God for whom thou sighest :
   Come, with thoughts to heaven upsoaring ;
   Come, with lowly knees adoring ;
     Come, angelic anthems singing.

Therefore, on this feast of glory,
When on earth began his story,
   Round our Jesus praises ringing ;
Sing to God in heaven paternal,
Sing the Word-made-flesh supernal :
   Come, with thoughts to heaven upsoaring ;
   Come, with lowly knees adoring ;
     Come, angelic anthems singing.
                       C. Kent.

Part Four.

Jesu, Redemptor omnium.

Jesus, the Ransomer of man,
Who, ere created light began,
Didst from the sovereign Father spring,
His power and glory equalling ;
   Thou brightness of thy Father's rays,
   The hope and end of all our ways,
With gracious ear the prayers attend
Which round the world to thee ascend.
   Remember, Lord, that heretofore,
When thee thy Virgin-mother bore,
Thou from her womb didst breathe our air,
And human nature for us wear.
   To thee, this present solemn day,
We yearly adorations pay ;
The world's Redeemer thee we own,
Descending from thy Father's throne.

The joyful heavens, earth and main,
With whatsoever they contain,
In new harmonious accents sing
New life restored by the new-born king.

We, ransomed by that bloody tide
That issued from thy sacred side,
With double hymns of heart and voice
For this thy birth-day now rejoice.

Jesus, to thee the Virgin's Son,
Be everlasting homage done ;
To God the Father we repeat
The same, and to the Paraclete.

' *Evening Office*, 1710.

Victis sibi cognomina.

To earthly kings fresh names accrue
From nations whom their arms subdue ;
A better title, Christ, to thee,
Is drawn from those whom thou dost free.

For other name has not been given
For man's salvation under heaven ;
No other shall the dead awake,
Or title to their glory make.

What cost so much—the blood divine,
E'en precious blood, Redeemer, thine—
Shall evil to such madness grow
This priceless treasure to forego ?

Rather to suffer for that name,
Be the best honour we may claim ;
By it death's bitterness doth pass,
And lovely seems which dreadful was.

O thou that dost vouchsafe to bear
The name of Jesus, Saviour dear,
Our only boast therein we place,
Receive our prayer for thy name's grace.

Lord Braye.

Christmas: Part Four.

A solis ortus cardine.

From the far-blazing gate of morn
    To earth's remotest shore,
Let every tongue confess to him
    Whom holy Mary bore.

Lo, the great maker of the world,
    Lord of eternal years,
To save his creatures, veiled beneath
    A creature's form appears.

A spotless Maiden's virgin-breast
    With heavenly grace he fills;
In her pure womb he is conceived,
    And there in secret dwells.

That bosom, chastity's sweet home,
    Becomes, oh, blest reward,
The shrine of heaven's immortal king,
    The temple of the Lord.

And Mary bears the Babe, foretold
    By an archangel's voice;
Whose presence made the Baptist leap,
    And in the womb rejoice.

A manger scantly strewn with hay
    Becomes the Eternal's bed;
And he, who feeds each little bird,
    Himself with milk is fed.

Straightway with joy the heavens are filled,
    The hosts angelic sing;
And shepherds hasten to adore
    Their shepherd and their king.

Praise to the Father, praise to him,
    The Virgin's holy Son,
Praise to the Spirit Paraclete,
    While endless ages run.

E. Caswall.

Puer nobis nascitur.

A Child for us is born this day,
   The angels' king is he;
The Lord who over all has sway,
   Nurst here vouchsafes to be.
In a manger where asses fed
   This divine Child is laid;
Whom they as Christ acknowledged,
   As king and Lord obeyed.
With joy the angels fillèd were,
   And with the Lord do sing;
'Glory to God above the sphere,'
   In tuneful notes does ring.
Then Herod, who with fear was seized,
   His envy great displays;
With slaughtered babes must be appeased,
   Whose gore his fear allays.
Thou who wast born as on this day
   Of Virgin Mary pure,
Lead and conduct us in the way
   To joys which e'er endure.
O Virgin-flower of virgins blest,
   Pardon for us obtain,
That we our Lord in heavenly rest
   May bless and bless again.
                        Evening Office, 1748.

Adeste fideles.

   Oh come, all ye faithful,
     Adoring, triumphant,
Oh joyful, oh joyful, to Bethlehem repair;
     Behold in a manger
     The monarch of angels;
With glad alleluias his glory declare.

Christmas: Part Four.

God eternal of God,
Light eternal of Light,
'Twas thine in thy womb, blessed Maiden, to bear;
True God uncreated,
Not made but begotten;
With glad alleluias his glory declare.

Ye chorus of angels,
From heaven descending,
Oh haste ye, oh haste ye, our triumph to share;
Singing, 'Glory to God
In the highest for ever';
With glad alleluias his glory declare.

All glory for ever
To thee, blessed Jesus,
Born to rescue the fallen from woe and despair;
True Word of the Father,
Eternal, incarnate;
With glad alleluias his glory declare.

R. Campbell.

Epiphany and Season after.

Epiphany and Octave.

Crudelis Herodes, Deum.

WHY, ruthless Herod, why should fear
    Thus in thy jealous bosom rise?
He seizes not on kingdoms here
    Who grants the kingdom of the skies.

Forth sped the Magian kings, whilst bright
    The star of mystery lured their view;
'Twas thus they sought the fount of light,
    And owned him God with offerings due.

Behold, the Lamb of heaven to-day
    To touch the limpid wave goes down;
Thus cleansing us, he cleansed away
    The guilt-spots that were not his own.

Oh, wondrous power; a conscious blush
    Hath tinged the waters ruby-red;
From them he bade the wine-stream gush;
    The wine-stream gushed, the water fled.

To thee, O Lord, be glory given,
    Whose light so brightly shines to-day,
And to the eternal Sire of heaven,
    And to the Holy Ghost, for aye.

                    J. D. Aylward.

Quæ stella sole pulchrior.

What beauteous sun-surpassing star
    O'er Bethlehem's lonely road,

Reveals a rising brighter far,
 And shows the cradled God.
The star from Jacob see arise,
 By prophets long foretold;
Ye Eastern nations, in the skies
 His messenger behold.
While thus the star its light imparts,
 A ray within doth shine,
Which leads a few but faithful hearts
 To seek the glorious sign.
No dangers can their purpose shake;
 Love suffers no delay;
Home, kindred, country they forsake;
 God calls, and they obey.
Jesu, bright morning Star, our hearts
 Cleanse with thy light within;
And suffer not the tempter's arts
 To lure us back to sin.
The Light of Gentile lands adore,
 The Day-spring from on high,
Alike the Father evermore,
 And Spirit magnify.
R. Campbell.

Fac, Christe, nostri gratia.

Thou from the cradle to the grave
 For us to pain condemned,
A grateful heart thy people give
 To praise their suffering friend—
That friend who longed for man to die,
 While yet in Mary's womb;
That God who took humanity,
 To lay it in the tomb.
He comes a Babe, though Lord of all,
 In cold and want to lie;

His cradle is the oxen's stall,
    The straw his drapery:
'Tis love that makes the innocent
    The pains of guilt to bear,
The giver of the law content
    Its penalty to share.

That precious blood which gently flows
    And speaks the law obeyed,
Foreshadoweth his dying woes
    A little while delayed.
The sword that slays the sucklings now
    Unsheathèd must remain,
To pierce his heart and lay him low
    With those already slain.

His chosen race their God expel—
    An exile poor he flies;
In heathen lands he seeks to dwell
    Who made the earth and skies.
O king of suffering, king of love,
    All praise be paid to thee,
With Father, Spirit, God above,
    Eternal Trinity.

R. Campbell.

O sola magnarum urbium.

Bethlehem, of noblest cities
    None can once with thee compare;
Thou alone the Lord from heaven
    Didst for us Incarnate bear.

Fairer than the sun at morning
    Was the star that told his birth;
To the lands their God announcing,
    Hid beneath a form of earth.

By its lambent beauty guided,
    See, the Eastern kings appear;

Epiphany: Second Week.

See them bend, their gifts to offer—
Gifts of incense, gold and myrrh.

Solemn things of mystic meaning—
Incense doth the God disclose;
Gold a royal Child proclaimeth;
Myrrh a future tomb foreshows.

Holy Jesu, in thy brightness
To the Gentile world displayed;
With the Father and the Spirit,
Praise eterne to thee be paid.

E. Caswall.

Second Week after Epiphany.
MOST HOLY NAME OF JESUS.
Part One.
Jesu, dulcis memoria.

THE memory sweet of Jesus' name
True joy brings to the breast;
But far above all honied sweets
Is his dear presence blest.

No tuneful song, no pleasant sound,
No fancy ever won
Upon the senses, like the name
Of Jesus, God's dear Son.

Jesu, the contrite sinner's hope
To suppliants how kind;
How good art thou to those who seek—
But what to those who find?

No tongue can tell, no pen can write
How sweet it is to love
This sweetest Lord; the hearts that try
Alone this sweetness prove.

Jesu, thy love delights the soul,
   With sweets that never tire;
They fill, yet cloy not, but enhance
   The keenness of desire.
J. D. Aylward.

Jesu, rex admirabilis.

O Jesu, Lord, most mighty king
   And conqueror divine,
Sweetness unspeakable, for whom
   Our souls unceasing pine.

When thou art in my heart, the world
   With its vain pomp decays;
Bright shines the truth, and love lights up
   Its ready kindled blaze.

Jesu, thou sweetness of all hearts,
   Thou living spring of light,
So far exceeding all desire,
   All joys of sense or sight.

Ah, sweetest Jesu, let me feel
   The fulness of thy love;
Cleanse thou mine eyes to see thy face
   In thy bright courts above.

O Jesu, brighter than the sun,
   Balm with all healing blest,
Of all things sweet, of all things fair,
   Thou sweetest, fairest, best.
J. D. Aylward.

Jesu, decus angelicum.

Crown of the angels, thy sweet name
   Excels all tuneful art;
'Tis very honey to the lips,
   And nectar to the heart.

Who taste thee hunger still; who drink
   Still feel a thirst intense;

Epiphany: Second Week.

They yearn for thy delights alone
  And loathe the joys of sense.

Stay with us, Lord, and round our souls
  Still shed thy radiance bright;
Oh, chase the shadows, and rejoice
  The world with thy sweet light.

Flower of a Virgin-stem, to thee,
  My lover true, be given
Honour and praise and kingly rule
  O'er all the realms of heaven.

J. D. Aylward.

Part Two.

Jesu, dulcis memoria.

Thy sweet remembrance, Lord, imparts
Serenest joy to faithful hearts;
But far above all sweetest things,
The sweetness that thy presence brings.

What song so tuneful to the ear,
What earthly sound so sweet to hear,
What thought can such delight supply,
As Jesus, Son of God most high?

Jesu, of penitents the stay,
And refuge in the evil day;
To those that seek thee ever kind,
But oh, what joy to those that find.

No tongue can speak, no thought conceive,
Nor they who have not known believe;
The heart that feels alone can tell,
What 'tis in Jesus' love to dwell.

Then, Jesu, while on earth we tread,
Thy love within our bosom shed;
And be, dear Lord, when time is o'er,
Our crown of glory evermore.

R. Campbell.

Jesu, rex admirabilis.

Jesu, king o'er all adored,
Jesu, our victorious Lord,
Sweetness thou that speech transcends,
Hope of earth's remotest ends.

Coming to the faithful heart,
Light and love thou dost impart,
Earth's deceitful pleasures fall,
Thou alone art All in all.

Jesu, Lord of pure delight,
Cleanser of the inward sight,
Every joy thou dost excel,
Sweetest love's o'erflowing well.

Unto thee let us repair,
Seek thy face with earnest prayer;
Earnest seek thy love to know;
Seeking, still more earnest grow.

Jesu, let our lips proclaim,
And our lives confess thy name;
Thou our joy and portion be,
Now and in eternity.

R. Campbell.

Jesu, decus angelicum.

Jesu, highest heaven's completeness,
Name of music to the ear,
To the lips surpassing sweetness,
Wine the fainting heart to cheer.

Eating thee the soul may hunger,
Drinking, still athirst may be;
But for earthly food no longer,
Nor for any stream but thee.

Jesu, all delight exceeding,
Only hope of heart distrest;

Weeping eyes and spirit mourning
Find in thee a place of rest.

Stay, O beauty uncreated,
Ever ancient, ever new;
Banish deeds of darkness hated,
With thy sweetness all bedew.

Jesu, fairest blossom springing
From a Maiden ever-pure,
May our lips thy praise be singing
While eternal years endure.
R. Campbell.

Third Week after Epiphany.
Crudelis Herodes, Deum.

What makes thee, cruel Herod, shake
For fear that Christ thy crown should take?
He will not seize an earthly throne
Who heavenly kingdoms makes our own.

The sages coming from afar
Follow the new-appearing star;
With light they seek a better light;
Their gifts confess the God of might.

The heavenly Lamb in Jordan stood
To sanctify the crystal flood;
Our sins with that baptismal dew
Were washed in him who sin ne'er knew.

A strange unusual power is shown—
The water-pots are ruddy grown,
Whose waters, by command divine,
Their nature change and run pure wine.

To Christ, who did the Gentiles call,
Be endless glory given by all;
To God the Father we repeat
The same, and to the Paraclete.
Evening Office, 1710.

Clamantis, ecce, vox sonans.

Hark, in the wilderness
The Lord's forerunner pleads,
While crowds of mourners press
To show their wicked deeds;
And with the guilty throng draws nigh
The Lamb of God, so soon to die.

But since the brightest star
Grows pale before the sun,
How shall the Baptist dare
To cleanse the Holy One?
This God declares to be his will:
' All righteousness I must fulfil.'

O Baptist, 'tis thy part
That cleanser to confess,
Whose Spirit comes the heart
To purify and bless;
Then, Saviour, in thy name we boast;
Praise Father, Son and Holy Ghost.

R. Campbell.

Linquunt tecta Magi principis urbis.

The princely city passing by,
  The Magi turn to greet
The goal of all their toilsome march
  In Bethlehem's lowly street;
And while, from many tuneful lips,
  Spontaneous anthems rise,
Triumphant faith takes wings of hope,
  And wafts them to the skies.

Transporting joy, when once again
  The star that they had lost,
With heavenly light and promise bright,
  Their eager pathway crossed;

Nor stayed its radiant course until
    It took its golden rest,
Above the place where Jesus lay
    Upon his Mother's breast.

No glint is here of ivory,
    No blaze of burnished gold,
No purple robes the infant limbs
    In gorgeous hues enfold :
His palace is a stable rude,
    His throne a manger wild,
And raiment rough in web and woof,
    The purple of that Child.

Let pomp and splendour other kings
    Luxuriously adorn ;
For better proves he thus his reign
    Supreme the Babe new-born :
In peasant-garb and culture mean,
    He sways the realms of thought ;
And 'neath the sceptre of his will
    The hearts of men are brought.

Beside the cradle where he sleeps,
    They worship on their knees ;
And in the Child the eye of faith
    The present Godhead sees ;
Let us, their offspring in the faith,
    Adore the Infant here ;
And offer him our best of gifts,
    Hearts filled with sacred fear.

Let chaste and ardent love supply
    The gold of Eastern kings,
And bodies penance-chastened yield
    The myrrh devotion brings :
Our vows and prayers, like frankincense
    And myrrh, shall sweetly rise

To hail the Babe recumbent here
　　As ruler of the skies.

To God the Father, fount of light,
　　Be glory evermore;
To God the Son, whose light and grace
　　Extend from shore to shore,
Be equal glory given here
　　And in the realms above,
In never-ending songs of praise
　　Commensurate with love.

J. C. Earle.

Fourth Week after Epiphany.
Crudelis Herodes, Deum.

Why, cruel Herod, dost thou fear,
Lest our great God and king appear?
He who can heavenly crowns bestow
Comes not to seize thy throne below.

　The Wise-men followed that bright star,
Which shone to them in realms afar;
While light itself by light they seek,
Their gifts, their faith and love bespeak.

　The heavenly Lamb the waters lave,
He sanctifies the crystal wave;
And he, whom sin could never stain,
Bids none upon our souls remain.

　Behold a new display of might,
The pallid waters redden bright;
The mandate for the change once heard,
Wine flows obedient at the word.

　Jesus, to Gentile kings displayed,
Glory to thee and praise be paid,
With Father and with Holy Ghost,
Enthroned above the heavenly host.

F. C. Husenbeth.

Verbum quod ante sæcula.

Word of God, eternal Son,
From thy throne by pity won,
Let us at thy cradle kneel,
And thine infant sorrows feel.
Holy Babe, the sinner's woe
Guiltless thou art doomed to know;
Sobs that from thy cradle rise
Tell before of dying cries.

Poor art thou, that we may be
Blest by thy hard poverty;
Thou art weeping, and thy grief
Flows that we may find relief.
Thou art clothed in raiment mean,
Dwelling in a cave unclean;
Man is proud—the only great
Scorneth not the lowliest state.

Jesu, thee the Father gave,
Such his love, the earth to save;
Ransomed at so vast a cost,
Let us not, good Lord, be lost.
Offspring of the holy Maid,
Endless praise to thee be paid;
Equal praise, O Father, be
With the Spirit paid to thee.
R. Campbell.

Qua lapsu tacito stella loquacibus.

The beauteous star that beams on high
The wanderers watch with anxious eye,
And strive with careful step to tread
The path o'er which its light is shed.

At length arrived at Salem's walls,
The Lord his messenger recalls;

And as a bark they seem to stray,
Which hath no star to guide her way.

But nothing can the heart affright
Which walks by faith and not by sight;
To Herod's court they boldly bring
The tidings of a new-born king.

Hope ne'er deceives the faithful mind;
Who meekly seeks is sure to find;
In him on whom his people trod,
The Gentiles see their king and God.

Then let us praise our heavenly king,
To Father, Son and Spirit sing;
That Spirit is the star divine
Which will in faithful bosoms shine.

R. Campbell.

Fifth Week after Epiphany.
Crudelis Herodes, Deum.

Why, cruel Herod, dost thou fear
Lest Christ should seize thy crown so dear?
He needeth not thy earthly throne
Who heavenly kingdoms makes our own.

The sages hastening from afar,
With joy pursue their guiding star;
By its bright beams they seek the light,
And humbly own the God of might.

Behold, the spotless Lamb hath stood
In Jordan's purifying flood;
And he, who sin's foul stains ne'er knew,
Our sins hath washed with healing dew.

A new and wondrous sign we see;
From her fixed laws doth nature flee;
And water, by command divine,
Is quickly changed to ruddy wine.

Epiphany: Fifth Week. 55

To Christ, who did the Gentiles call,
Be endless glory paid by all;
To God the Father we repeat
The same, and to the Paraclete.
T. J. Potter.

Christus tenebris obsitam.

The bright and morning-star arose
  And brought the glorious morn;
But Israel's blind and hardened seed
  The Lord of glory scorn.
He feeds their poor, he heals their sick,
  The dumb, the blind, the lame;
He calls their dead to life—these signs
  The mighty God proclaim.
A stiff-necked race with hearts of stone
  Delighting in the night,
Refused to hear the Holy One
  And fled his loving light.
Let us, O Day-spring from on high,
  Pursue thy radiance pure,
And suffer not the night of sin
  Thy presence to obscure.
Thou art the truth, and thou the love,
  The life, the light are thine;
Oh, grant that with thy love and truth
  Our hearts may live and shine.
To God the Father, God the Son
  And God the Holy Ghost,
Be glory from the Church on earth
  And from the heavenly host.
R. Campbell.

Non abluunt lymphæ Deum.

God needeth not the cleansing wave,
But giveth it the power to save;

His sinless flesh, baptized therein,
Hath hallowed it to cleanse from sin.

The sacred fountain long foretold
For all uncleanness here behold;
For thus the Lord his death applies,
And with his blood the spirit dyes.

For bathed in that baptismal flood,
The soul is dyed with Jesus' blood;
And clothed in robes which brightly glow,
Surpassing far the purest snow.

As once the Spirit brooded o'er
The Maid who our Redeemer bore,
So broods he o'er that mystic flood—
The womb from which we rise to God.

Mysterious womb, the Spirit's shade
That rested on the holy Maid—
His quickening power to thee bestows,
And sons of God from thee we rose.

Jesu, to thee all praise we pay,
For thou hast washed our sins away;
The Father equally adore,
And Holy Spirit evermore.

R. Campbell.

O sola magnarum urbium.

Let other cities strive, which most
Can of their strength or heroes boast;
Bethlem alone is chose to be
The seat of heaven-born majesty.

 Here, while our God incarnate lay,
The officious stars their homage pay;
A sun-like meteor quits its sphere
To show the Sun of justice here.

 Hither the faithful sages ran
To own their king, both God and Man;

Epiphany: Fifth Week.

And with their incense, myrrh and gold
The mysteries of their vows unfold.

To God the censer's smoke ascends ;
The gold the sovereign king attends ;
In myrrh the bitter type we see
Of suffering and mortality.

Glory to thee, O Christ, whose rays
Illustrated the Gentiles' ways ;
Whilst equal praises still repeat
The Father, and the Paraclete.

Primer, 1706.

Alleluia, dulce carmen.

Alleluia, sweetest lay,
Sung through heaven's eternal day ;
Alleluia, angel choir,
Now ye wake the golden lyre ;
Throned on God's own holy hill,
Alleluia, sing ye still.

Alleluia, souls set free
Join the heavenly melody ;
Far from earthly woe and wrong,
Alleluia, be your song ;
We who exiles yet remain,
Faint and feeble flows our strain.

Alleluia, now we sing,
Lenten hours will sorrow bring ;
Then must cease the voice of joy,
Penitence our hearts employ ;
We are fallen—sin and woe
Cast their shade on all below.

R. Campbell.

Septuagesima, Sexagesima and Quinquagesima.

Septuagesima.

PRAYER OF OUR LORD JESUS CHRIST.

Aspice, ut Verbum Patris a supernis.

SEE the eternal Word descending
   From the throne of bliss supreme,
Love-constrained, his way now wending
   Adam's children to redeem.

Pitying the world's disaster,
   Yearning to repair its fall,
Prone upon the earth, our master
   Prays for pardon for us all.

Oh, what anguish, what affliction
   Hemmed him round on every side ;
Who shall tell his dereliction
   While his suppliant accents cried :

'O my Father, O my Father,
   Let this chalice pass away ;
Yet not my will, thy will rather,
   Be accomplishèd this day.'

'Neath that load of anguish sinking,
   Drops of blood stood on his brow ;
Wondering earth in silence drinking,
   One by one, the drops that flow.

But an angel, swiftly gliding,
   Comes from heaven to his aid ;
And that form the Godhead hiding,
   Comfort seeks from those he made.

Septuagesima.

To the Father praise be given ;
Praise the Son, whose name is greater
Than all names beneath the heaven ;
Praise the Spirit, every creature.
W. Wallace.

Te læta, mundi conditor.

Thou, Creator, art possest
Of unbroken endless rest ;
Choirs angelic sing to thee
With unceasing melody.
We who lost fair Eden's bowers,
Shame and painful toil are ours ;
Mourning exiles, how shall they
Sing their distant country's lay?
Thou who never dost despise
Contrite hearts and weeping eyes,
Teach us our offence to know,
Bid the tears of sorrow flow—
Blessèd tears that bring relief,
Faith and hope assuaging grief ;
Peace the broken heart regains,
Sweetly flow the joyful strains.
God the Father, God the Son,
God the Spirit, Three in One,
Honour, glory, love and praise,
Be to thee through endless days.
R. Campbell.

Venit e cœlo Mediator alto.

Daughter of Sion, cease thy bitter tears
    And calm thy breast ;
Foretold through ages past, lo, now appears
    Thy Mediator blest.

That garden, where of old our guilt began,
    Wrought death and pain ;

But this, where Jesus prays by night for man,
    Brings life and joy again.

Hither, of his own will, the Lord for all
    Comes to atone;
And stays the thunderbolts about to fall
    From the dread Father's throne.

So shall he break the adamantine chain
    Of hell's abyss;
And opening heaven long closed, call us again
    To his eternal bliss.

Praise to the Son, to whom a name above
    All names is given;
Praise to the Father and the Spirit of love
    From all in earth and heaven.

E. Caswall.

Sexagesima.
COMMEMORATION OF THE PASSION.

Mærentes oculi, spargite lacrymas.

With sorrow deep oppressed, now let us sadly wail,
And fill our very hearts with bitter grief and shame,
Whilst pondering the wounds, the shame and torments dread,
    Which cruel man for God did frame.

Behold, the impious band with deadly haste draw nigh;
See, how with swords and staves upon the Lord they rush:
Then madly strike the Lamb; and then with savage blows
    That head divine they fiercely crush.

But yet comes not the end: now bound with cruel cords,
Unto the savage scourge the Lord of life they give;

Sexagesima. 61

And then without remorse, fierce ruffian hands are raised
    'Gainst him who causeth all to live.
List, O ye people, list ; the good and loving God
In gentlest meekness stands beneath the lash severe ;
And while his blood runs down, all guiltless though he be,
    No word he speaks his fame to clear.
What man who would not weep? Not even yet the race
Of sin, the vipers' brood, their bitter hate have quenched ;
Upon his brow divine a thorny crown they press,
    And all his face with gore is drenched.
Then—blackest, deadliest sin—with rude and cutting cords
They drag our loving Lord unto the place of death ;
Upon the cross he dies, and to his Father's care
    Resigns his soul with his last breath.
To him who freely died upon the bitter cross,
To gain for sinful man sweet mercy, peace and grace,
Be honour, fame and praise, be glory ever sung
    In notes of joy by all our race.

T. J. Potter.

Aspice, infami, Deus ipse, ligno.

Behold our God upon the rood ;
    All drenched in gore thereon he hangs ;
His hands are nailed unto the wood,
    Pierced through with cruel iron fangs.
See how he hangs betwixt two thieves,
    As though a partner in their guilt ;
Behold the treatment he receives
    From those for whom his blood is spilt.
How pale the face ; the drooping head

Is bowed in death. His eyelids close;
Forth from his breast his spirit fled
  Unto its well-deserved repose.
O heart of man, more hard than brass
  If thou thy crime dost not bewail;
For thine own guilty crime it was
  Which Christ unto the cross did nail.
Eternal praise to God be given
  Through every age, who loved us so,
That by his blood our souls are shriven
  From sin, which works such bitter woe.
W. Wallace.

Sævo dolorum turbine.

O'erwhelmed in depths of woe,
  Upon the tree of scorn
Hangs the Redeemer of mankind,
  With racking anguish torn.

See, how the nails those hands
  And feet so tender rend;
See, down his face and neck and breast
  His sacred blood descend.

Hark, with what awful cry
  His Spirit takes its flight;
That cry, it smote his Mother's heart,
  And wrapt her soul in night.

Earth hears, and to its base
  Rocks wildly to and fro;
Tombs burst; seas, rivers—mountains quake;
  The veil is rent in two.

The sun withdraws his light;
  The midday heavens grow pale;
The moon, the stars, the universe,
  Their maker's death bewail.

Shall man alone be mute?
  Come, youth and hoary hairs;

Quinquagesima.

Come, rich and poor; come, all mankind,
 And bathe those feet in tears.
Come, fall before his cross,
 Who shed for us his blood;
Who died the victim of pure love,
 To make us sons of God.
Jesu, all praise to Thee,
 Our joy and endless rest:
Be thou our guide while pilgrims here,
 Our crown amid the blest.
E. Caswall.

Quinquagesima.

HOLY CROWN OF THORNS OF OUR LORD.

Exite, Sion filiæ.

Go forth, ye Sion's daughters, now,
 A monarch's bashful train,
To see the crown on Jesus' brow—
 Your mother wrought that pain.
His hair is plucked; the piercing thorns
 Red with his blood appear;
The deathly pallor of his face
 Shows that the end is near.
What barren tract produced those thorns
 Bristling with bush and brier?
What ruthless hand hath gathered in
 So stern a crop and dire?
Each thorn now steeped in Jesus' blood,
 Becomes a blooming rose,
Bears sweeter fruit than any palm,
 His triumph better shows.
O Christ, the thorns which wound thy brow
 Were sown in our great sin;
Pluck from our hearts our guilty thorns,
 And plant thine own thorns in.

Strength, honour, praise and glory be
  To Father and to Son
And to the Spirit Paraclete,
  While endless ages run.
W. Wallace.

Rebus creatis nil egens.
Thou didst not need creation's aid,
  All blest thyself within,
When coming from thy secret shade
  Creation to begin.
The morning stars together sing,
  The sons of God rejoice,
For earth and skies to being spring
  At thy creating voice.
But while so fair to outward view
  Arose the earth and skies,
A fairer world thy will foreknew
  Hereafter to arise.
Its maker, Christ our Lord and God ;
  Its frame, his truth and grace ;
And far as foot of man hath trod,
  It finds a resting place.
But soon, its earthly travail o'er,
  'Twill hear his loving call,
And rise to dwell for evermore
  With him, the Lord of all.
Thy new creation, Lord, direct,
  Till raised above secure ;
O Father, from its foes protect ;
  Oh, cleanse it, Spirit pure.
R. Campbell.

Legis figuris pingitur.
Christ's peerless crown is pictured in
  The figures of the law—
The ram entangled in the thorns ;
  The bush which Moses saw ;

Quinquagesima.

The rainbow girding round the ark;
    The table's crown of gold;
The incense that in waving wreaths
    Around the altar rolled.

Hail, circlet dear, that didst the pangs
    Of dying Jesus feel;
Thou dost the brightest gems outshine,
    And all the stars excel.

Praise, honour, to the Father be,
    And sole-begotten Son;
Praise to the Spirit Paraclete,
    While endless ages run.

E. Caswall.

Lent.

PART I.—SUNDAYS IN LENT.

First Sunday in Lent.

Audi, benigne Conditor.

O GRACIOUS Lord, Creator dear,
In mercy lend a pitying ear
Unto the mournful prayer we pour
In this our solemn Lenten hour.

Thou who our secret thoughts canst trace
And knowst the frailty of our race—
Like wandering sheep we went astray—
Oh, take us back, we meekly pray.

Black is our guilt and great our shame;
But for the glory of thy name,
Forgive the wickedness we own,
And heal the wounds for which we groan.

Grant us by holy abstinence
To mortify each carnal sense;
That so our souls, from sin set free,
May rise all-holy unto thee.

Blest Three in One, with grief sincere,
Before thy footstool we appear;
Oh, bless our fast, that it may prove
The source of pardon, peace and love.
R. Campbell.

Ex more docti mystico.

Now with the slow-revolving year,
Again the fast we greet,

Lent: First Sunday.

Which in its mystic circle moves
    Of forty days complete;
That fast, by law and prophets taught,
    By Jesus Christ restored—
Jesus, of seasons and of times
    The maker and the Lord.

Henceforth, more sparing let us be
    Of food, of words, of sleep;
Henceforth, beneath a stricter guard
    The roving senses keep.

And let us shun whatever things
    Distract the careless heart;
And let us shut our souls against
    The tyrant tempter's art;

And weep before the judge, and strive
    His vengeance to appease;
Saying to him with contrite voice,
    Upon our bended knees:

'Much have we sinned, O Lord, and still
    We sin each day we live;
Yet look in pity from on high,
    And of thy grace forgive.

Remember that we still are thine,
    Though of a fallen frame;
And take not from us in thy wrath
    The glory of thy name.

Undo past evil; grant us, Lord,
    More grace to do aright;
So may we now and ever find
    Acceptance in thy sight.'

Blest Trinity in Unity,
    Vouchsafe us, in thy love,
To gather from these fasts below
    Immortal fruit above.

E. Caswall.

O Sol salutis, intimis.

O sovereign Sun, diffuse thy light,
And clear our inmost minds of night;
Thy beams drive all that's dark away,
And give the world a better day.
Now days of grace with mercy flow,
O Lord, the gift of tears bestow,
To wash our stains in every part,
Whilst heavenly fire consumes the heart.
Rise, crystal tears from that same source
From whence our sins derive their course;
Nor cease, till hardened hearts relent,
And softened by your streams, repent.
Behold, the happy days return,
The days of joy for them that mourn;
May we of their indulgence share,
And bless the God that grants our prayer.
May heaven and earth aloud proclaim
The Trinity's almighty fame;
And we, restored to grace, rejoice
In newness both of hearts and voice.

Primer, 1706.

Second Sunday in Lent.

Audi, benigne Conditor.

O gracious Lord, incline thine ears
To prayers accompanied with tears,
Which in this sacred fast of Lent
Are offered by the penitent.

   Searcher of hearts, whose piercing eyes
See clearly man's infirmities;
To convert-sinners grant the grace
Of pardon, and their sins efface.

   Our crimes are grievous to excess,
But spare us who our guilt confess,

Lent: Second Sunday.

And for thy greater praise apply
To our sick souls a remedy.
    May saving fasts observed this Lent
Become the body's punishment ;
That sin may thus unfed remain,
And so the heart from sin abstain.
    Grant, O most sacred Trinity,
Grant, O most perfect Unity,
That this our solemn abstinence
May fruitful prove to mind and sense.
Evening Office, 1710 *and* 1748.

Quod lex adumbravit vetus.
The fast that, in the ancient law
Prefigured, Israël foresaw,
And Christ, the high-priest of the new,
Ordained—that fast observe we too.
Be ours then sparingly to use
The sleep and rest we yet may choose—
The talk, the meat, the drink ; and stand
More watchful against foes at hand.
    Oh, let the earnest mind control
Those passions which assault the soul,
And guard the fortress of the heart
Against the crafty tempter's art.
With faces towards the altar bent,
Let prayers and sighs to heaven be sent ;
That so God's just displeasure may
Pass by us in the reckoning-day.
    Tremendous judge, thou know'st the sense
Of sin to us is weight immense :
Immense—yet, clement Father, say,
' My mercy all your sins shall slay.'
Though formed of dust, we still are thine,
Created by thy power divine ;

And bought again at such a cost,
Let not thy people, Lord, be lost.

Send pardon from thy mercy seat
And give the good which we entreat;
Bestow on us that broken heart
To which thy grace thou dost impart.
Blest Three in One, with grief sincere
Before thy footstool we appear;
Oh, bless our fast, that it may prove
The source of pardon, peace and love.

R. Campbell and J. C. Earle.

Lugete, pacis angeli.

Angels, look down and weep;
The Lord of glory dies;
He bleeds to save his wandering sheep,
On him our vileness lies.

Oh, spare that flesh so pure;
That sacred form, oh, spare;
So marred, what can it yet endure?
What blood remaineth there?

We know 'tis not the nails
That hold him to the tree;
But love more strong than death prevails
O'er all his agony.

Oh, miracle of love,
O man, more hard than stone—
God comes to die from heaven above,
But man loves earth alone.

Jesu, thy cross alone
Can save from endless pain;
Nailed to thy cross here let us groan,
But joy at length attain.

Awhile the flesh may shrink,
But looking up we pray,

Lent: Third Sunday.

'Help us, good Lord, thy cup to drink;
  Oh, help us to obey.'
Healed by thy stripes within,
  And cleansed from every stain,
Oh, suffer not returning sin
  To torture thee again.

To God who gave his Son,
  To him who came to die,
And to the Spirit, Three in One,
  Be praise eternally.
R. Campbell.

Third Sunday in Lent.

Audi, benigne Conditor.

Creator, bounteous and benign,
With tears we pray, thine ear incline,
As in these hallowed days of Lent,
Our contrite sighs to heaven are sent.

Great searcher of the reins and heart,
Thou seest us frail, thy grace impart;
We turn to thee, thy mercy show,
And pardon for our sins bestow.

Our sins are multiplied and great,
But spare us in our helpless state;
And for thy name's renown and praise
Our souls to health and virtue raise.

May we, by wholesome penance, now
Compel our sinful flesh to bow;
That tutored in this sacred time,
Our humbled hearts may fast from crime.

Grant us, O blessed Three in One,
To end with fruit our course begun;
May contrite fasts and ardent love
Secure us endless joys above.
F. C. Husenbeth.

Fando quis audivit, Dei.

Who hath heard what God hath wrought?
　Who hath heard it and believed?
Far surpasseth speech and thought
　What his mercy hath achieved.
Christ, the Lamb, the victim meet,
　Slain before creation's day,
Hastes his offering to complete,
　And the price for all to pay.

But, O Lord, why overthrown
　Dost thou on the cold earth lie?
Whence those tears, that dreadful groan,
　Bloody sweat and agony?
'Tis for man he hides his face;
　'Tis for man his soul's dark gloom—
Standing in the sinner's place,
　Trembling at the sinner's doom.

Is the cup by thee abhorred,
　With God's anger running o'er?
Yet, unless thou drain it, Lord,
　We must drink it evermore.
Love, more strong than death prevails;
　'Father, I thy will obey;'
Welcome thorns and scourge and nails;
　Power of darkness, take thy prey.

Now endured each dreadful pain,
　See he bows his head and dies;
Christ, the Lamb of God, is slain—
　Christ, our perfect sacrifice.
Glory be to God above,
　To the Father and the Son
And the Spirit, God of love,
　While eternal ages run.

　　　　　　　　　R. Campbell.

Lent: Fourth Sunday.

Solemne nos jejunii.

Again the time appointed see,
   That calls to fast and sigh;
Let priest and people bend the knee,
   And loud for mercy cry.
But vain all outward form of grief,
   And vain the word of prayer,
Unless the heart desire relief,
   And penitence be there.
The forehead prostrate in the dust,
   The hair and garments torn,
Can never stay the vengeance just,
   Unless the conscience mourn.
Then, let us to the Lord draw near
   With tears that contrite flow;
By reverence and godly fear
   We may escape the woe.
O holy judge, O Christ, relent,
   Thine arm uplifted stay;
And grant a season to repent,
   A time in which to pray.
Great Three in One, thy name we bless,
   Thy praises ever sing;
Oh, grant that fruits of righteousness
   From Lenten tears may spring.
                       R. Campbell.

Fourth Sunday in Lent.

Audi, benigne Conditor.

O gracious Maker, bend thine ears
Unto our prayers and bitter tears;
May we this fast in truth now keep,
Whilst thus we pray and humbly weep.
Thy piercing eye our hearts doth scan,
And measure all the woes of man;
Whilst now, we sorrowing turn to thee,
From sin's foul burden set us free.

Much have we sinned, and to excess,
But spare us, Lord, who thus confess;
And for the glory of thy name,
Thy saving mercy now proclaim.

Whilst saving fasts our flesh subdue,
May thy sweet grace our hearts renew,
That vice may thus unfed remain,
And we from sin and guilt abstain.

Grant us, O sacred Trinity,
Grant us, O perfect Unity,
That these our fasts may fruitful prove
Of endless bliss, in realms above.

T. J. Potter.

Ex more docti mystico.

From heaven's own school's mysterious ways
We're taught a fast of forty days;
Let humble sufferings, whilst we fast,
Atone for our disorders past.

'Tis this the law and prophets preach,
Both Moses and Elias teach;
And Christ, in whom they both are joined,
This great example left behind.

Each sense and power must then abstain,
And e'en allowances restrain;
Whilst watching and reserve augment
The wholesome abstinence of Lent.

Let's fly the baits that hell designed
For snares to catch the heedless mind;
Nor leave the foe one fenceless way
By which he may our souls betray.

With prostrate hearts let's lay before
Our judge the miseries we deplore;
And bowed beneath the threatening rod
Disarm the just revenge of God.

O God, O Father, our excess
Has long provoked thy tenderness;

Preserve for us the same good-will—
Though rebels, we're thy children still.
  Remember, though we're brittle earth,
'Tis thou, O Lord, that gav'st us birth;
Then let us not those works defame
That bear thy image and thy name.
  Forget our crimes, and grant increase
Of faith and hope, of love and peace;
That we may live as pleases thee,
Both here and in eternity.
  Grant, O most sacred Trinity,
One undivided Unity,
That abstinence may here improve
Our claim to reign with thee above.
Primer, 1706.

O Sol salutis, intimis.

The darkness fleets, and joyful earth
  Welcomes the newborn day;
Jesu, true Sun of human souls,
  Shed in our souls thy ray.
Thou who dost give the accepted time,
  Give tears to purify,
Give flames of love to burn our hearts
  As victims unto thee.
That fountain, whence our sins have flowed,
  Shall soon in tears distil,
If but thy penitential grace
  Subdue the stubborn will.
The day is near when all re-blooms,
  Thy own blest day, O Lord;
We too would joy, by thy right hand
  To life's true path restored.
All glorious Trinity, to thee
  Let earth's vast fabric bend;
And evermore from souls renewed
  The saints' new song ascend.
E. Caswall.

Fifth Sunday in Lent.

Audi, benigne Conditor.

Benignant Maker, hear at last
   Our supplications, drowned in tears,
And through our forty days of fast
   Assuage our woes, disperse our fears.

Heart-searcher, whose all-piercing eyes
   The infirmities of men behold,
Forgiving, grant to suppliant cries
   Thy wondrous graces manifold.

Though many be our sins of shame,
   Spare all confessing here their guilt;
Exalt the glory of thy name,
   Sin washing with thy blood once spilt.

So may our tempered bodies feel
   The chastening aid of abstinence;
That sins no nutriment may steal,
   And hearts may fast from all offence.

Most blessèd Trinity in heaven,
   Most perfect Unity in bliss,
May boundless recompense be given
   In thy world, for our fasts in this.

C. Kent.

Opprobriis, Jesu, satur.

Like faithful Abraham's holy child
   Bearing his painful load,
The Lord, forsaken and reviled,
   Pursues his last sad road.
Nailed to the cross and raised on high,
   He pours his precious blood;
To him be turned every eye—
   To him, the Lamb of God.
O landless sea of charity,
   That flows to earth from heaven;

Lent: Fifth Sunday.

God's sinless Son expires, and we,
   The guilty, are forgiven.
No blood less precious can atone
   For our rebellious race,
And mercy by the cross alone,
   With justice may embrace.
It is the cross that breaks our chain,
   Unlocks the prison-cell,
And heaven with earth unites again
   In harmony to dwell.
To him who died that all might live,
   Let all their praises pour,
Like glory to the Father give,
   And Spirit evermore.
                              R. Campbell.

   O splendor æterni Patris.

O Christ, the true and endless Day,
Eternal Light's co-equal ray ;
And hope of all from pole to pole,
Dispel the darkness of the soul.

   The brightness of the sun is past,
And evening shades are gathering fast ;
O thou whose mercy blessed the light,
Defend us in the gloom of night.

   Though closed in sleep our eyelids be,
Arouse our souls to watch with thee ;
Thy loving servants shield from harm
By thy right hand and holy arm.

   Our mortal body's heavy load
Impedes us in the narrow road ;
Blest Lord, to us thy succour lend,
That all our thoughts may heaven-ward tend.

   O Christ, our only Saviour dear,
Our supplications deign to hear ;
Thy blood-bought children e'er protect,
And to a peaceful end direct.

O merciful and mighty Lord,
Be thou for evermore adored,
Who sparest all that unto thee
In fasting, prayer and weeping flee.
R. Campbell.

Palm Sunday.

Gloria, laus et honor.

Glory and praise to thee, Redeemer blest,
Whom children with hosannas glad confessed.

Hail, Israel's king, hail, David's son adored,
Who comest in the name of Israel's Lord.

Thy praise in heaven the host angelic sings;
On earth mankind, with all created things.

Thee with their palms the Jews went forth to meet;
Thee now with prayers and holy hymns we greet.

Thee, on thy way to die, they crowned with praise;
To thee, now king on high, our song we raise.

Thee their poor homage pleased, O gracious king;
Ours too accept—the best that we can bring.
E. Caswall.

Gloria, laus et honor.

To thee, O Christ, be glory, praises loud,
To thee Hosanna, cried the Jewish crowd.

We, Israel's monarch, David's son proclaim;
Thou com'st, blest king, in God's most holy name.

Angels and men in one harmonious choir,
To sing thy everlasting praise conspire.

Thee, Israel's children met with conquering palms;
To thee our vows we pay in loudest psalms.

For thee on earth with boughs they strewed the ways,
To thee in heaven we sing melodious praise.

Accept this tribute which to thee we bring,
As thou didst theirs, O good and gracious king.
Evening Office, 1738.

PART II.—WEEK DAYS IN LENT.

First Week in Lent.

HOLY SPEAR AND NAILS OF OUR LORD.

Quænam lingua tibi, O lancea.

On Calvary with what a mystery gleams
 The spear that, at the ninth hour of the day,
Made for the precious blood toward the earth,
 Out of the pulseless heart, its last strange way.
As the first Adam by the tree of life
 Lay still and silent in sleep's deep repose,
Mother of all that live, from his cleft side
 Eve, guileful bride, to life and beauty rose.
So, when upon the cross' quickening tree,
 In death's deep sleep, the Second Adam hung,
Mother of all that live by faith, the Church
 From his cleft side in blood and water sprung.
There too the nails that pierced him—there they were,
 Wherewith the Saviour to the bitter wood
Whereto his hands and feet were nailed, nailed too
 The dark hand-writing that against us stood.
Praise to the Father, and the Holy Ghost,
 And him who, where earth's feeble vision fails,
Amid the glory of the eternal throne
 Still bears the marking of the spear and nails.
Roman Breviary, 1879.

Salvete, clavi et lancea.

Hail, holy nails ; hail, blessed spear,
 Once stained with rude ignoble rust ;
What ruby tints on you appear,
 When in Christ's body you were thrust.

The treacherous Jews chose you to aid
The accomplishment of their foul crime;
And God in heaven of you hath made
The instruments of grace sublime.
For, from the wounds which you did trace
Upon those members all divine,
As many founts of heavenly grace,
With all their ruby treasures, shine.
To Jesus, pierced with nails and spear,
Be glory, with the Father blest,
And with the Spirit ever dear,
Both now and always still confessed.

W. Wallace.

Tinctam ergo Christi sanguine.

Oh, turn those blessed points, all bathed
   In Christ's dear blood, on me;
Mine were the sins that wrought his death,
   Mine be the penalty.

Pierce through my feet, my hands, my heart;
   So may some drop distil
Of blood divine, into my soul,
   And all its evils heal.

So shall my feet be slow to sin,
   Harmless my hands shall be;
So from my wounded heart shall each
   Forbidden passion flee.

Thee, Jesu, pierced with nails and spear,
   Let every knee adore;
With thee, O Father, and with thee,
   O Spirit, evermore.

E. Caswall.

Second Week in Lent.

HOLY WINDING SHEET OF OUR LORD.

Gloriam sacræ celebremus omnes.

Jesus, when on thy fatal day
   Thy people turn their awe-struck eyes,
Thy latest vesture's history dread
   Distinct before their memory lies.

Thy suffering o'er, from hands and feet
   They drew the nails who loved thee well;
Into the linen's spotless folds
   Thy soul-less body gently fell.

O Word of God, the conquest won,
   Thy trophies still around thee lay;
Clothed in a vesture dipped in blood,
   Thou restedst victor from the fray.

With our salvation's awful price,
   Still wet upon thy gaping side
And mangled feet and hands and brow,
   The virgin web was redly dyed.

If blood from thee, let tears from us
   In spirit on thy grave-clothes fall;
The price was thine, the debt was ours;
   For us, for us, was suffered all.

Thou who thine own blest life didst give
   A sacrifice for ours to be,
Teach us, O God, in least return
   Our blood-bought lives to give to thee.

Word of the self-existent One,
   Word, uttered with the breath divine,
Word, clad in vesture dipped in blood,
   All praise eternally be thine.

Roman Breviary, 1879.

Mysterium mirabile.

A wondrous mystery this day
   Reveals itself before our eyes;
The true Son of the living God
   Upon the cross in torment dies.
To advocate a servant's cause,
   He takes that servant's guilty guise;
The master suffers for the slave;
   The just man for the sinner dies.
The emblems of his cruel death
   And triumph, we behold impressed
Upon the robe, which with its folds
   His mangled body did invest.
These are the signs of victory won
   O'er death, o'er hell and o'er the world;
These are the trophies which our chief
   Displays triumphantly unfurled.
This gratitude at least we owe
   To him who brought eternal life—
That 'neath this banner we should stand,
   And fight and conquer in the strife.
Then let us die to all our sin,
   And let us rise to life of grace;
That by the cross we may deserve
   To see the glory of his face.
Grant this, O Father merciful,
   And thou, his own co-equal Son;
Grant this, O Spirit, who dost bear
   The sceptre, while the ages run.

W. Wallace.

Jesu, dulcis amor meus.

Jesu, as though thyself wert here,
I draw in trembling sorrow near;
And hanging o'er thy form divine,
Kneel down to kiss these wounds of thine.

Lent: Third Week.

Ah me, how naked art thou laid,
Blood-stained, distended, cold and dead—
Joy of my soul, my Saviour sweet—
Upon this sacred winding-sheet.

Hail, awful brow; hail, thorny wreath;
Hail, countenance now pale in death;
Whose glance but late so brightly blazed,
That angels trembled as they gazed.

And hail to thee, my Saviour's side;
And hail to thee, thou wound so wide—
Thou wound more ruddy than the rose,
True antidote of all our woes.

Oh, by those sacred hands and feet
For me so mangled, I entreat,
My Jesu, turn me not away,
But let me here for ever stay.

E. Caswall.

Third Week in Lent.

SACRED WOUNDS OF OUR LORD JESUS CHRIST.

Ecce tempus idoneum.

Behold the appointed time to win
The balm which heals the wounds of sin,
Of thoughts and words and actions base,
That hide from us our Father's face.

In mercy and forbearance long,
The day of grace he doth prolong;
Lest, should he raise the avenging hand,
'Twould crush us with our guilty land.

Then to his throne let us repair,
With fasting, tears and humble prayer;
And holy deeds unite with these,
His just resentment to appease.

So may he cleanse our sins away,
In virtue's robe our souls array,

And us to heavenly mansions bring,
With angels evermore to sing.

Praise to the Father of our Lord ;
Praise to his only Son and Word ;
Like praise, O Holy Ghost, to thee—
Eternal One, eternal Three.
R. Campbell.

Prome vocem, mens, canoram.

Slow and mournful be our tone,
Telling of the grief unknown—
Grief that on the sinless weighed,
When the sinner's debt he paid.
   'Twas for man the lash he bore,
And the thorns his temples tore ;
Bound and helpless on the tree,
Man enslaved he setteth free.
   Pierced for us, a double tide
Flows from his most precious side ;
Awful mysteries revere,
Hail the font and altar here.
   Blessed streams for ever flow,
Bringing grace to all below—
Here our cup of blessing prove,
And our cup of bliss above.
   Man of sorrows, Man of grief,
Let us find in thee relief ;
'Till the night of sorrow o'er,
Sadly flows thy praise no more.
R. Campbell.

Quæ te pro populi criminibus nova.

O thou who, though high-priest, art victim made,
What price for sin has innocence not paid?
What load immense has not thy Father laid
    On thee, his only Son?

Those cruel nails that tore thy sacred feet
Release the captive souls whom devils cheat:
Those piercèd hands the ancient yoke unseat
    That rides a world undone.

The midwife-lance that perforates thy side,
And children from thy loving breast supplied,
Has opened for our souls a healing tide
    To cleanse them and set free.

O juice and source of spiritual life;
O entrance into gates with marvel rife;
O riven rock, which, far from the world's strife,
    We penetrate—e'en we.

Father, if we provoke thee by our guilt,
Behold the precious blood thy Son has spilt:
The lightnings flash: he spreads his palms: thou wilt
    Quench all thy fires divine.

Yea, Father, for his cross and passion's sake,
Thy children of his glory partners make;
And God the Spirit only shall partake
    His honour—his and thine.
                      J. C. Earle.

Fourth Week in Lent.

PRECIOUS BLOOD OF OUR LORD JESUS CHRIST.

Festivis resonent compita vocibus.

With glad and joyous strains now let each street resound,
And let the laurel wreath each Christian brow entwine;
With torches waving bright let old and young go forth,
    And swell the train in solemn line.

Whilst we with bitter tears, with sighs and grief profound,
Wail o'er the saving blood poured forth upon the tree,
Oh, deeply let us muse, and count the heavy price
    Which Christ hath paid to make us free.

The primal man of old, who fell by serpent's guile,
Brought death and many woes upon his fallen race;
But our New Adam, Christ, new life unto us gave,
    And brought to all ne'er-ending grace.

To heaven's highest height, the wailing cry went up
Of him, who hung in pain, God's own eternal Son;
His saving, priceless blood, his Father's wrath appeased,
    And for his sons full pardon won.

Whoe'er in that pure blood his guilty soul shall wash,
Shall from his stains be freed—be made as roses bright—
Shall vie with angels pure, shall please his king and Lord,
    And precious shine in his glad sight.

Oh, from the path of right ne'er let thy steps depart,
But haste thee to the goal in virtue's peaceful ways;
Thy God who reigns on high will e'er direct thy steps,
    And crown thy deeds with blissful days.

Father of all things made, to us propitious be,
For whom thy own dear Son his saving blood did spill;
O Holy Spirit, grant the souls by thee refreshed
    Eternal bliss may ever fill.

T. J. Potter.

Ira justa conditoris.

He who once, in righteous vengeance,
    Whelmed the world beneath the flood,
Once again in mercy cleansed it
    With the stream of his own blood,

Coming from his throne on high
  On the painful cross to die.
Blest with this all-saving shower,
  Earth her beauty straight resumed;
In the place of thorns and briers,
  Myrtles sprang and roses bloomed :
    Bitter wormwood of the waste
    Into honey changed its taste.
Scorpions ceased ; the slimy serpent
  Laid his deadly poison by ;
Savage beasts of cruel instinct
  Lost their wild ferocity ;
    Welcoming the gentle reign
    Of the Lamb for sinners slain.
Oh, the wisdom of the Eternal ;
  Oh, its depth and height divine ;
Oh, the sweetness of that mercy
  Which in Jesus Christ doth shine ;
    Slaves we were condemned to die—
    Our king pays the penalty.
When before the judge we tremble,
  Conscious of his broken laws,
May this blood, in that dread hour,
  Cry aloud and plead our cause :
    Bid our guilty terrors cease ;
    Be our pardon and our peace.
Prince and author of salvation,
  Lord of majesty supreme,
Jesu, praise to thee be given
  By the world thou didst redeem ;
    Who with the Father and the Spirit,
    Reignest in eternal merit.
                                E. Caswall.

Salvete, Christi vulnera.
Hail, holy wounds of Jesus, hail,
  Sweet pledges of the saving rood,

Annus Sanctus.

Whence flow the streams that never fail,
    The purple streams of his dear blood.
Brighter than brightest stars ye show,
    Than sweetest rose your scent more rare,
No Indian gem may match your glow,
    No honey's taste with yours compare.
Portals ye are to that dear home
    Wherein our wearied souls may hide,
Whereto no angry foe can come,
    The heart of Jesus crucified.
What countless stripes our Jesus bore,
    All naked left in Pilate's hall:
What copious floods of purple gore
    Through rents in his torn garments fall.
His beauteous brow, oh, shame and grief,
    By the sharp thorny crown is riven;
Through hands and feet, without relief,
    The cruel nails are rudely driven.
But when for our poor sakes he died,
    A willing priest by love subdued,
The soldier's lance transfixed his side,
    Forth flowed the water and the blood.
In full atonement of our guilt,
    Careless of self, the Saviour trod—
Even till his heart's best blood was spilt—
    The wine-press of the wrath of God.
Come, bathe you in that healing flood,
    All ye who mourn, by sin opprest;
Your only hope is Jesus' blood,
    His sacred heart your only rest.
All praise to him, the eternal Son,
    At God's right hand enthroned above,
Whose blood our full redemption won,
    Whose Spirit seals the gift of love.

H. N. Oxenham.

Fifth Week in Lent.
Part One.

SEVEN DOLOURS OF THE BLESSED VIRGIN MARY.

Stabat Mater dolorosa.

By the cross, on which suspended,
With his bleeding hands extended,
   Hung that Son she so adored,
Stood the mournful Mother weeping,
She whose heart, its silence keeping,
   Grief had cleft as with a sword.

Oh, that Mother's sad affliction—
Mother of all benediction—
   Of the sole-begotten One ;
Oh, the grieving, sense-bereaving,
Of her heaving breast, perceiving
   The dread sufferings of her Son.

What man is there so unfeeling,
Who, his heart to pity steeling,
   Could behold that sight unmoved?
Could Christ's Mother see there weeping,
See the pious Mother keeping
   Vigil by the Son she loved?

For his people's sins atoning,
She saw Jesus writhing, groaning,
   'Neath the scourge wherewith he bled ;
Saw her loved one, her consoler,
Dying in his dreadful dolour,
   Till at length his spirit fled.

O thou Mother of election,
Fountain of all pure affection,
   Make thy grief, thy pain, my own ;

Make my heart to God returning,
In the love of Jesus burning,
   Feel the fire that thine has known.

Blessed Mother of prediction,
Stamp the marks of crucifixion
   Deeply on my stony heart,
Ever leading where thy bleeding
Son is pleading for my needing,
   Let me in his wounds take part.

Make me truly, each day newly
While life lasts, O Mother, duly
   Weep with him, the Crucified;
Let me, 'tis my sole demanding,
Near the cross, where thou art standing,
   Stand in sorrow at thy side.

Queen of virgins, best and dearest,
Grant, oh, grant the prayer thou hearest,
   Let me ever mourn with thee;
Let compassion me so fashion
That Christ's wounds, his death and passion,
   Be each day renewed in me.

Oh, those wounds do not deny me;
On that cross, oh, crucify me;
   Let me drink his blood I pray:
Then on fire, enkindled, daring,
I may stand without despairing
   On that dreadful judgment-day.

May the cross be my salvation;
Make Christ's death my preservation;
   May his grace my heart make wise:
And when death my body taketh,
May my soul when it awaketh
   Ope in heaven its raptured eyes.

D. F. MacCarthy.

Lent: Fifth Week.

Part Two.

Stabat Mater dolorosa.

Weeping sore, the Mother stood
Nigh the cross, the fatal wood,
   Whereon hung her dying Son.

Through her soul for anguish crying,
Sunk in sorrow, spent with sighing,
   The prophetic sword had run.

Oh, how sad, how heavy laden,
Was that meek and blessed Maiden,
   God's true Mother undefiled:

Trembling, grieving, whelmed in woes,
When she saw the dying throes
   Of her own immortal Child.

Who is he whose weeping eyes
Would not choose but sympathise
   With the Mother of our Lord?

Who is he that would refuse
Pity for such Mother's woes,
   Weeping o'er her Son adored?

Tortured for his sinful race,
She beheld each ghastly trace
   Of his scourging at the post.

She beheld her Son so sweet
Dying and all desolate
   When he yielded up the ghost.

Come, dear Mother, love's sweet spring,
Let me share thy sorrowing,
   Let my tears unite with thine,

Let my heart be wrapt in fire
Still to seek with fond desire
   Christ my God, my love divine.

Holy Mother, this impart,
Deeply print upon my heart
   All the wounds he dying bore.

Let me share his pains with thee,
Who so tenderly for me
   Deigned those sorrows to endure.

Let our tears in one same tide
Flow for Jesus crucified,
   Long as life shall warm my breast.

By the cross to take my station,
Share thy tender lamentation,
   This is my most fond request.

Brightest of the virgin-train,
Do not thou my suit disdain,
   Come and share thy grief with me.

Let me trace his sufferings o'er,
Bear the very death he bore,
   When they nailed him to the tree :

Feel the wounds he felt for us,
Drink the chalice of his cross,
   All for love of thy dear Son.

Screened by thee from flames divine,
Mary, guard this soul of mine
   When the judgment-day comes on.

Christ, when these my days are done,
Let thy Mother lead me on
   To the palm of victory :

Yea, when this frail flesh hath died,
Let my soul be glorified
   Safe in paradise with thee.

J. D. Aylward.

Lent: Fifth Week.

Part Three.
Stabat Mater dolorosa.

By the cross of expiation
The Mother stood, and kept her station,
  Weeping for her Son and Lord:
With the nails his hands were riven;
Through her heart the sword was driven,
  Simeon's dread, predicted sword.
Oh, that blessed one grief-laden,
Blessed Mother, blessed Maiden,
  Mother of the All-holy One;
Oh, that silent, ceaseless mourning,
Oh, those dim eyes never turning
  From that wondrous, suffering Son.
Who is he of nature human
Tearless that could watch that Woman?
  Hear unmoved that Mother's moan?
Who, unchanged in shape and colour,
Who could mark that Mother's dolour,
  Weeping with her Son alone?
For his people's sins the All-holy
There she saw, a victim lowly,
  Bleed in torments, bleed and die:
Saw the Lord's Anointed taken;
Saw her Child in death forsaken;
  Heard his last expiring cry.
Fount of love and sacred sorrow,
Mother, may my spirit borrow
  Sadness from thy holy woe;
May it love—on fire within me—
Christ, my God, till great love win me
  Grace to please him here below.
Those five wounds of Jesus smitten,
Mother, in my heart be written
  Deeply as in thine they be;

Thou my Saviour's cross who bearest,
Thou thy Son's rebuke who sharest,
   Let me share them both with thee.

In the passion of my maker
Be my sinful soul partaker;
   Let me weep till death with thee:
Unto me this boon be given,
By thy side, like thee bereaven,
   To stand beneath the atoning tree.

Virgin holiest, Virgin purest,
Of that anguish thou endurest
   Make me bear with thee my part;
Of his passion bear the token
In a spirit bowed and broken,
   Bear his death within my heart.

May his wounds both wound and heal me;
His blood enkindle, cleanse, anneal me;
   Be his cross my hope and stay:
Virgin, when the mountains quiver,
From that flame which burns for ever,
   Shield me on the judgment-day.

Christ, when he that shaped me calls me,
When advancing death appals me,
   Through her prayer the storm make calm:
When to dust my dust returneth
Save a soul to thee that yearneth;
   Grant it thou the crown and palm.

A. de Vere.

PART III.—PASSION-TIDE.

Part One.

Vexilla regis prodeunt.

Banners of our King are streaming,
Blazoned with the cross redeeming,

Passion-Tide: Part One.

Mystic sign of death life stealing,
And of death new life revealing.

At the dreadful spear-point's wounding,
Forth from sacred heart came drowning
Floods that marked our sin-stains' ending,
Water, blood, together blending.

Now fulfilled those words astounding,
Sung in David's psalms resounding,
When to nations prophesying
God from tree should reign in dying.

Beauteous tree, with royal splendour
Purpled by those life-streams tender,
Fair, 'mid ignominious scorning,
Thee, those lovely limbs adorning.

Blessed tree, with arms upbearing
Earth's great ransom from despairing,
God's stupendous balance, weighing
The world's price o'er hell dismaying.

O sweet cross, our hope in anguish,
In this time ere sorrows languish,
Shed thy flood of heavenly graces,
That man's foulest crime effaces.

Threefold fountain of salvation,
God, supreme in exaltation,
Grant to all thy cross here guarding
Thy celestial crowns rewarding.
C. Kent.

Pange lingua gloriosi, lauream.
(*Crux fidelis.*)

O faithful cross, of trees the fairest,
O tree among them all the rarest,
'Mid sylvan bowers no nobler towers,
Or yields such leaves, such fruit, such flowers.

Sweet nails, sweet wood, God's love declaring,
So sweet a load to heaven up-bearing.

(*Pange lingua.*)

O sing my tongue, God's glory sing,
Triumphant palms and laurels bring;
That noblest victory proclaim,
Achieved upon the cross of shame;
When earth's Redeemer gave his breath,
By immolation conquering death.

Our lost progenitors, when God,
Beneath his dread avenging rod,
Saw planting first sin's upas root
On eating the forbidden fruit—
The pitying Lord this holy rood
Placed where the tree of evil stood.

This work benign, of sovereign grace,
Ordained to save the human race,
In spite of hellish arts combined
Wins heaven by arts in heaven designed;
From fiercest foes wrings holiest calm;
In deadliest wound pours healing balm.

For God's own sacrifice sublime,
When came the dread appointed time,
Christ, from the Father's bosom torn,
Creator of the world was born;
God from a Virgin's womb, in tears,
A creature of the flesh appears.

Mere wailing Babe to human eyes—
Lo, God in narrow manger lies;
His limbs in swathing-bands enrolled,
His Virgin-mother's arms enfold;
Almighty—feet, hands, tightly bound,
In lowly girdling-clothes enwound.

(*Lustra sex.*)

Already thirty years have shed
Their humble glory on his head,
When earth's Redeemer freely goes
Through death to dissipate our woes,
On cross, by deadliest wrath assailed,
In awful immolation nailed.

Behold him fainting—gall his drink;
His heart, his strength in anguish sink;
While nails and spear and thorn-crown wound,
His limbs in blood and water drowned;
Wherewith the seas, the stars, the earth
Washed clean, resume their primal worth.

Bend low thy branches, lofty tree,
Let thy stiff sinews loosened be,
The native toughness of thy grain
Be melted 'neath so sweet a strain;
And gently stretch, on tender board,
The limbs of heaven's eternal Lord.

Alone thou art thus fit to bear
The Lamb, earth saving from despair;
Alone, to form salvation's ark
For nations drowning in the dark—
Now safely borne across the flood,
Anointed by that paschal blood.

(*Sempiterna sit.*)

Now everlasting homage be
To God, the holy Trinity;
To God, in whom co-equal meet,
The Father, Son and Paraclete;
The glory of whose triune name
Creation's thousand realms proclaim.

C. Kent.

Part Two.

Vexilla regis prodeunt.

Behold the royal ensigns fly,
Bearing the cross' mystery,
Where life itself did death endure,
And by that death did life procure.

A cruel spear let out a flood
Of water mixed with saving blood,
Which, gushing from the Saviour's side,
Drowned our offences in the tide.

The mystery we now unfold,
Which David's faithful verse foretold
Of our Lord's kingdom; whilst we see
God ruling nations from a tree.

O lovely tree, whose branches wore
The royal purple of his gore,
How glorious does thy body shine,
Supporting members so divine.

The world's blest balance thou wert made,
Thy happy beam its purchase weighed,
And bore his limbs, who snatched away
Devouring hell's expected prey.

Hail cross, our hope; on thee we call,
Who keep this mournful festival;
Grant to the just increase of grace,
And every sinner's crimes efface.

Blest Trinity, we praises sing
To thee, from whom all graces spring;
Celestial crowns on those bestow
Who conquer by the cross below.

Evening Office, 1710.

Passion-Tide: Part Two.

Pange lingua gloriosi, lauream.
(*Crux fidelis.*)
O faithful cross, O noblest tree,
In all our woods there's none like thee;
No earthly groves, no shady bowers,
Produce such leaves, such fruit, such flowers.

Sweet are the nails, and sweet the wood
That bears a weight so sweet, so good.

(*Pange lingua.*)
Sing, O my tongue, devoutly sing
The glorious laurels of our king;
Sing the triumphant victory
Gained on the cross erected high;
Where man's Redeemer yields his breath,
And dying conquers hell and death.

With pity our creator saw
His noble work transgress his law,
When our first parents rashly eat
The fatal tree's forbidden meat;
He then resolved the cross' wood
Should make that tree's sad damage good.

By this wise method, God designed
From sin and death to save mankind;
Superior art with love combines,
And arts of Satan countermines;
And where the traitor gave the wound,
There healing remedies are found.

When the full time decreed above
Was come, to show this work of love,
The eternal Father sends his Son,
The world's creator from his throne;
Who on our earth, this vale of tears,
Clothed with a Virgin's flesh appears.

Thus God made Man an Infant lies,
And in the manger weeping cries;
His sacred limbs by Mary bound,
The poorest tattered rags surround;
And God's incarnate feet and hands
Are closely bound with swathing-bands.

(Lustra sex.)
Full thirty years were freely spent
In this our mortal banishment;
And then the Son of Man decreed
For the lost sons of men to bleed;
And on the cross a victim laid,
The solemn expiation made.

Gall was his drink; his flesh they tear
With thorns and nails; a cruel spear
Pierces his side, from whence a flood
Streams forth of water mixed with blood;
With what a tide are washed again
The sinful earth, the stars, the main.

Bend, towering tree, thy branches bend,
Thy native stubbornness suspend;
Let not stiff nature use its force,
To weaker sap have now recourse;
With softest arms receive thy load,
And gently bear our dying God.

On thee alone the Lamb was slain
That reconciled the world again;
And when on raging seas was tossed
The shipwrecked world and mankind lost,
Besprinkled with his sacred gore,
Thou safely broughtst them to the shore.

(Sempiterna sit.)
All glory to the sacred Three,
One undivided Deity;

To Father, Holy Ghost and Son
Be equal praise and homage done ;
Let the whole universe proclaim
Of One and Three the glorious name.

Divine Office, 1763.

Part Three.

Vexilla regis prodeunt.

Behold, the royal banners fly,
Now shines the awful mystery
Of the dread cross, whereon in death
Incarnate God resigned his breath.

While from his deeply wounded side,
Pierced with the cruel lance, a tide
Of mingled blood and water ran
To cleanse the stains of guilty man.

Then was fulfilled the faithful song
Chaunted of old by David's tongue,
'Lo, from the tree our God commands,
And reigns a king o'er all the lands.'

O glorious tree, all decked with light,
And with the royal purple bright,
Thy branches bear a blessed load,
The price that ransomed us to God.

Blest are thine arms, for what they bear—
Our forfeit nature's ransom dear—
Thou balance which his love weighed down,
To claim what hell had made its own.

Dear cross, best hope o'er all beside,
That cheers the solemn passion-tide,
Give to the just increase of grace,
Give to each contrite sinner peace.

To thee, O Trinity, be given
All the high songs of earth and heaven,
And rule us thou who savest us,
Through the sweet mystery of the cross.
J. D. Aylward.

Pange lingua gloriosi, lauream.
(*Crux fidelis.*)

O faithful cross, O peerless tree,
  In shadiest grove, in greenest bower,
There groweth none to show like thee
  For germ and leaf, for bud and flower.

Sweet are the nails and sweet the wood,
  But sweeter far thy sacred load.

(*Pange lingua.*)

Sing loud the conflict, O my tongue,
  The victory that repaired our loss;
Exalt the triumph of thy song
  To the bright trophy of the cross;
Tell how the Lord laid down his life
To conquer in the glorious strife.

Our pitying maker saw the waste
  Caused by our ancient father's fall,
Through the forbidden fruit, whose taste
  Had made him Satan's helpless thrall;
God then decreed the tree should save
Him whom the tree had made a slave.

Such was the deep and needful scheme
  That rescued man from death's strong toils,
A plan devised by love supreme
  To rend asunder Satan's coils;
That where the foe had dealt the wound,
There might the healing balm be found.

Soon as the destined season came,
  The Father's sole-begotten Son,
Creator of this mighty frame,
  Was sent commissioned from his throne;
Made flesh within the Virgin's womb,
He came to free us from our doom.

Behold, within the manger lying,
  And wrapt in meanest swaddling-clothes,
The heavenly Babe all feebly crying,
  Acquainted even now with woes;
See, how the Virgin-mother sweet
Doth fondly bind his hands and feet.

(*Lustra sex.*)

Now, when full thirty annual suns
  Had seen him draw this mortal breath,
Born to the glorious work, he runs—
  Willing and dedicate to death—
Runs to the cross, the Lamb of God,
And sheds his sacrificial blood.

The bitter drink, the cruel thorn,
  The smiting reed, the nails, the spear,
His tender side all rent and torn,
  The blood and water flowing clear—
With what a strange mysterious tide
Earth, sea and sky are purified.

Bend, lofty tree, thine arms; and let
  The twining fibres of thy frame
All their ungentleness forget,
  Which from thy sterner nature came;
Receive thy God; grow mild for him;
And gently touch each suffering limb.

O cross, deemed worthiest him to bear,
  Who raised us when in ruin hurled;

O ark divine, which floating there,
  Where lay a wrecked and sinking world;
O ark, anointed o'er with blood
Shed by the suffering Lamb of God.

(Sempiterna sit.)
Glory and honour still be done
  To him who reigns o'er all most high;
Alike to Father and to Son
  And Holy Ghost eternally;
To whom alone be power and praise
Through an eternity of days.
J. D. Aylward.

Part Four.
Vexilla regis prodeunt.

The King of kings his banner rears,
The mystery of love appears,
The Lord of life resigns his breath,
And dying ransoms all from death.

Though bowed his head and closed his eyes,
The love he bears us never dies;
And mingled now, more living flows
The stream that life on all bestows.

What prophets sang in heavenly strain,
A king who should for ever reign,
Behold upon his purple throne,
Let all the earth his sceptre own.

O honoured cross, O beauteous tree,
In Eden's bowers was none like thee;
What glory may with thine compare
The Lord, the King of kings to bear?

Blest balance, on whose arms is weighed
The price for our redemption paid—

Passion-Tide: Part Four.

The ransom dear of sinful men,
To bring us back to God again.

Hail, tree of life, whose leaves supply
New life to nations doomed to die;
Beneath thy shade let us abide,
Through hours of holy passion-tide.

To thee, O Christ, for man betrayed,
Be endless praise and glory paid;
The Father equally adore,
And Holy Spirit evermore.
R. Campbell.

Pange lingua gloriosi, lauream.
(*Crux fidelis.*)

Holy cross, blest tree, outvying
   All that's fair in loveliest bowers,
God's own blood thy bloom supplying,
   Sweet thy leaves, thy fruit, thy flowers.

Medicine of the sick and dying,
   Tree of life, thy balm be ours.
R. Campbell.

(*Pange lingua.*)

Sing, my tongue, with glowing accents,
   Of thy Saviour's death the strain;
Sing the great and noble triumph
   Of thy God by sinners slain;
How, upon the cross triumphing,
   He for man did mercy gain.

Grieving in his tender mercy
   O'er his fallen creatures' sin,
He their woes to soothe and soften
   Did in loving haste begin;
And the tree marked out, which later
   Should for sinners mercy win.

Such the order of redemption
  By the Lord our God decreed,
O'er the wily serpent's projects,
  Thus in triumph to succeed;
That the fatal tree of Eden
  Man to glory bright should lead.

When the time of grace and mercy
  In its fulness had drawn nigh,
He, the world's Redeemer, coming
  From his Father's throne on high,
Clad in flesh of purest Virgin,
  Came to suffer and to die.

See the new-born Infant Jesus,
  In a lowly manger lie;
See his Mother's gentle fingers
  His poor humble garments tie;
As with loving hand she swathes him,
  List her fond maternal sigh.

Bright and everlasting glory,
  To the sacred Triad be;
To the Father, Son and Spirit,
  Equal glory ever be;
Heaven, earth and all creation,
  Praise you ever, One in Three.

T. J. Potter.

(*Lustra sex.*)

Soon the sweetest blossom wasting,
  Droops its head and withered lies;
Early thus to Calvary hasting,
  On the cross the Saviour dies;
Freely death for all men tasting,
  There behold our sacrifice.

Finishing his tribulation,
  Now his head he boweth low;

From his side for our salvation,
  Blood and water mingling flow;
Hail the Lamb, from earth's foundation
  Slain to bear the sinner's woe.

Yet bend thine arms, O lofty tree,
  To ease the sufferer's agony;
O bitter tears, O dying groans—
  Why melt ye not, ye rocks, ye stones;
Blest cross, some kind relief accord,
  And gently bear our dying Lord.

Borne on thee the storm we weather,
  Thou dost ride the billows o'er,
And though floods around us gather,
  Safe on thee we reach the shore,
Where the mansions of our Father
  Shelter us for evermore.

(Sempiterna sit.)
Now all praise and adoration
  To the blessed Trinity;
Co-eternal in duration,
  And in power co-equal Three;
Honour, worship and salvation,
  Evermore be paid to thee.

R. Campbell.

Canonical Hours.

PART I.—DAYS OF THE WEEK.

Sunday.

Primo die, quo Trinitas.

TO-DAY the blessed Three in One
  Began the earth and skies;
To-day death's conqueror, God the Son,
  Did from the grave arise:
We too will wake, and, in despite
Of sloth and languor, all unite,
As psalmists bid, through the dim night
  Waiting with wistful eyes.

So may he hear, and heed each vow
  And prayer to him addrest;
And grant an instant cleansing now,
  A future glorious rest:
So may he plentifully shower,
On all who hymn his love and power,
In this most still and sacred hour,
  His sweetest gifts and best.

Father of purity and light,
  Thy presence if we win,
'Twill shield us from the deeds of night,
  The burning darts of sin;
Lest aught defiled or dissolute
Relax our bodies or imbrute,
And fires eternal be the fruit
  Of fire now lit within.

Fix in our hearts, Redeemer dear,
  The ever-gushing spring
Of grace to cleanse, of life to cheer
  Souls sick and sorrowing:
Thee, bounteous Father, we entreat,
And only Son, awful and sweet,
And life-creating Paraclete,
    The everlasting king.

Cardinal Newman.

Æterne rerum conditor.

Maker of the earth and sky,
  Ruler of the day and night,
At thy word the shadows fly,
  Morn returns and all is bright.

Through the midnight-hours forlorn,
  Thou, the Lord of light, art near;
Taught by thee, the bird of morn
  Tells that day will soon appear.

Tossed upon the stormy tide,
  Seamen hail the morning-ray;
He, who thrice his Lord denied,
  Found repentance with the day.

Let us then our hearts arouse,
  Morning calls us to awake,
Bids us haste to pay our vows,
  And our meek confession make.

Jesu, Master, when we fall,
  Turn on us thy healing face;
With that look our souls recall
  Unto penitential grace.

Glory to the Father be,
  Equal glory to the Son,
With the Spirit, One and Three,
  While eternal ages run.

R. Campbell.

Lucis creator optime.

Blest Maker of the radiant light,
Who from the darksome womb of night
Didst make the sun, at nature's birth,
To show the beauteous face of earth :
Who, of the morn and evening ray,
Madst measured light and call'dst it day;
Whilst sable night involves the spheres,
Vouchsafe to hear our vocal tears.
Lest our frail mind on creatures bent,
Should hug its chain and banishment ;
And whilst it thus supinely lies,
Forgets to use its wings and rise.
Oh, may we then our souls exert,
And shake their pinions from the dirt,
To soar on high, and like the dove
Find nought to fix on but above.
In this, most gracious Father, hear,
Through Christ thy equal Son, our prayer,
Who, with the Holy Ghost and thee,
Resides and reigns eternally.

Primer, 1706.

Monday.

Somno refectis artubus.

Sleep has refreshed our limbs, we spring
   From off our bed, and rise ;
Lord, on thy suppliants, while they sing,
   Look with a Father's eyes.

Be thou the first on every tongue,
   The first in every heart ;
That all our doings all day long,
   Holiest, from thee may start.

Cleanse thou the gloom, and bid the light
   Its healing beams renew ;

The sins which have crept in with night,
  With night shall vanish too.
Our bosoms, Lord, unburden thou,
  Let nothing there offend;
That those who hymn thy praises now,
  May hymn them to the end.
Grant this, O Father, only Son
  And Spirit, God of grace,
To whom all worship shall be done
  In every time and place.

Cardinal Newman.

Splendor Paternæ gloriæ.

Splendour of the Father's glory,
  Source of all things fair to sight,
Light of Light, let all adore thee,
  Day in whom the day is bright.

Truest Sun, upon us brighten
  With thy pure and constant gleam;
Fill our hearts, our spirits lighten
  With thy Spirit's cleansing stream.

Christ, be thou our bread from heaven
  And our cup, faith's holy light,
Whence the Spirit, freely given,
  Shall with us himself unite.

So our day serenely flowing,
  Pure will be as morning dawn;
Bright our faith like noon-tide glowing,
  O'er our eve no darkness drawn.

Now all praise and adoration
  To the blessed Trinity;
Praise our God through time's duration;
  Praise him through eternity.

R. Campbell.

Immense cœli conditor.

Creator, God immense and wise,
At whose command the liquid skies
Around the world in order flow,
With streams above and streams below.
To each assigning veins and ways,
By which that element allays
The wasting fires of barren earth,
And fits the soil for fruitful birth.
So, gracious God, mayst thou impart
Thy streams of grace to enrich our heart,
Lest sin's consuming fires decay
Our tenement of fruitless clay.
May faith improve our inward sight,
And guide our wills with heavenly light,
That no vain fires may lead astray,
Nor errors shroud that glorious ray.
In this, most gracious Father, hear,
Through Christ thy equal Son, our prayer,
Who, with the Holy Ghost and thee,
Resides and reigns eternally.

Primer, 1706.

Tuesday.

Consors Paterni luminis.

O God from God, and Light from Light,
   Who art thyself the day,
Our chants shall break the clouds of night ;
   Be with us while we pray.

Chase thou the gloom that haunts the mind,
   The thronging shades of hell,
The sloth and drowsiness that bind
   The senses with a spell.

Lord, to their sins indulgent be,
   Who, in this hour forlorn,

By faith in what they do not see,
With songs prevent the morn.

Grant this, O Father, only Son
And Spirit, God of grace,
To whom all worship shall be done
In every time and place.
Cardinal Newman.

Ales diei nuntius.

The herald of the morn
  Salutes the brightening skies;
Then, let us to our Saviour turn,
  Who calls us to arise.

He calls—ye slothful hear;
  His call brooks no delay;
The Son of Man approaches near—
  Be sober, watch and pray.

If closed on us the gate,
  'Tis closed for evermore;
Prepared his coming then await,
  Nor long for joy before.

O Christ, our souls awake,
  Disperse the clouds of night;
Of former sins the bondage break,
  And give us life and light.

Glory to God above,
  The Father and the Son
And Spirit, source of peace and love,
  While endless ages run.
R. Campbell.

Telluris alme conditor.

O God who, when at nature's birth
The waters hid the face of earth,

Didst make the shores their floods restrain,
And raise the land above the main;
That teeming earth might herbage yield,
And flowers and fruit adorn the field,
At once to charm the taste and eye
With pleasure and variety;
Grant thus our souls may rise from sin,
To bear the fruits of grace again,
Whilst floods of tears resort, to kill
The passions that inflame our will.
May we in all that's good rejoice,
At every call obey thy voice;
And strangers to the ways of death
Untainted yield our parting breath.
In this, most gracious Father, hear,
Through Christ thy equal Son, our prayer,
Who, with the Holy Ghost and thee,
Resides and reigns eternally.

Primer, 1706.

Wednesday.
Rerum creator optime.

Who madest all and dost control,
   Lord, with thy touch divine
Cast out the slumbers of the soul,
   The rest that is not thine.

Look down, eternal holiness,
   And wash the sins away,
Of those who, rising to confess,
   Outstrip the lingering day.

Our hearts and hands by night, O Lord,
   We lift them in our need;
As holy psalmists give the word,
   And holy Paul the deed.

Each sin to thee of years gone by,
   Each hidden stain lies bare;

We shrink not from thine awful eye,
But pray that thou wouldst spare.

Grant this, O Father, only Son
 And Spirit, God of grace,
To whom all worship shall be done
 In every time and place.
Cardinal Newman.

Nox et tenebræ et nubila.

Swift as shadows of the night
Haste before the morning-light;
Powers of darkness quickly fly,
See the Day-spring from on high.

To thy light, O heavenly King,
Undivided hearts we bring;
Seek in praise and prayer thy grace,
Hide not, Lord, from us thy face.

Many stains our souls defile;
Many snares to sin beguile;
Much we need thy light divine—
Light of angels on us shine.

Glory be to God on high,
Father, thee we magnify;
Equally the Son adore,
And the Spirit evermore.
R. Campbell.

Cæli Deus sanctissime.

O source of light, whose glorious ray
Improves the fiery noon of day;
And paints the lucid realms more bright
With beauteous gleams of burnished light;
Who round the world, twice-two days old,
The burning luminary rolled;

And taught the moon and stars to steer
Their roving course around the sphere.
That certain periods thus might show
How time's alternate seasons flow;
How days and nights and months succeed,
And years supply each other's stead.
Restore in us thy heavenly day,
And drive the night of sin away;
That man like them, from darkness free,
May end this course and rest in thee.
In this, most gracious Father, hear,
Through Christ thy equal Son, our prayer,
Who, with the Holy Ghost and thee,
Resides and reigns eternally.
Primer, 1706.

Thursday.

Nox atra rerum contegit.

All tender lights, all hues divine,
   The night has swept away;
Shine on us, Lord, and we shall shine
   Bright in an inward day.

The spots of guilt, sin's wages base,
   Searcher of hearts, we own;
Wash us and robe us in thy grace,
   Who didst for sins atone.

The sluggard soul that bears their mark,
   Shrinks in its silent lair,
Or gropes amid its chambers dark
   For thee, who art not there.

Redeemer, send thy piercing rays,
   That we may bear to be
Set in the light of thy pure gaze,
   And yet rejoice in thee.

Grant this, O Father, only Son
And Spirit, God of grace,
To whom all worship shall be done
In every time and place.
Cardinal Newman.

Lux ecce surgit aurea.

As at morn's golden ray
  Flee the shadows of night,
Thou true Light of the day,
Shades of ill chase away,
  Give thy people thy light.

To thine all-seeing eye
  Every secret is known,
And recorded on high
As each hour passes by
  Are the deeds we have done.

Let our thoughts then be clean,
  And our actions be love;
Let no strife intervene;
All be pure and serene
  As the ray from above.

To the Father be praise,
  And praise to the Son,
And the Spirit always,
While the infinite days
  Of eternity run.
R. Campbell.

Magnæ Deus potentiæ.

O God, whose watery stores supply
The liquid realms of seas and sky
With fruitful stocks of fish and fowl,
To fly the air and swim the pool.
Who taught the birds to soar on high,
Whilst fish their finny pinions ply;

That each, though born of one descent,
Might fill its several element.
Grant that our souls, now past the flood
Of Christ's redeeming tears and blood,
May raise themselves on wing and fly
The dangers of mortality.
That none may sink beneath their fate,
Nor soar on wings of self-conceit;
Lest earthly minds sink once for all,
Or raised too high, increase their fall.
In this, most gracious Father, hear,
Through Christ thy equal Son, our prayer,
Who, with the Holy Ghost and thee,
Resides and reigns eternally.

Primer, 1706.

Friday.

Tu Trinitatis Unitas.

May the dread Three in One, who sways
    All with his sovereign might,
Accept us for this hymn of praise,
    His watchers in the night.

For in the night, when all is still,
    We spurn our bed and rise,
To find the balm for ghostly ill,
    His bounteous hand supplies.

If e'er by night our envious foe
    With guilt our souls would stain,
May the deep streams of mercy flow,
    And make us white again;

That so, with bodies braced and bright,
    And hearts awake within,
All fresh and keen may burn our light,
    Undimmed, unsoiled by sin.

Shine on thine own, Redeemer sweet,
  Thy radiance increate
Through the long day shall keep our feet
  In their pure morning state.

Grant this, O Father, only Son
  And Spirit, God of grace,
To whom all worship shall be done
  In every time and place.
                              Cardinal Newman.

Æterna cœli gloria.

Christ, the glory of the sky,
  Christ, of earth the hope secure,
Only Son of God most high,
  Offspring of a Maiden pure.

Help us now thy praise to sing,
  Praise for this returning day;
Light and life let morning bring,
  Clouds and darkness flee away.

Purest light, within us dwell,
  Never from our souls depart;
Come, the shades of earth expel,
  Fill and purify the heart.

Faith in him whose name we bear,
  In our heart of hearts abound;
Hope, thy brightest torch prepare;
  All with holy love be crowned.

Praise the Father; praise the Son;
  Spirit blest, to thee be praise;
To the eternal Three in One
  Glory be through endless days.
                              R. Campbell.

Hominis superne conditor.

Man's sovereign God, to whom we owe
Both all we are and all we do;

Who, from the teeming womb of earth,
Gavst servile brutes and reptiles birth ;
That monsters of the land and deep
Awaked to life from realms of sleep,
By turns might their obedience pay
To nobler man's imperial sway ;
Suppress whate'er by sensual arts,
Like insects, breeds in earthly hearts;
Before those sins to monsters grow
And move the wheels of all we do.
From noisy strife our souls release ;
Cement the ties of heavenly peace ;
Shower down thy streams of grace, till we
Meet our reward and bliss in thee.
In this, most gracious Father, hear,
Through Christ thy equal Son, our prayer,
Who, with the Holy Ghost and thee,
Resides and reigns eternally.
Primer, 1706.

Saturday.
Summæ parens clementiæ.

Father of mercies infinite,
   Ruling all things that be,
Who, shrouded in the depth and height,
   Art One, and yet art Three :

Accept our chants, accept our tears,
   A mingled stream we pour ;
Such stream the laden bosom cheers,
   To taste thy sweetness more.

Purge thou with fire the o'ercharged mind,
   Its sores and wounds profound ;
And with the watcher's girdle bind
   The limbs which sloth has bound.

That they who with their chants by night
   Before thy presence come,

All may be filled with strength and light
  From their eternal home.
Grant this, O Father, only Son
  And Spirit, God of grace,
To whom all worship shall be done
  In every time and place.
                Cardinal Newman.

Aurora jam spargit polum.
Morning shines with Eastern light,
  Earth is glad the day to see,
Flee ye phantoms of the night,
  Thoughts and deeds of darkness flee.

So, when breaks our latest morn,
  And we rise our Lord to meet,
Songs shall welcome in its dawn,
  Shouts of joy its coming greet.

Glory to the Father be,
  Equal glory to the Son,
With the Spirit, One and Three,
  While eternal ages run.
                R. Campbell.

Jam sol recedit igneus.
The fiery sun now rolls away,
And hastens to the close of day;
Thy brightest beams, O Lord, impart,
And rise in our benighted heart.
To us the praises of thy name
Are morning-song and evening-theme;
Thus may we sing ourselves to rest
Amidst the music of the blest.
To God, the Father and the Son
And Holy Spirit, Three in One,
Be endless glory, as before
The world began, so evermore.
                Primer, 1706.

PART II.—HOURS OF THE DAY.

Matins.
Nocte surgentes.

Let us arise, and watch by night,
    And meditate always ;
And chant, as in our maker's sight,
    United hymns of praise.

So, singing with the saints in bliss,
    With them we may attain
Life everlasting after this,
    And heaven for earthly pain.

Grant it to us, O Father, Son
    And Spirit, God of grace,
To whom all worship shall be done
    In every time and place.
                   Cardinal Newman.

Lauds.
Ecce jam noctis.

Paler have grown the shades of night,
    And nearer draws the day,
Checkering the sky with streaks of light,
    Since we began to pray :

To pray for mercy when we sin,
    For cleansing and release,
For ghostly safety, and within
    For everlasting peace.

Praise to the Father, as is meet,
    Praise to the only Son,
Praise to the holy Paraclete,
    While endless ages run.
                   Cardinal Newman

Prime.

Jam lucis orto sidere.

The star of morn to night succeeds;
  We therefore meekly pray,
May God, in all our words and deeds,
  Keep us from harm this day:
May he in love restrain us still
From tones of strife and words of ill,
And wrap around and close our eyes
To earth's absorbing vanities.

May wrath, and thoughts that gender shame
  Ne'er in our breasts abide;
And cheerful abstinences tame
  Of wanton flesh the pride:
So, when the weary day is o'er,
And night and stillness come once more,
Strong in self-conquering purity,
We may proclaim, with choirs on high:

  Praise to the Father, as is meet,
    Praise to the only Son,
  Praise to the holy Paraclete,
    While endless ages run.

Cardinal Newman.

Terce.

Nunc sancte nobis Spiritus.

Come, Holy Ghost, who ever One
Reignest with Father and with Son;
It is the hour, our souls possess
With thy full flood of holiness.

Let flesh and heart and lips and mind
Sound forth our witness to mankind;
And love light up our mortal frame,
Till others catch the living flame.

Now to the Father, to the Son
And to the Spirit, Three in One,

Be praise and thanks and glory given
By men on earth, by saints in heaven.

Cardinal Newman.

Sext.
Rector potens, verax Deus.

O God, who canst not change nor fail,
   Guiding the hours, as they roll by,
Brightening with beams the morning pale,
   And burning in the mid-day sky,

Quench thou the fires of hate and strife,
   The wasting fever of the heart;
From perils guard our feeble life,
   And to our souls thy peace impart.

Grant this, O Father, only Son
   And Holy Spirit, God of grace,
To whom all glory, Three in One,
   Be given in every time and place.

Cardinal Newman.

None.
Rerum Deus tenax vigor.

O God, unchangeable and true,
   Of all the life and power,
Dispensing light in silence through
   Every successive hour.

Lord, brighten our declining day,
   That it may never wane,
Till death, when all things round decay,
   Brings back the morn again.

This grace on thy redeemed confer,
   Father, co-equal Son
And Holy Ghost, the Comforter,
   Eternal Three in One.

Cardinal Newman.

Vespers.
Lucis creator optime.

Father of lights, by whom each day
   Is kindled out of night,

Who, when the heavens were made, didst lay
  Their rudiments in light ;
Thou, who didst bind and blend in one
  The glistening morn and evening pale,
Hear thou our plaint, when light is gone,
  And lawlessness and strife prevail.

Hear, lest the whelming weight of crime
  Wreck us with life in view ;
Lest thoughts and schemes of sense and time
  Earn us a sinner's due :

So may we knock at heaven's door,
  And strive the immortal prize to win,
Continually and evermore
  Guarded without and pure within.

Grant this, O Father, only Son
  And Spirit, God of grace,
To whom all worship shall be done
  In every time and place.
Cardinal Newman.

Compline.

Te lucis ante terminum.

Now that the daylight dies away,
  By all thy grace and love,
Thee, maker of the world, we pray
  To watch our bed above.

Let dreams depart and phantoms fly,
  The offspring of the night ;
Keep us, like shrines, beneath thine eye,
  Pure in our foe's despite.

This grace on thy redeemed confer,
  Father, co-equal Son
And Holy Ghost, the Comforter,
  Eternal Three in One.
Cardinal Newman.

Easter.

First Week.

Ad regias Agni dapes.

SING, for the dark Red Sea is past,
The Lamb's high feast is won at last ;
In snow-white stoles to Christ our king
Loud paschal alleluias sing.

Victim and priest—his flesh our food,
The chalice crowned with his dear blood ;
His love divine, in death made known,
That royal feast for us hath won.

Of old the avenging angel fled
The blood upon the lintel spread,
For Israel's sons the waves divide,
Closed o'er their foes the refluent tide.

The Church this day in heavenlier strain
Hymns the true paschal victim slain,
Pure bread of truth to pure souls given,
The unleavened bread that came from heaven.

Hail, heavenly victim, Lord of life,
True conqueror in the unearthly strife,
True Lord of life's unfailing crown,
Whom death and hell their sovereign own.

See, Christ his spoils victorious show,
The rebel host in chains laid low ;
Dragged to the portals of the sky,
See, hell's dark king a captive lie.

Easter: First Week.

O Christ, from death of sin set free
The sons of life new-born to thee,
So, on our inmost souls shalt thou
Unceasing paschal joy bestow.

Father of heaven, all praise to thee;
To Jesus risen all glory be;
Dread Paraclete, to thee we raise
Through endless years the song of praise.
H. N. Oxenham.

Chorus novæ Hierusalem.

Jerusalem, thy song be new,
To-day a gladlier strain is due;
Let chastened joy in floods descend
The paschal morning to befriend.
   Lion of Judah, ere this hour
Rising, thou break'dst the serpent's power;
Ere light be born, thy voice so clear
Those saved from death shall joyous hear.
   Hell yields his prey he held amain,
And those he snared are freed again;
In willing thraldom, bound by love,
Onwards as Jesus' band they move.
   His triumph all in splendour is,
Passing the heart's best ecstasies,
Of earth and yon bright heaven to come
He makes one commonwealth, one home.
   To him as soldiers all belong,
Blend we a lowly prayer with song,
That in his palace wondrous bright
The king may place us in his sight.
   Through ages that a goal have none
To Father homage shall be done,
To Son and Spirit honour be,
And equal praise eternally.
Lord Braye.

Rex sempiterne cœlitum.

O thou, the heavens' eternal King,
    Lord of the starry spheres,
Who with the Father equal art
    From everlasting years:
All praise to thy most holy name,
    Who, when the world began,
Yoking the soul with clay, didst form
    In thine own image, man.
And praise to thee, who, when the foe
    Had marred thy work sublime,
Clothing thyself in flesh, didst mould
    Our race a second time;
When from the tomb new-born, as from
    A Virgin born before,
Thou raising us from death with thee
    Didst us in thee restore.
Eternal shepherd, who thy flock
    In thy pure font dost lave,
Where souls are cleansed, and all their guilt
    Buried as in a grave;
Jesu, who to the cross wast nailed,
    Our hopeless debt to pay;
Jesu, who lavishly didst pour
    Thy blood for us away:
Oh, from the wretched death of sin
    Keep us; so shalt thou be
The everlasting paschal joy
    Of all new-born in thee.
To God the Father, with the Son
    Who from the grave arose,
And thee, O Paraclete, be praise
    While age on ages flows.
                  E. Caswell.

Easter: First Week.

Aurora cœlum purpurat.

Aurora spreads her cheerful rays,
The heavens rejoice in hymns of praise;
The earth resounds in tuneful strains
More loud than hell can shake its chains;
    To see the mighty Jesus lead
The patriarchs ransomed from the dead,
Late sons of shades and heirs of night,
To people realms of endless light.

    The dead's first-born resumes his breath,
And forces through the gates of death,
To come victorious, and increase
The triumphs of his own decease.
    Cease, mournful tears; behold, relief;
Enough you have indulged in grief:
The herald-angels now proclaim
Life's reign restored, and sound his fame.

    From death of sin, O Jesus, free
Them that are born again to thee;
Be thou alone our chosen guest
And everlasting paschal feast.
    May endless worlds the glories tell
Of Christ, who vanquished death and hell;
And one eternal praise repeat
The Father and the Paraclete.

Primer, 1706.

O filii et filiæ.

O maids and striplings, hear love's story:
The King of heaven, the king of glory
This day hath risen from cerements gory.

At gleam of east, earth's blush resembling,
Around the tomb, with awe and trembling,
The Lord's disciples were assembling.

At dawn, with love their anguish calming,
Three Maries, stifling sobs and psalming,
Came bent upon the Lord's embalming.

An angel, clad in garments glowing,
There sat who spoke thus: 'Fear not; knowing
To Galilee the Lord is going.'

And John, of all the twelve belovèd,
Outstripping Peter who fast movèd,
First reached the tomb as love behovèd.

But they and theirs while grief yet wrung them,
Behold, Christ one day stood among them :
'Peace,' when he breathed, joy pain-like stung them.

But Didymus, not present, hearing
Of his, their Jesus' re-appearing,
Withheld his faith, deception fearing.

'Behold, O Thomas unbelieving,
My feet, my hands, my side; and grieving,
Mark well these wounds no sight deceiving.'

Who, when he saw his Lord's flesh keeping,
Those brands of death, his heart upleaping,
'My Lord, my God,' cried he there weeping.

Yea, rather, blessèd they who see not,
Yet whose undoubting faith will flee not,
Though visual proof, e'en one, there be not.

Upon this holy feast, now raising
Our hearts to heaven in songs of praising,
Sing him of glory, sun-like blazing.

In hushed humility avowing,
With knees and hearts and senses bowing,
All his great mercies life endowing.

C. Kent.

Second Week.
Ad regias Agni dapes.

The Red Sea now is passed, and now
Around the Lamb's great feast we bow;
Now clothed in white and purified,
We praise our king—the Christ who died.

So great his love, that for our good,
He bids us drink his sacred blood;
And gives us in the mystic feast,
Himself—the sacrifice and priest.

Blood sprinkled on the posts of yore
Scared death's sad angel from the door;
The sea was parted too, and gave
To the pursuing foe a grave.

But Christ is now the pasch by whom
We triumph o'er impending doom;
Sincere and pure, we now are fed
By Christ, the pure prefigured bread.

Hail, truest victim, truly given—
By whom the thrall of hell is riven;
Who makest death itself as nought—
By whom the joys of life are bought.

Hell now is vanquished; Christ displays
To the wide world his trophies. Gaze
On heaven laid open—while the foe,
The king of shades, he drives below.

Jesus, be thou our paschal joy;
Be thoughts of thee our sole employ;
From deadly sin, we pray thee, free
Those born again to life by thee.

To God the Father loudly sing,
And Jesus, who rose triumphing,

And to the Holy Ghost upraise
For evermore melodious praise.
J. R. Beste.

Rex sempiterne cœlitum.

Eternal King, whose equal reign
With God before the world began;
And from the darksome womb of night
Brought'st all created things to light.

When first thou gav'st to nature birth,
And framd'st the globe of heaven and earth—
Of that same earth, a narrow span,
Thou mad'st thy own resemblance, man.

And when hell's black prevailing art
Had changed the hue and turned the heart;
Thou cam'st to rescue and restore
The image thou hadst framed before.

Then wert thou born of Virgin's womb;
And now in thee the sacred tomb
Restores the grave's first-fruits to breath,
To lead us from the realms of death.

He leads through the baptismal flood—
A stream he tinctured with his blood—
By which, as from the grave of sin,
The soul revives and lives again.

The cross he freely underwent,
And took on him our punishment;
His wounds like springs of mercy bled,
And plentiful redemption shed.

From death of sin, O Jesus, free
Them that are born again to thee;
Be thou alone our chosen guest,
And everlasting paschal feast.

May endless worlds the glories tell
Of Christ, who vanquished death and hell;

And one eternal praise repeat
The Father and the Paraclete.
Primer, 1706.

Aurora cælum purpurat.
The dawn was purpling o'er the sky;
　With alleluias rang the air;
Earth held a glorious jubilee;
　Hell gnashed its teeth in fierce despair:
When our most valiant mighty king
　From death's abyss, in dread array,
Led the long-prisoned Fathers forth,
　Into the beam of life and day:

When he, whom stone and seal and guard
　Had safely to the tomb consigned,
Triumphant rose, and buried death
　Deep in the grave he left behind.
'Calm all your grief, and still your tears';
　Hark, the descending angel cries;
'For Christ is risen from the dead,
　And death is slain, no more to rise.'

O Jesu, from the death of sin
　Keep us, we pray; so shalt thou be
The everlasting paschal joy
　Of all the souls new-born in thee.
To God the Father, with the Son
　Who from the grave immortal rose,
And thee, O Paraclete, be praise
　While age on endless ages flows.
E. Caswall.

Victimæ paschali laudes.
The holy paschal work is wrought,
　The victim's praise be told,
The loving shepherd back hath brought
　The sheep into his fold:

The just and innocent was slain
To reconcile to God again.

Death from the Lord of life hath fled—
    The conflict strange is o'er ;
Behold, he liveth that was dead,
    And lives for evermore :
'Mary, thou soughtest him that day ;
Tell what thou sawest in the way.'

'I saw the empty cavern's gloom,
    The garments of the prison,
The angel-guardians of the tomb,
    The glory of the Risen.'
We know that Christ hath burst the grave,
Then, victor King, thy people save.
                              R. Campbell.

Third Week.
Ad regias Agni dapes.

Come to the regal feast displayed
In robes of purest white arrayed,
The Red Sea's threatening perils past,
And sing to Christ secure at last.

The Lamb's pure blood, the pledge of love,
Is freely given us from above ;
His body now in glorious state,
As priest, his love will immolate.

The doors which show the sanguine dye
The avenging angel passes by :
The waters of the deep divide—
The foe is whelmed beneath the tide.

Christ is the pasch we sacrifice,
Pure victim to the Father's eyes,
Approaching with unsullied mind,
May all his grace and mercy find.

Celestial victim, spotless, true,
Who hell's dark kingdom overthrew,
From chains of death our souls relieved,
And life's perennial crown received.

Victor of hell, Christ risen displays
His trophies bright with glory's rays;
And opening heaven, he binds his chain
Around the king of hell's domain.

O Jesus, that our faithful mind
In thee pure paschal joy may find,
From deadly sin redeem us free,
And grant us life renewed in thee.

To God the Father, to the Son
Who rose from death, his victory won,
And Holy Spirit, hymns of praise
And glory sempiternal raise.

F. C. Husenbeth.

Aurora lucis rutilat.

The ruddy light now newly born,
With newest praise awakes the morn;
The whole bright world with joy is gay,
The night, death's type, has passed away.

And now the king, the Lord of strength,
Bursting the bars of death at length,
Breaks down the prison—hell and sin—
To free the captives chained therein.

E'en he, beneath the sealèd stone,
Whom soldiers guarded as death's own,
Leading a triumph nobly bright,
Rises resplendent o'er death's night.

Man's every sigh finds solace near,
Comes comfort for man's every fear,
An angel clothed in robes from heaven
Proclaims on earth, 'The Lord is risen.'

The apostles' hearts were filled with pain—
The Lamb by evil men was slain ;
The apostles mourned o'er that fierce woe
Their Lord had deigned to undergo.

We pray thee, Lord of heaven and earth,
In this unbounded paschal mirth,
To save the people of thine arm
From taint of sin, hell's ready harm.

We pray thee, maker of all things,
While Easter's note in gladness rings,
Thy people from sin's power defend,
From power of death save to the end.

Lord Braye.

Rex sempiterne cœlitum.

High heaven's eternal Lord,
  Maker of earth and sky,
Co-equal Son, co-equal Word,
  From all eternity.

From thee our being flowed
  When this fair world began,
Thy breath a living soul bestowed
  Thine image formed in man.

And when by guilt undone
  We marred that form so fair,
Our nature frail thou didst not shun
  The ruin to repair.

Once born from Mary's womb,
  Now rising from the dead,
Thou callest us to thee to come,
  To thee our living head.

Good shepherd, from whose side
  Baptismal waters pour,
Thy ransomed flock to cleanse and hide
  The guilt that we deplore.

The penalty we owed,
'Twas thine, O Lord, to bear ;
The blood that from thy body flowed
Has paid our ransom here.

Lord, that our paschal joy
May never find an end,
The breath of sin and death destroy,
Our new-born souls defend.

Praise to the Father sing,
Our risen Lord adore,
Like praises to the Spirit bring,
One God for evermore.

R. Campbell.

O filii et filiæ.

Young men and maids, rejoice and sing,
The King of heaven, the glorious king,
This day from death rose triumphing.

On Sunday morn by break of day,
His dear disciples haste away
Unto the tomb, wherein he lay.

Nor Magdalen, nor Salomè,
Nor James' mother now delay
To embalm the precious corpse straightway.

An angel clothed in white they see,
When thither come ; and thus spoke he :
'The Lord is gone to Galilee.'

The dear beloved apostle John
Much swifter than Saint Peter run,
And first arrivèd at the tomb.

While in a room the apostles were,
In midst of them Christ did appear,
And said : 'Peace be unto all here.'

When Didymus had heard it said
That Christ was risen from the dead,
His feeble faith yet staggerèd.

'O Thomas, view my side and see
The wounds in hands and feet that be;
Renounce thine incredulity.'

When Thomas Jesus had surveyed,
And on his wounds his fingers laid;
'Thou art my Lord and God,' he said.

Blessed are they who have not seen,
And yet whose faith entire hath been,
Them endless life from death shall screen.

On this most solemn feast let's raise
Our hearts to God in hymns of praise,
And let us bless the Lord always.

Our grateful thanks to God let's give
In humble manner, while we live,
For all the favours we receive.

*Evening Office, 1748 and
Divine Office, 1763.*

Fourth Week.

Ad regias Agni dapes.

At the Lamb's high feast we sing
Praise to our victorious king;
Washed our garments in the tide
Flowing from his pierced side.

Praise we him whose love divine
Gives the guests his blood for wine,
Gives his body for the feast—
Love the victim, love the priest.

Where the paschal blood is poured,
Death's dark angel sheathes his sword;

Israel's hosts triumphant go
Through the wave that drowns the foe.

Christ, the Lamb whose blood is shed,
Paschal victim, paschal bread;
With sincerity and love
Eat we manna from above.

Mighty victim from the sky,
Powers of hell beneath thee lie;
Death is conquered in the fight;
Thou hast brought us life and light.

Now thy banner thou dost wave;
Vanquished Satan and the grave;
Angels join his praise to tell—
See o'erthrown the prince of hell.

Paschal triumph, paschal joy,
Only sin can this destroy;
From the death of sin set free,
Souls re-born, dear Lord, in thee.

Hymns of glory, songs of praise,
Father, unto thee we raise;
Risen Lord, all praise to thee,
Ever with the Spirit be.
R. Campbell.

Aurora cœlum purpurat.

The morn had spread her crimson rays,
When rang the skies with shouts of praise;
Earth joined the joyful hymn to swell,
That brought despair to vanquished hell.

He comes victorious from the grave,
The Lord omnipotent to save,
And brings with him to light of day
The saints who long imprisoned lay.

Vain is the cavern's three-fold ward—
The stone, the seal, the armèd guard;
O death, no more thine arm we fear,
The victor's tomb is now thy bier.

Let hymns of joy to grief succeed,
We know that Christ is risen indeed;
We hear his white-robed angel's voice,
And in our risen Lord rejoice.

With Christ we died, with Christ we rose,
When at the font his name we chose;
Oh, let not sin our robes defile,
And turn to grief the paschal smile.

To God the Father let us sing,
To God the Son, our risen king,
And equally let us adore
The Spirit, God for evermore.
R. Campbell.

Jesu, Redemptor sæculi.

Jesu, the earth's Redeemer thou,
In death thy head didst meekly bow,
Uprising from the grave again,
Death's victor evermore to reign;

Night's veil is covering all below;
Lord, shield us from our crafty foe;
While needful rest our bodies take,
Oh, keep our souls in thee awake.

This blessing, Lord, thy people give—
With thee to die, with thee to live;
For thee, things earthly to despise,
And have our treasure in the skies.

To God the Father praises sing;
Sing praises to our risen king,
Great leader of the Christian host;
Sing praises to the Holy Ghost.
R. Campbell.

Victimæ paschali laudes.

Bring, all ye dear-bought nations, bring
Your richest praises to your king—
That spotless Lamb, who more than due
Paid for his sheep, and those sheep you;
That guiltless Son, who wrought your peace,
And made his Father's anger cease.
Life and death together fought,
Each to a strange extreme were brought.
Life died, but soon revived again,
And even death by it was slain.
Say, happy Magdalen, oh say,
What didst thou see there by the way?
'I saw the tomb of my dear Lord;
I saw himself and him adored;
I saw the napkin and the sheet,
That bound his head and wrapt his feet;
I heard the angels witness bear,
"Jesus is risen; he is not here:
Go, tell his followers, they shall see
Thine and their hope in Galilee."'
We, Lord, with faithful heart and cheerful voice,
On this thy glorious rising-day rejoice;
O thou, whose conquering power o'ercame the grave,
By thy victorious grace us sinners save.
W. K. Blount, 1670.

Fifth Week.
Ad regias Agni dapes.

Now to the Lamb's high festival,
    Clad in our dazzling robes we haste,
And all the Red Sea's dangers o'er,
    His deep and tender love we taste.

Behold his love, so deep, so high,
   His blood he gives instead of wine;
Whilst his own flesh so sweet and pure,
   Doth crown the feast of love divine.

As Israel's lintels stained with gore
   Quick doth the 'venging angel pass;
Or as the rough and surging sea,
   Doth merge all Egypt's struggling mass;

So Jesus Christ, our paschal feast,
   Brings us safe through dangers dread,
Food for pure and holiest souls,
   Jesu, our pure unleavened bread.

Of victims high the highest, hail,
   Hell's hosts do bend in awe to thee,
Thou dost the chains of death unloose,
   And man doth gain his crown through thee.

Hail, thou our victim, Christ our Lord,
   Clad in bright trophies of thy might;
Thou hast the gates of heaven unbarred,
   And scattered all the powers of night.

From the sad death of sin and guilt
   Keep us, O Jesu, ever free;
Be thou the paschal joy divine
   Of the pure souls new-born in thee.

To God the Father endless praise,
   To God his co-eternal Son
Who rose from death, may homage glad,
   With God the Holy Ghost, be done.

T. J. Potter.

Chorus novæ Hierusalem.

Ye choirs of new Jerusalem,
   Your sweetest notes employ,
The paschal victory to hymn
   In strains of holy joy;

How Judah's Lion burst his chains,
    And crushed the serpent's head,
And brought with him, from death's domains,
    The long-imprisoned dead.

From hell's devouring jaws the prey
    Alone our leader bore ;
His ransomed hosts pursue their way
    Where he hath gone before.

Triumphant in his glory now,
    His sceptre ruleth all ;
Earth, heaven and hell before him bow,
    And at his footstool fall.

While joyful thus his praise we sing,
    His mercy we implore,
Into his palace bright to bring,
    And keep us evermore.

Through times unknown to earthly thought,
    O Father, praise to thee ;
To him who our salvation wrought,
    And to the Spirit be.
                  R. Campbell.

Sermone blando angelus.

The angel's gracious message came
Upon the women's hearts like flame ;
Haste, haste, for ye shall surely see
Your risen Lord in Galilee.

While quick they speed along the road
The master's steps had lately trod,
Behold, he lives and speaks, he stands,
And they adore his feet and hands.

And when they had discerned him, lo,
To Galilee the brethren go,
Intent to see the glorious face
Desired of all the human race.

The sun with paschal joy is bright,
The air becomes a flood of light,
When his apostles see the true
And risen Lord exposed to view.

His sacred wounds how clear they shine
In frame of lucid flesh divine;
While every voice extols the might
That raised it from the couch of night.
O Lord of all, defend, we pray,
In this glad resurrection-day,
Thy people from assault of ill,
And all thy promises fulfil.

Arise, O Lord, into thy rest,
And make thine ark in every breast,
That unto thee we render praise
And blessing all our peaceful days.
To thee, O Lord, be glory given,
Who didst arise from earth to heaven,
And who, with Sire and Spirit one,
Dost reign eternal—God the Son.

J. C. Earle.

O filii et filiæ.

Ye sons and daughters of the Lord,
The king of glory, king adored,
This day himself from death restored.

All in the early morning grey
Went holy women on their way,
To see the tomb where Jesus lay.

Of spices pure a precious store
In their pure hands those women bore,
To anoint the sacred body o'er.

Then straightway one in white they see,
Who saith, 'Ye seek the Lord; but he
Is risen, and gone to Galilee.'

This told they Peter, told they John ;
Who forthwith to the tomb are gone,
But Peter is by John outrun.

That self-same night, while out of fear
The doors were shut, their Lord most dear
To his apostles did appear.

But Thomas, when of this he heard,
Was doubtful of his brethren's word ;
Wherefore again there comes the Lord.

' Thomas, behold my side,' saith he ;
' My hands, my feet, my body see,
And doubt not, but believe in me.'

When Thomas saw that wounded side,
The truth no longer he denied ;
' Thou art my Lord and God,' he cried.

Oh, blest are they who have not seen
Their Lord, and yet believe in him :
Eternal life awaiteth them.

Now let us praise the Lord most high,
And strive his name to magnify
On this great day, through earth and sky :

Whose mercy ever runneth o'er ;
Whom men and angel hosts adore ;
To him be glory evermore.

E. Caswall.

Sixth Week.

Ad regias Agni dapes.

The Red Sea's dangers now are past,
In robes of white come let us taste
The Lamb's most royal feast, and sing
A hymn of praise to Christ our king.

His blood with charity divine
He to us drinks, instead of wine ;

His body for this mystic feast
Is sacrificed by love, as priest.

The posts thus stained with sacred gore
The wasting angel passes o'er;
The yielding sea divides its waves—
Egyptians float in liquid graves.

Our paschal feast and sacrifice
Is Christ the Lamb, that for us dies;
Christ is the pure unleavened bread,
By which the purest minds are fed.

O true celestial sacrifice,
By thee hell's power vanquished lies:
Relentless death unlocks his chains,
And life eternal man regains.

The tyrant-prince of hellish night
Thus conquered, and the infernal fight
Thus won, victorious Christ displays
His trophies, and to heaven conveys.

That we for ever may possess
This joyful paschal happiness,
From death of sin, O Jesus, free
Those that are born again of thee.

To God the Father, and the Son
Who rose from death, be homage done;
This praise for ever let's repeat
To God the holy Paraclete.

Evening Office, 1710.

Adeste, cœlitum chori.

Heavenly choirs with anthems sweet
Haste the risen Lord to greet;
Victor he of death and hell—
Join with us his praise to tell.

Vain the seals, the soldiers vain,
Life himself takes life again;
All in vain the guarded tomb—
Clave he not the Virgin-womb?

Yield not with degrading fear,
None his body shall come near;
He who fought and vanquished death,
Will renew the body's breath.

Crowds insulting cried, 'Descend,
And to thee our knees we bend;'
But, resolving to fulfil
Unto death his Father's will,

Mightier triumph he achieves—
Dying and behold he lives;
Rising from his dark abode,
Hail him, Christ, the Son of God.

Hark, what notes of bitter scorn
Through the thickening gloom are borne,
While the Roman and the Jew
Mock their Lord, their Saviour too.

He, the victim and the priest,
Has the world from guilt released;
Though not from the cross set free,
Gain untold was his to be.

Grant us, Lord, with thee to die,
Earth's temptations to deny;
Grant us, Lord, with thee to rise
Rich with treasures of the skies.

Hymns of glory, songs of praise,
Father, unto thee we raise;
Risen Lord, all praise to thee
With the Spirit ever be.

R. Campbell and
J. C. Earle.

Sermone blando angelus.

How sweet those words of soothing were,
Whereby an angel calmed their fear
Who sought the Lord : 'Him ye shall see'—
'Twas thus he spake—'in Galilee.'
   Swift in their joy such words to tell,
The women seek the apostles' cell ;
When, lo, midway the Lord appears—
They kiss his feet and bathe with tears.
   Swift too, when first the tidings came,
His dear disciples ran to claim
A vision there in Galilee
Of that lost face they yearned to see.
   For very paschal gladness gay,
Brighter the sun shines down to-day—
This day on which the apostles see
The risen Saviour bodily.
   Refulgent with a splendour new
His wounded flesh they touch and view ;
To all the nations under heaven
This is their message, 'Christ is risen.'
   King Christ, whose mercy is thy crown,
These hearts of ours make thou thine own ;
So bounden praises we may pour
Before thy throne for evermore.
   We pray thee, Lord of heaven and earth,
In this unbounded paschal mirth,
To save the people of thine arm
From taint of sin, hell's ready harm.
   We pray thee, maker of all things,
While Easter's note of gladness rings,
Thy people from sin's power defend,
From power of death save to the end.

Lord Braye.

Easter: Sixth Week.

Jesu, Redemptor sæculi.

Jesus, who didst redeem mankind,
And on the third day thence unbind
The bands of death, sharp throes of strife
Thou changest for the crown of life.
    Again will fall the shades of night,
Again deep sleep will veil our sight;
Oh, scatter thou each noxious air,
And bring to light each hidden snare.
    O Christ, the light of life, renew
Our bodies with sleep's balmy dew;
And by thy grace our souls inspire
From thy perennial altar fire.
    We ask the mystic life to live,
Which thou alone hast power to give;
To rise from earth and live above
In thy transporting realm of love.
    Praise to the Father and the Son
Who hast for us the victory won;
And equal praise to thee be given,
The Spirit guiding man to heaven.
J. C. Earle.

Victimæ paschali laudes.

    Christians, your voices raise,
And to the paschal victim give
    A sacrifice of praise.
    Man's ransom hath been paid,
A guiltless Lamb hath bled and died
    To save the sheep that strayed.
    Christ, source of every grace,
Hath to his Father reconciled
    Eve's fallen, guilty race.
    How marvellous the strife;
How dread the combat, hand to hand,
    When death confronted life.

That combat now is o'er;
The Lord of life triumphant reigns;
He lives to die no more.

'Say, Magdalen, oh say,
What saw you when you hurried forth
At early dawn of day?'

'I saw the empty tomb;
And saw again in glory risen
The fruit of Mary's womb:

'I saw the cloths, the sheet,
And angels sent, with tidings glad,
Our drooping hearts to greet:

'"But haste to Galilee,
And there, for he hath gone before,
Our life, our hope you'll see."'

Great Lord, we thee adore;
With joy we hail thee truly risen;
Thy mercy we implore.

Anonymous.

Ascension.

Part One.
Salutis humanæ Sator.

SAVIOUR of Men, who dost impart
Pure pleasure to the faithful heart,
Creator of our world redeemed,
Thy light on loving souls has beamed.

O victim of triumphant love,
The bearer of our sins to prove,
All guiltless to resign thy breath,
To free our souls from endless death.

Forcing the gloomy gates of hell,
Thou freest its slaves from bondage fell,
Victorious with thy ransomed band,
Enthroned on high at God's right-hand.

May kind compassion move thee now,
Repair the ills with which we bow,
Grant us to see thy radiant face,
Enrich our souls with light and grace.

Be thou our heavenly guide and way,
The leader whom our hearts obey,
The joy that bids our weeping cease,
Our sweet reward in life and peace.
F. C. Husenbeth.

Æterne rex altissime.

O thou eternal King most high,
Who didst the world redeem;

And conquering death and hell, receive
  A dignity supreme.
Thou, through the starry orbs, this day
  Didst to thy throne ascend;
Thenceforth to reign in sovereign power,
  And glory without end.

There, seated in thy majesty,
  To thee submissive bow
The heaven of heavens, the earth beneath,
  The realms of hell below.
With trembling there the angels see
  The changed estate of men;
The flesh which sinned by flesh redeemed;
  Man in the Godhead reign.

There, waiting for thy faithful souls,
  Be thou to us, O Lord,
Our joy of joys while here we stay,
  In heaven our great reward.
Renew our strength; our sins forgive;
  Our miseries efface;
And lift our souls aloft to thee,
  By thy celestial grace.

So, when thou shinest on the clouds,
  With thy angelic train,
May we be saved from deadly doom
  And our lost crowns regain.
To Christ returning gloriously
  With victory to heaven,
Praise with the Father evermore
  And Holy Ghost be given.

E. Caswall.

Tu, Christe, nostrum gaudium.

O Christ, the source of our delight,
Enthroned on thy celestial height,

Thou rulest all these lower skies
That far above them we may rise.
 Hence, thee once more we pray, forgive,
That through thy pardon we may live;
Oh, raise our hearts by grace divine
To thee, their only worthy shrine.
 That so, when thou shalt come in flame
To judge men in thy Father's name,
Thou mayest call thy children blest,
And summon them to perfect rest.
 Be thou our joy, in whom is stored
Our hope and promise of reward;
Be thou our glory, 'till the age
Of heaven shall reach a final stage.
 To thee, O Lord, be glory given,
Who climbest high the starry heaven,
With Sire and Spirit, Three in One,
As long as endless ages run.
J. C. Earle.

Part Two.
Salutis humanæ Sator.

Jesus, who man's Redeemer art,
Delight of every pious heart,
Creator of this earthly frame,
The lover's chaster light and flame.

 What strange excess of clemency
Prevailed, that thou wouldst satisfy
For sinful man? and guiltless give
Thy life to make the guilty live?

 Hell's dark abodes are forced by thee,
Its captives from their chains set free;
And thou, with this triumphant train,
At God's right-hand dost victor reign.

Let mercy there with thee prevail,
To cure the wounds we here bewail;
And by enjoyment of thy sight,
Enrich us with eternal light.

O guide and way to heavenly rest,
Be thou the aim of every breast,
Be thou the comfort of our tears,
And sweet reward above the spheres.
Evening Office, 1710.

Opus peregisti tuum.

Thy sacred race, O Lord, is run,
Thy work is wrought, thy victory won;
The glory thou didst leave requires
Thy presence in supernal choirs.
The clouds thy chariot, earth afar
Beneath thy feet, a little star;
Ten thousand thousand angels sing,
To welcome their returning king.

The gates of heaven obey the call,
And open to the Lord of all;
His throne receives the eternal Son,
Both God and Man for ever one.
Thou Mediator and high-priest,
Fresh from the sacrifice released,
By love constrained dost hither bring
Thy smitten heart's best offering.

And she who from thy opened side
Her being took, thy holy Bride,
Still nourished from thy side survives,
And life and all from thee derives.
Hence, in the thickest of the fight,
Thy warriors win their heavenly might;
And hence, thy martyrs sing their psalms,
And joyous wave triumphal palms.

Where thou, the head, art gone, thy voice
Calls all thy members to rejoice;
Ah, let them cleave the shining way,
Thy footprints through the ether fray.
To thee be glory, conquering king,
Who unto heaven thy way dost wing,
Great Son of the eternal Sire,
Whose Spirit is our one desire.
*R. Campbell and
J. C. Earle.*

Sensus quis horror percutit?
Fearful thought of endless doom—
Skies are rent, the judge is come;
Clouds his throne; around him stand
Angel-guards, a countless band.

Hear the voice from shore to shore,
Tells that time shall be no more;
See the dead from dust arise,
Summoned to the great assize.

On his right are placed the just,
To the left the wicked thrust;
Well to him are sinners known—
Known, but severed from his own.

These a blest retreat have won,
Earth's delights who learned to shun;
Chose affliction, pain and loss,
Followed him who bore the cross.

Cross, from which the Hebrew turned,
Cross, by haughty Gentiles spurned,
Thee with joy the righteous see,
But the lost with agony.

Deeper still their shame and dread,
Seeing him whose blood they shed;
Lord, from sin thy people keep,
Lest its dreadful fruit they reap.

Mingling joy with holy fear,
Praise we him whose day is near;
Bless alike the Father's name,
And the Spirit's praise proclaim.
R. Campbell.

Part Three.
Salutis humanæ Sator.

Jesu, slain for earth's release,
Source of pardon, source of peace,
Corner-stone for ever sure,
Purest light of spirits pure;

Saviour, say what love unknown
Brought thee here for us to groan;
Guiltless thee to bear our sin,
Dying, us from death to win.

Souls that long imprisoned lay,
At thy word returned to-day;
Now thy earthly travail o'er,
Heaven thy throne for evermore.

Risen and exalted Lord,
Unto us thy grace accord;
Thou who didst our nature take,
Never leave us, nor forsake.

Thou the guide and thou the way,
Thou the drooping spirit's stay;
Solace in the vale of tears,
Only joy that earth endears.

Jesu, heaven-exalted now,
At thy holy name we bow;
Father, equal praise to thee,
With the Spirit, ever be.
R. Campbell.

Ascension: Part Three.

Jesu, nostra redemptio.

Jesu, our ransom from above,
Our sole desire, our sweetest love,
Creator-God, o'er all supreme,
Yet shrined within our fleshly frame.

What urgent mercy moved thy breast
To bear the heavy weight that pressed
Our souls, and seek a death of pain
To free us from death's ghastly reign?

Piercing the shadowy depths of hell,
Thou didst redeem thy captives well,
Arising with thy triumph train
The Father's right-hand seat to gain.

Oh, let that mercy move thee still
To fence us round from every ill,
And give our souls the crowning grace,
To see the glories of thy face.

Be thou our present bliss, O Lord,
Who art our future blest reward;
And let our crown and glory be
In thee, good Jesu, only thee.

J. D. Aylward.

Æterne rex altissime.

O Saviour Christ, O God most high,
Whose glorious triumph decks the sky,
Arising from the world's defeat,
With tyrant-death beneath your feet:
Called from above, you, as your own,
In right of God resume the throne;
And thence this universe survey,
Whilst all your creatures homage pay.

Both heaven and earth, nay, death and hell
And all that in their confines dwell,

With bended knees fall down before
The general victor and adore.

 The angels stand amazed to see
Such change in our mortality;
That human flesh, the root of sin,
Should serve their God to triumph in.

May he our great reward bestow,
Whose influence o'er this world below
Makes heaven alone seem worth our care,
And all things else insipid here.

 Then Lord, with the release of sin,
Let thy triumphant grace begin;
And sweetly draw our hearts to thee,
Our centre and felicity;

That when our judge in clouds shall come,
Clothed like a storm and armed with doom,
Our lot may be to 'scape the rod,
And meet with a rewarding God.

 May endless worlds Christ's triumphs own,
Ascending his immortal throne;
And one eternal praise repeat
The Father and the Paraclete.

Primer, 1706.

Part Four.

Salutis humanæ Sator.

Hail thou, who man's Redeemer art,
Jesu, the joy of every heart;
Great maker of the world's wide frame,
And purest love's delight and flame:

What nameless mercy thee o'ercame,
To bear our load of sin and shame,
For guiltless, thou thy life didst give,
That sinful erring man might live?

The realms of woe are forced by thee,
Its captives from their chains set free ;
And thou, amid thy ransomed train,
At God's right-hand dost victor reign.

Let mercy sweet with thee prevail,
To cure the wounds we now bewail ;
Oh, bless us with thy holy sight,
And fill us with eternal light.

Our guide, our way to heavenly rest,
Be thou the aim of every breast ;
Be thou the soother of our tears,
Our sweet reward above the spheres.

T. J. Potter.

Felix dies mortalibus.

O day, so dear to man once lost,
When through his blood, our ransom-cost,
The Lord unfolds the eternal door
Which closed so long, is closed no more.

Our head and leader up hath gone,
The members left, but not alone ;
United here in holy love,
One glory shall be theirs above.

Though far beyond the starry sky,
Unseen his Spirit dwelleth nigh ;
He constant with his Church resides,
And in each member still abides.

But oh, that day, that awful day,
To those who would not him obey,
When God, descending from his throne,
As an avenger will come down.

The innocent, who once did die
That man might live eternally,
To judge his judges will appear ;
His death despised—what may we fear?

Himself to death the Lord resigned,
To ransom man to death consigned;
Then, what shall be the endless pain
Of those for whom he died in vain?

O thou our judge and Saviour too,
Jesu, to thee all praise is due,
With Father, Spirit, One and Three,
Both now and through eternity.

R. Campbell.

Jesu, nostra redemptio.

O Jesu, our redemption,
    Loved and desired with tears,
God, of all worlds creator,
    Man, in the close of years;
What wondrous pity moved thee
    To make our cause thine own,
And suffer death and torments,
    For sinners to atone?
O thou, who piercing Hades,
    Thy captives didst unchain,
Who gloriously ascendedst
    Thy Father's throne again,
Subdue our many evils
    By mercy all divine;
And comfort with thy presence
    The hearts that for thee pine.
Be thou our joy, O Jesu,
    In whom our prize we see;
Always, through all the ages,
    In thee our glory be.

E. Caswall.

Whit-Sunday.

Part One.
Veni, creator Spiritus.

CREATOR-SPIRIT, all-divine,
Come visit every soul of thine,
And fill with thy celestial flame
The hearts which thou thyself didst frame.

O gift of God, thine is the sweet
Consoling name of Paraclete—
And spring of life and fire and love
And unction flowing from above.

The mystic seven-fold gifts are thine,
Finger of God's right-hand divine;
The Father's promise sent to teach
The tongue a rich and heavenly speech.

Kindle with fire brought from above
Each sense, and fill our hearts with love;
And grant our flesh, so weak and frail,
The strength of thine which ne'er may fail.

Drive far away our deadly foe,
And grant us thy true peace to know;
So we, led by thy guidance still,
Safely may pass through every ill.

To us, through thee, the grace be shown
To know the Father and the Son;
And Spirit of them both, may we
For ever rest our faith in thee.

To Sire and Son be praises meet,
And to the holy Paraclete;

And may Christ send us from above
That Holy Spirit's gift of love.

J. D. Aylward.

Jam Christus astra ascenderat.

Above the starry spheres
To where he was before
Christ had gone up, soon from on high
The Father's gift to pour.

And now had fully come,
On mystic cycle borne
Of seven-times-seven revolving days,
The pentecostal morn :

When, as the apostles knelt
At the third hour in prayer,
A sudden rushing sound proclaimed
The God of glory near.

Forthwith a tongue of fire
Alights on every brow ;
Each breast receives the Father's light,
The Word's enkindling glow.

The Holy Ghost on all
Is mightily outpoured ;
Who straight in divers tongues declare
The wonders of the Lord.

While strangers of all climes
Flock round from far and near,
And with amazement, each at once
Their native accents hear.

But faithless still, the Jews
Deny the hand divine ;
And madly jeer the saints of Christ,
As drunk with new-made wine.

Till Peter in the midst
Stood up, and spake aloud;
And their perfidious falsity
By Joel's witness showed.

Praise to the Father be;
Praise to the Son who rose;
Praise, holy Paraclete, to thee,
While age on ages flows.

E. Caswall.

Beata nobis gaudia.

The rolling year pursues its way,
And now turns up the joyful day
Whereon the Holy Ghost possest
And reigned in each apostle's breast.

The sudden flames, like tongues of fire,
Their hearts and speech at once inspire
To kindle love, and to dispense
The gift of heavenly eloquence.

They speak; and mingling nations throng
Amazed to hear their native tongue;
Whilst strangers to the gospel think
The mind's excess, excess of drink.

But here mysterious terms appear—
And as the Jewish fiftieth year
Declared the legal debtors free,
This day's the Christian jubilee.

Now gracious God, with bended knee,
The Spirit's gifts we ask of thee;
Make all the seven-fold fountains flow
And shed their grace on us below.

Long since thy grace thou didst impart,
To rule in each disciple's heart;

With the same grace our crimes release,
And grant us everlasting peace.

May endless worlds Christ's triumphs own
Ascending his immortal throne ;
And one eternal praise repeat
The Father and the Paraclete.

Primer, 1706.

Veni, sancte Spiritus.

Come, O Spirit, Lord of grace,
From thy heavenly dwelling-place,
Bring pure light our gloom to chase.

Come, the friend of all brought low ;
Fountain whence all graces flow,
On the heart thy light bestow.

Thine to wipe the bitter tear ;
Thine the lonely heart to cheer ;
Fainting spirits find thee near.

In our labour thou art rest ;
Tears by thee are solaced best ;
Raging heat by thee refreshed.

Come, O light most pure and blest,
Come and fill each longing breast ;
Be thy people's constant guest.

If thy Deity be hence,
Nothing brings man honour thence,
Nothing is without offence.

Come, to cleanse the guilty stain,
On the hardened heart to rain,
Wounds of sin to heal again.

To thy will the stubborn mould ;
Warm and melt the bosom cold ;
Bring the erring to the fold.

Whit-Sunday: Part Two.

Unto us who seek thy face,
And in thee reliance place,
Give thy seven-fold gifts of grace.

Pardon grant if we offend ;
Grant us space till we amend,
Joy above that knows no end.

R. Campbell and
J. C. Earle.

Part Two.

Veni, creator Spiritus.

Creating-Spirit, come, possess
Our souls, and with thy presence bless ;
And in our hearts framed by thy hand,
Let thy celestial grace command.

Thou who art called the Paraclete,
The almighty Father's gift complete ;
The living fountain, fire and love
And sacred unction from above ;

Thou finger of the Father's hand,
Who dost a seven-fold grace command ;
Thou promise from the Highest sent,
In various language eloquent ;

Purge with thy light our earthly parts,
And with thy love inflame our hearts ;
Thus human weakness fortify
With everlasting constancy.

Far from us drive the infernal foe,
And peace, the fruit of love, bestow ;
Thus having thee our safest guide,
Let not our feet to evil slide.

Let us by thee the Father own,
And to us let the Son be known ;
Let us believe in thee who dost
From both proceed, the Holy Ghost.

To God the Father and the Son,
Who rose from death, be homage done;
This praise for ever let's repeat
To God the holy Paraclete.

Evening Office, 1710.

Beata nobis gaudia.

Hail, this joyful day's return;
Hail, the pentecostal morn,
Morn when our ascended head,
On his Church his Spirit shed.
Like to cloven tongues of flame
On the twelve the Spirit came;
Tongues, that earth may hear their call;
Fire, that love may burn in all.

Hear the speech before unknown,
Trembling crowds the wonder own;
What though hardened some abide,
And the holy work deride?
Lord, to thee thy people bend,
Unto us thy Spirit send;
Blessings of this sacred day
Grant us, dearest Lord, we pray.

Thou who didst our fathers guide,
With their children still abide;
Grant us pardon, grant us peace,
Till our earthly wanderings cease.
To the Father praises sing,
Praise to Christ our risen king,
Praise to thee, the Lord of love,
Blessed Spirit, holy Dove.

R. Campbell.

Veni, sancte Spiritus.

Come, Holy Ghost, to us send down,
Like rays of light from heavenly throne,
    Thy guiding influence, pure and bright.

Thou poor man's Father, hear our call;
Come, thou who givest good to all;
   Come, thou the spirit's joy and light.

Come, thou of all consolers best,
The soul's delightful, bounteous guest,
   Refreshment through the strife of years.

'Mid every toil thou givest rest;
Sweet calm to man's o'er-heated breast;
   True comforter in all his tears.

O blessed Light, come down and fill
The inmost wants of heart and will
   Of all who firmly trust in thee.

Without thy grace, can man attain
No single good; he strives in vain;
   He cannot even harmless be.

Wash every stain sin leaves behind;
Rain dew upon the arid mind;
   The spirit's wounds and bruises heal.

Make stubborn reason humbly bow;
Inflame it with a heavenly glow;
   To thee make doubt obedient kneel.

Oh, grant thy faithful, dearest Lord,
Whose only trust is thy sure word,
   Thy seven-fold gifts of grace and love.

Grant patience, peace, forbearance mild,
Meek charity, joy undefiled,
   Hope here and lasting bliss above.

J. R. Beste.

Part Three.

Veni, creator Spiritus.

Creator-Spirit, from thy throne
Descend to make our souls thine own,

And with thy heavenly grace possest
Be every Christian's glowing breast.

O Paraclete, to thee we sigh,
Thou splendid gift of God most high,
The living spring, our heart's desire,
Celestial unction, love and fire.

Gifts seven-fold spring at thy command,
Finger of God's paternal hand,
Promise, whom man had learnt to seek,
Teaching with gifted tongues to speak.

To every sense thy light impart,
Kindle thy love in every heart,
The weakness of our frame supply
With lasting virtue from on high.

Command our restless foe to cease,
Bid us repose in lasting peace;
And led by thee, celestial guide,
Turn from the paths of vice aside.

Grant us, while banished yet below,
The Father and the Son to know;
Thee, Holy Spirit, may our creed
Profess, who dost from both proceed.

To God the Father, to the Son
Who rose from death, his victory won,
And Holy Spirit, hymns of praise
And glory be for endless days.

F. C. Husenbeth.

Jam Christus astra ascenderat.

Now, far above the starry plain
Our Lord had reached his throne again,
To send from his celestial seat
The Father's promised Paraclete.

Whit-Sunday: Part Three.

For time its link of years had wound
The mystic seven-times-seven around—
A sign that now at length was given
The happy day marked out by heaven.

When the third hour of morn was told,
Sudden the wondrous tidings rolled
Of the descending Spirit, where
The twelve pursued their patient prayer.

Thus from the Father's fount of light
Was sent a fire divinely bright,
To warm each faithful breast below
With Christ the Lord's all-quickening glow.

Warm breathings of that Spirit blest
Have all their inmost souls possest;
Their tongues a varied speech intone
And all God's mighty works make known.

Strangers from Greece, and they that come
From barbarous lands and purple Rome,
Amazed they stand around, for each
Can hear his own familiar speech.

To Sire and Son be praises meet,
And to the holy Paraclete;
May Christ the Spirit's gift send down,
Soft-streaming from the mercy-throne.

J. D. Aylward.

Veni, sancte Spiritus.

Come, Holy Ghost, send down those beams
Which sweetly flow in silent streams
   From thy bright throne above.

Come, thou the Father of the poor,
Thou bounteous source of all our store,
   Come, fire our hearts with love.

Come, thou of comforters the best;
Come, thou the soul's delicious guest,
   The pilgrim's sweet relief.

Thou art our rest in toil and sweat,
Refreshment in excessive heat,
   And solace in our grief.

O sacred light, shoot home thy darts;
Oh, pierce the centre of these hearts
   Whose faith aspires to thee.

Without thy Godhead, nothing can
Have any price or worth in man,
   Nothing can harmless be.

Lord, wash our sinful stains away;
Water from heaven our barren clay;
   Our wounds and bruises heal.

To thy sweet yoke our stiff necks bow;
Warm with thy fire our hearts of snow;
   Our wandering feet repeal.

Oh, grant thy faithful, dearest Lord,
Whose only hope is thy sure word,
   The seven gifts of thy Spirit.

Grant us in life to obey thy grace;
Grant us at death to see thy face;
   And endless joys inherit.
Divine Office, 1763.

Part Four.

Veni, creator Spiritus.

Creator-Spirit, Lord of grace,
Make thou our hearts thy dwelling-place,
And with thy might celestial, aid
The souls of those whom thou hast made.

Come from the throne of God above,
O Paraclete, O holy Dove;
Come, oil of gladness, cleansing fire
And living spring of pure desire.

O finger of the hand divine,
The seven-fold gifts of grace are thine,
And touched by thee the lips proclaim
All praise to God's most holy name.

Then to our souls thy light impart,
And give thy love to every heart;
Turn all our weakness into might,
O thou the source of life and light.

Far from us keep our cruel foe,
And peace from thine own hand bestow;
Upheld by thee, our strength and guide,
No evil can our steps betide.

Spirit of faith, on us bestow
The Father and the Son to know;
And of the twain, the Spirit, thee—
Eternal One, eternal Three.

To God the Father let us sing;
To God the Son, our risen king;
And equally with these adore
The Spirit, God for evermore.

R. Campbell.

Jam Christus astra ascenderat.

Now Christ had pierced the skies to claim
His Father's throne, from whence he came;
About to send the sacred Dove,
The Holy Ghost, true God of love.
The day was come on which the sun
Had seven-times-seven glad courses run;

To usher in the seven-fold rays
With a mysterious term of days.

Three hours from the sun-rise were past,
When lo, in a surprising blast,
The twelve at prayers, the ghostly God
Came down to take his new abode.
Thus from the Father's Light there came
A sacred warmth and living flame,
To make their faithful hearts reveal,
By fiery tongues, their ardent zeal.

They filled with God, in transports bless
With various tongues and languages,
The God that taught those wondrous ways
To preach his works and speak his praise.
The Romans, Greeks, and barbarous sects,
All nations and all dialects,
Their native tongues perceive, and praise
The author of their strange amaze.

Whilst Jews alone, of all mankind
The most supinely deaf and blind,
Revile God's greatest works with sin,
And call the gift excess of wine.
But Peter thwarts their impious spite,
And brings the sacred truth to light;
A truth which though from them concealed,
The prophets taught and God revealed.

May endless worlds Christ's triumphs own
Ascending his immortal throne;
And one eternal praise repeat
The Father and the Paraclete.

Primer, 1706.

Beata nobis gaudia.

Again the slowly circling year
  Brings round the blessed hour,

Whit-Sunday: Part Four.

When on the saints the Paraclete
   Came down in grace and power.

In fashion of a fiery tongue
   On each and all he came;
Their lips with eloquence he strung,
   And filled their hearts with flame.

Straightway with divers tongues they speak,
   Instinct with grace divine;
While wondering crowds the cause mistake,
   And deem them drunk with wine.

These things were mystically wrought,
   The paschal time complete,
When Israel's law remission brought
   Of every legal debt.

God of all grace, to thee we pray,
   To thee adoring bend;
Into our hearts this sacred day
   Thy Spirit's fulness send.

Thou who in ages past didst pour
   Thy graces from above,
Thy grace in us where lost restore,
   And stablish peace and love.

All glory to the Father be,
   And to the Son who rose;
Glory, O Holy Ghost, to thee,
   While age on ages flows.
E. Caswall.

Veni, sancte Spiritus.

Holy Spirit, come and shine
On our souls with beams divine,
   Issuing from thy radiance bright.

Come, O Father of the poor,
Ever bounteous of thy store,
   Come, our hearts unfailing light.

Come, consoler, kindest, best,
Come, our bosom's dearest guest,
   Sweet refreshment, sweet repose.

Rest in labour, coolness sweet,
Tempering the burning heat,
   Truest comfort of our woes.

O divinest light, impart
Unto every faithful heart
   Plenteous streams from love's bright flood.

But for thy blest Deity,
Nothing pure in man could be;
   Nothing harmless, nothing good.

Wash away each sinful stain;
Gently shed thy gracious rain
   On the dry and fruitless soul.

Heal each wound and bend each will,
Warm our hearts benumbed and chill,
   All our wayward steps control.

Unto all thy faithful just,
Who in thee confide and trust,
   Deign the seven-fold gift to send.

Grant us virtue's blest increase,
Grant a death of hope and peace,
   Grant the joys that never end.

J. D. Aylward.

Trinity Sunday.

Part One.

Jam sol recedit igneus.

BEHOLD, the radiant sun departs
    In glory from our sight,
But, O our God, possess our hearts
    With thy celestial light.

By day, by night our hymns of love
    We offer, Lord, to thee ;
Oh, may we sing with saints above
    Thy praise eternally.

All praise to thee, blest Three in One,
    The God whom we adore ;
As hath been paid in ages gone,
    And shall be evermore.

R. Campbell.

Summæ parens clementiæ.

O God, by whose command is swayed
This ordered world which thou hast made ;
Parent of heavenly clemency,
In nature One, in persons Three ;
Assist us whilst our minds we raise,
Inflamed with thy immortal praise ;
That with our sober thoughts, we may
For ever our thanksgiving pay.
May age to age thy wonders tell,
Eternal praise thy works reveal,

And sing with the celestial host
The Father, Son and Holy Ghost.
Primer, 1706.

Part Two.

Jam sol recedit igneus.

The fiery sun now rolls away;
Blest Three and One, eternal day
Thy beams of light and love impart
To every cold benighted heart.

In morning and in evening verse
Thy glorious praises we rehearse;
May we, O God, the same express
Amidst thy saints in happiness.

To God, the Father and the Son
And Holy Spirit, Three in One,
Be endless glory, as before
The world began, so evermore
Evening Office, 1710.

Tu Trinitatis Unitas.

O thou, who dost all nature sway,
   Dread Trinity in Unity,
Accept the trembling praise we pour
   To thy eternal majesty.

The star that heraldeth the dawn
   Is slowly fading in the skies;
The darkness melts—O thou true light,
   Upon our darkened souls arise.

To God the Father glory be,
   And to the sole-begotten Son,
And Holy Ghost co-equally,
   While everlasting ages run.
E. Caswall.

Part Three.

HOURS OF THE HOLY TRINITY.

Jam sol recedit igneus.

Blest Light, eternal Trinity,
Sole, undivided Unity,
Now that the burning sun retires,
Light in our hearts thy sacred fires.

Our morning-lauds to thee we raise,
To thee our evening-songs of praise:
Oh, may it still our glory be
To hymn thy name eternally.

Blest Trinity, to thee be given—
The one co-equal God of heaven—
Now and henceforth that grace divine
Which from eternity is thine.

While shines the morning-star, whose ray
Gives tidings of the new-born day,
And westward glides the mighty gloom,
Let thy pure light our souls illume.

If thou assist our wakening eyes
The sobered heart shall grateful rise,
And kindling in thy gracious rays,
Pay its large debt of ceaseless praise.

O God, whose mercy passeth thought,
Whose power this world's vast fabric wrought;
One nature we adore in thee
And in one nature persons three.

O thou who rul'st this mighty sphere
Great Three in One, incline thine ear
Unto the songs of praise that we,
Thy wakeful suppliants, sing to thee.

These Hours, my humble offering
To thee, blest Trinity, I bring :
Oh, be thou gracious unto me,
Lord, in my final agony ;
And grant that we may all obtain
The glories of thy heavenly reign.

J. D. Aylward.

Part Four.
Jam sol recedit igneus.

Whilst fades the glowing sun away,
To thee, sole source of light, we pray ;
Blest Three in One, to every heart
The beams of life and love impart.

At early dawn, at close of day,
To thee our homage glad we pay ;
May we 'mid joys that never end,
With thy bright saints this homage tend.

To God the Father and the Son
And Holy Spirit, Three in One,
Be endless glory, as before
The world began, so evermore.

T. J. Potter.

Tu Trinitatis Unitas.

Thou great mysterious Three and One,
Whose power commands this world alone ;
Whilst we our nightly voices raise,
Awake and listen to thy praise.
The morning star now climbs the sky ;
The sun succeeds, the shadows fly ;
So may the dawn of inward light
Arise and chase the works of night.
May age to age thy wonders tell,
Eternal praise thy works reveal,
And sing with the celestial host
The Father, Son and Holy Ghost.

Primer, 1706.

Part Five.

Jam sol recedit igneus.

Behold the fiery sun recede :
Blest Unity, our light in need,
Blest Trinity, adored above,
Pour in our hearts celestial love.

Thee in our morning-hymn we praise,
To thee our prayer at eve we raise :
Oh, may our fervent praise ascend,
Where heavenly spirits lowly bend.

To God the Father, glory sing,
The like to God the Son our king,
The same, O Holy Ghost, to thee,
Which ever was, shall ever be.

F. C. Husenbeth.

Tu Trinitatis Unitas.

Blest Three in One and One in Three,
Great ruler of the world, to thee
   Thy suppliant people kneel ;
Oh, listen from thy throne on high,
And grant of thy great clemency
   Thy balm our wounds to heal.

Whate'er in us hath been decayed
By Satan's fraud, Lord, with thine aid
   Assist us to renew ;
With bodies pure and kindling hearts,
And shielded from temptation's darts,
   May we our path pursue.

O Light of Light, with thy blest ray,
Direct our steps throughout this day
   We humbly thee implore ;
Praise we the Father, praise the Son,
And Holy Ghost, blest Three in One,
   Both now and evermore.

R. Campbell.

Corpus Christi.

Part One.

Pange lingua gloriosi corporis.

SING, my joyful tongue, the mystery
    Of the glorious body slain,
And the blood all pure and precious
    Shed a lost world to regain,
By the king of nations, issuing
    From a womb that knew no stain.

Born unto us of a Virgin
    Purer than the purest snow,
And amongst mankind conversing
    Seeds of heavenly truth to sow,
He at length in wondrous order,
    Closed his sojourn here below.

Seated with his brethren round him
    On the night when last they met,
For the law's complete fulfilment,
    When the Lamb was duly ate,
Then before the twelve disciples
    For their food himself he set.

By a word the Word incarnate
    Simple bread to flesh divine,
Simple wine to blood converteth;
    But, if sense to doubt incline,
Under faith's sufficient teaching
    Simple hearts all doubts resign.

Corpus Christi: Part One.

(*Tantum ergo.*)
Wherefore this dread Host adoring,
 Let us bend with reverence due ;
Let the ancient rite departing
 Yield and fade before the new ;
Faith alone the proof supplying
 Which the senses fail to view.

Unto the Sire and Son eternal
 Praise and jubilation sing ;
Saving health, immortal honour,
 Glory, might and blessing bring ;
And the same unto the Spirit
 Who from both doth equal spring.

J. D. Aylward.

Sacris solemniis juncta sint gaudia.
 Let old things pass away ;
 Let all be fresh and bright ;
And welcome we with hearts renewed
 This feast of new delight.

 Upon this hallowed eve
 Christ with his brethren ate,
Obedient to the olden law,
 The pasch before him set.

 Which done, himself entire,
 The true incarnate God,
Alike on each, alike on all,
 His sacred hands bestowed.

 He gave his flesh ; He gave
 His precious blood ; and said,
' Receive, and drink ye all of this,
 For your salvation shed.'

 Thus did the Lord appoint
 This sacrifice sublime,
And made his priests its ministers
 Through all the bounds of time.

Farewell to types; henceforth
We feed on angels' food:
The slave—oh, wonder—eats the flesh
Of his incarnate God.
O blessed Three in One,
Visit our hearts, we pray;
And lead us on through thine own paths
To thy eternal day.
E. Caswall.

Verbum supernum prodiens.

The Word supernal, from the heavens descending,
  Nor ever from the Father's right hand gone,
To his great work, redeeming and defending,
  Came when the evening of his life had shone.
Ere unto death by a disciple given,
  Delivered falsely as to robber-band,
To his disciples, even as bread from heaven,
  He gave himself with his own loving hand.
In either form, himself on them bestowing,
  He gave to all his flesh, he gave his blood,
That with his flesh and with his life-blood glowing,
  He might for all men truly be the food.
As our companion on his first appearing,
  As our refection at the banquet-board,
In dying object for our fond revering,
  In heaven when reigning our divine reward.

(*O salutaris Hostia.*)

O Host, salvation bringing,
Heaven's gate wide open flinging,
Lest hellish foes confound us,
With strength and help surround us.
Lord, Three in One, transcending
In glory never ending,
Give man—o'er death victorious—
His home in heaven all glorious.
C. Kent.

Corpus Christi: Part One.

Lauda, Sion, Salvatorem.
Zion, thy Redeemer praising,
Songs of joy to him upraising,
　Laud thy pastor and thy guide:
Swell thy notes most high and daring;
For his praise is past declaring,
　And thy loftiest powers beside.

'Tis a theme with praise that gloweth,
For the bread that life bestoweth
　Goes this day before us out;
Which, his holy supper taking,
To the brethren twelve his breaking
　None hath ever called in doubt.

Full then be our praise and sounding,
Modest and with joy abounding
　Be our mind's triumphant state;
For the festal's prosecution,
When the first blest institution
　Of this feast we celebrate.

In the new king's new libation,
In the new law's new oblation,
　End the ancient paschal rite;
Ancient forms new substance chaseth,
Typic shadows truth displaceth,
　Day dispels the gloom of night.

What he did at supper seated,
Christ enjoined to be repeated,
　When his love we celebrate:
Thus, obeying his dictation,
Blood and wine of our salvation,
　We the victim consecrate.

'Tis for Christian faith asserted,
Bread is into flesh converted,
　Into blood the holy wine:

Sight and intellect transcending,
Nature's laws to marvel bending,
   'Tis confirmed by faith divine.

Under either kind remaining,
Form, not substance, still retaining,
   Wondrous things our spirit sees:
Flesh and blood thy palate staining,
Yet still Christ entire remaining,
   Under either species.

All untorn for eating given,
Undivided and unriven,
   Whole he's taken and unrent;
Be there one, or crowds surrounding,
He is equally abounding,
   Nor, though eaten, ever spent.

Both to good and bad 'tis broken,
But on each a different token
   Or of life, or death attends:
Life to good, to bad damnation;
Lo, of one same manducation
   How dissimilar the ends.

When the priest the victim breaketh,
See thy faith in nowise shaketh,
Know that every fragment taketh
   All that 'neath the whole there lies:
This in him no fracture maketh,
'Tis the figure only breaketh,
Form, or state, no change there taketh
   Place in what it signifies.

Bread, that angels eat in heaven,
Now becomes the pilgrim's leaven,
Bread in truth to children given,
   That must ne'er to dogs be thrown.

He, in ancient types disguisèd,
Was with Isaac sacrificèd,
For the feast a lamb devisèd,
    Manna to the fathers shown.
Bread, whose shepherd-care doth tend us,
Jesu Christ, thy mercy send us,
Do thou feed us, thou defend us,
Lead us where true joys attend us,
    In the land where life is given :
Thou all ken and might possessing,
Mercies aye to us largessing,
Make us share thy cup of blessing,
Heritage and love's caressing
    With the denizens of heaven.
                            A. D. Wackerbarth.

Part Two.
Pange lingua gloriosi corporis.

Hail, the body bright and glorious,
    Mystery of love divine ;
Hail, the blood that flows victorious
    From the true, the living vine ;
Hail, our ransom meritorious,
    Flower and root of David's line.

Given for us, for us assuming
    Purest flesh in Mary's womb ;
Earth with heavenly light illuming,
    Scattering seeds of heavenly bloom ;
More and more with love consuming,
    As he hastens to the tomb.

Love to man his breast o'erflowing,
    See him from the table rise,
Ancient symbols overthrowing—
    Mystery of mysteries—
With his hands himself bestowing,
    Food of life that never dies.

Earthly things to things of heaven
  Changed by God's incarnate Word,
Flesh and blood in mystery given,
  We believe with faith assured;
As the Word hath said it, even
  Be that word believed, adored.

(*Tantum ergo.*)
Then before his altar bending,
  Let our hearts the Lord revere;
Faith her aid to vision lending,
  Tells that he unseen is near;
Ancient types and shadows ending,
  Christ our paschal Lamb is here.

Praise and glory in the highest,
  Thine, O Father, ever be;
Thine, who unto us suppliest
  Food of immortality;
Thine, O thou who sanctifiest;
  Ever blessed One and Three.

R. Campbell.

Verbum supernum prodiens.

The eternal God, by human birth,
Unchanged pursues his task on earth;
Concluding his laborious strife
With wonders at the close of life.

Betrayed to Jews, betrayed to death,
His own disciple grudged him breath;
Yet he for his disciples' food,
Himself, the bread of life, bestowed.

Beneath the types of wine and bread,
They on his blood and body fed;
That man, of two-fold substance made,
For each might find respective aid.

He's born, to make himself our mate;
He eats, to make himself our treat;

He dies, to lay our ransom down ;
And reigns, to make himself our crown.

(*O salutaris Hostia.*)
O saving Host, that heaven's high gate
Lay'st open at so dear a rate ;
Intestine wars invade our breast,
Be thou our strength, support and rest.
May endless praise attend the throne
Of heaven's high ruler, Three and One ;
And he on us those joys bestow
That neither end, nor measure know.
Primer, 1706.

Adoro te devote, latens Deitas.
Thee prostrate I adore, the Deity that lies [eyes ;
Beneath these humble veils concealed from human
My heart doth wholly yield subjected to thy sway,
For contemplating thee it wholly faints away.
Hail, Jesus, hail ; do thou, good Shepherd of the sheep,
Increase in all true hearts the faith they fondly keep.
The sight, the touch, the taste, in thee are here deceived ;
But by the ear alone this truth is safe believed ;
I hold whate'er the Son of God hath said to me ;
Than this blest word of truth no word can truer be.
 Hail, Jesus, hail ; etc.
Upon the cross thy Godhead only was concealed ;
But here thy manhood too doth lie as deeply veiled ;
And yet, in both these truths confessing my belief,
I pray as prayed to thee the poor repentant thief.
 Hail, Jesus, hail ; etc.
I see not with mine eyes thy wounds, as Thomas saw ;
Yet own thee for my God with equal love and awe ;
Oh grant me, that my faith may ever firmer be,
That all my hope and love may still repose in thee.
 Hail, Jesus, hail ; etc.

Memorial sweet, that shows the death of my dear Lord;
Thou living bread, that life dost unto man afford;
Oh grant, that this my soul may ever live on thee,
That thou mayst evermore its only sweetness be.
   Hail, Jesus, hail; etc.

O mystic pelican, Jesu, my loving Lord,
Cleanse me of my defilements in thy blood adored,
Whereof one only drop, in thy sweet mercy spilt,
Would have the power to cleanse the world of all its guilt.
   Hail, Jesus, hail; etc.

O Jesu, lying here concealed before mine eye,
I pray thou grant me that for which I ceaseless sigh,
To see the vision clear of thine unvèilèd face,
Blest with the glories bright that fill thy dwelling-place.
Hail, Jesus, hail; do thou, good Shepherd of the sheep,
Increase in all true hearts the faith they fondly keep.
        J. D. Aylward.

Part Three.

Pange lingua gloriosi corporis.

Sing, my tongue, the body glorious,
 Mystery of mysteries,
And the blood our king victorious
 Poured in costly sacrifice,
Blood from Mary's veins drawn for us,
 Shed for our redemption's price.

Given for us, for our salvation
 Born of Maiden's stainless womb,
In the world for man's probation
 Tarried he, to speak his doom;
Then, with wondrous consummation
 Bade farewell to earthly home.

That last night at supper lying,
  Ere his chosen band he leaves,
To the ancient law complying
  Paschal meat he first receives,
With his own hands meat undying
  To the twelve himself he gives.
Word made flesh, his word transmuted
  Bread to flesh and wine to blood;
Though each sense the change disputed,
  Nor discerned the unearthly food,
In the true heart deeply rooted,
  Faith adores her present God.

(*Tantum ergo.*)
Prostrate, heart and knee, adore him,
  Jesus on the altar lies,
Ancient types have fled before him ;
  Hail, tremendous sacrifice :
To our sight shall faith restore him
  Veiled from gaze of mortal eyes.
To the Sire salvation's merit,
  To the sole-begotten Son,
To the consubstantial Spirit,
  Co-eternal Three in One :
Equal praise let each inherit,
  Honour, power and benison.

H. N. Oxenham.

Adoro te devote, latens Deitas.
Hidden God, devoutly I adore thee,
  Truly present underneath these veils :
All my heart subdues itself before thee,
  Since it all before thee faints and fails.
Not to sight, or taste, or touch be credit,
  Hearing only do we trust secure ;
I believe, for God the Son hath said it—
  Word of truth that ever shall endure.

On the cross was veiled thy Godhead's splendour,
  Here thy manhood lieth hidden too ;
Unto both alike my faith I render,
  And, as sued the contrite thief, I sue.

Though I look not on thy wounds, with Thomas,
  Thee, my Lord and thee, my God I call :
Make me more and more believe thy promise,
  Hope in thee, and love thee over all.

O memorial of my Saviour dying,
  Living bread, that givest life to man ;
May my soul, its life from thee supplying,
  Taste thy sweetness, as on earth it can.

Deign, O Jesus, pelican of heaven,
  Me, a sinner, in thy blood to lave,
To a single drop of which is given
  All the world from all its sin to save.

Contemplating, Lord, thy hidden presence,
  Grant me what I thirst for and implore,
In the revelation of thine essence,
  To behold thy glory evermore.

J. O'Hagan.

Verbum supernum prodiens.

Proceeding forth the Word supernal,
  Nor leaving yet the Father's side,
Bent on his task of love eternal,
  Now reached his life's sad even-tide.
But, ere the traitor-fiend had sold him
  To envious hands and deathful strife,
He bade his chosen twelve behold him,
  The food of their immortal life.

Concealed beneath the two-fold token,
  He gave his flesh, he gave his blood,
And thus in him, one and unbroken,
  Man's two-fold nature finds its food.

Our fellow, in the manger lying ;
  Our food, within the banquet-room ;
Our ransom, in his hour of dying ;
  Our prize, in his own kingly home.
      (*O salutaris Hostia.*)
O Victim of the world's salvation,
  That wide the gates of heaven hast thrown,
The foe brings war and desolation ;
  Give timely aid and guard thine own.
To thee, in triune Godhead dwelling,
  Be glory everlasting given ;
Be ours the joys, the bliss unfailing,
  That crown our endless life in heaven.
                              J. D. Aylward.

Part Four.

Pange lingua gloriosi corporis.
Of the glorious body bleeding,
  O my tongue, the mystery sing ;
And the blood all price exceeding,
  Which for this world's ransoming
From a noble womb proceeding
  Jesus shed, the Gentiles' king.
Given for us, for us descended
  Of a Maid from evil freed,
And his life on earth expended
  Scattering the Word's blest seed,
His career at length he ended
  Wonderful in word and deed.
At the last sad supper seated,
  Circled by his chosen band,
Moses' law in full completed
  In the food it doth command,
To the twelve as food he meted
  Forth himself with his own hand.
At the incarnate Word's high bidding
  Bread to very flesh doth turn,

Wine becometh Christ's blood-shedding;
And if sense cannot discern,
Guileless spirits never dreading
May from faith sufficient learn.

(*Tantum ergo.*)
To the sacred Host inclining
In adoring awe we bend,
Ancient forms their place resigning
Unto rites of nobler end;
Faith the sense's dark refining
Mysteries to comprehend.

Sire and Son all power possessing,
God, to thee all glory be,
Might, salvation, honour, blessing,
Unto all eternity,
Holy Ghost from both progressing
Equal glory be to thee.

A. D. Wackerbarth.

Sacris solemniis juncta sint gaudia.

Welcome with jubilee
This glad solemnity
From the full heart singing clear and high;
Let the old types of grace
To the new things give place,
New hearts, new works and new songs of joy.

Sing of that solemn eve
When, as true hearts believe,
Christ gave the lamb and the paschal bread
Unto the chosen band,
Met for the high command
God had of old on their fathers laid.

Now, when the feast was done,
To each belovèd one
Gave he his body—the Lord of heaven—

Yea, by those hands so blest
Unto each single guest,
E'en as to all, the whole Christ was given.

Weak and unstable
They ate at that table
His flesh; whilst he cheered their drooping hearts
With the new mystic wine
Of his own blood divine :
'Drink ye the cup which my love imparts.'

Thus did our blessed King
Trust his new offering
Only to men of his priestly line;
Thus they receive it
And faithfully give it
To all who draw near for the gift divine.

Types are now banished,
Shadows are vanished,
Man eats the bread of the angels of heaven;
Yea, the thrice-holy
To servants so lowly—
Strange love—e'en himself for their food hath given.

O triune Deity,
Hear how we cry to thee,
Come thou to us who here kneel to adore thee;
Lead us on thine own way
Up to the realms of day,
Where is thy dwelling, the place of thy glory.

J. D. Aylward.

Verbum supernum prodiens.

Word of God to earth descending,
   With the Father present still,
Near his earthly journey's ending
   Hastes his mission to fulfil.

Well the traitor's kiss foreknowing—
    Miracle of love divine—
See his hands himself bestowing
    In the hallowed bread and wine.
Holy body, blood all precious,
    Given by him to be our food,
With them both he doth refresh us,
    Formed like him of flesh and blood.
Born, a brother dear he gave us;
    At his board the banquet he;
On the cross he died to save us;
    Reigneth our felicity.

    (O salutaris Hostia.)
Mighty Victim, earth's salvation,
    Heaven's own gate unfolding wide,
Help thy people in temptation,
    Feed them from thy bleeding side.
Unto thee, the hidden manna,
    Father, Spirit, unto thee,
Let us raise the loud hosanna,
    And adoring bend the knee.

R. Campbell.

Lauda, Sion, Salvatorem.
Sing forth, O Sion, sweetly sing
The praises of thy Shepherd-king,
    In hymns and canticles divine:
Dare all thou canst, thou hast no song
Worthy his praises to prolong,
    So far surpassing powers like thine.

To-day no theme of common praise
Forms the sweet burden of thy lays—
    The living, life-dispensing food—
That food which at the sacred board,
Unto the brethren twelve our Lord
    His parting legacy bestowed.

Corpus Christi: Part Four.

Then be the anthem clear and strong,
Thy fullest note, thy sweetest song,
　The very music of the breast:
For now shines forth the day sublime
That brings remembrance of the time
　When Jesus first his table blest.

Within our new king's banquet-hall
They meet to keep the festival
　That closed the ancient paschal rite:
The old is by the new replaced;
The substance hath the shadow chased;
　And rising day dispels the night.

Christ willed what he himself had done
Should be renewed while time should run,
　In memory of his parting hour:
Thus, tutored in his school divine,
We consecrate the bread and wine;
　And lo—a Host of saving power.

This faith to Christian men is given—
Bread is made flesh by words from heaven;
　Into his blood the wine is turned:
What though it baffles nature's powers
Of sense and sight? This faith of ours
　Proves more than nature e'er discerned.

Concealed beneath the two-fold sign
Meet symbols of the gifts divine,
　There lie the mysteries adored:
The living body is our food;
Our drink the ever-precious blood;
　In each, one undivided Lord.

Not he that eateth it divides
The sacred food, which whole abides
　Unbroken still, nor knows decay:

Be one, or be a thousand fed,
They eat alike that living bread
   Which, still received, ne'er wastes away.
The good, the guilty share therein,
With sure increase of grace or sin,
   The ghostly life, or ghostly death :
Death to the guilty ; to the good
Immortal life. See how one food
   Man's joy or woe accomplisheth.
We break the Sacrament; but bold
And firm thy faith shall keep its hold :
Deem not the whole doth more enfold
   Than in the fractured part resides :
Deem not that Christ doth broken lie ;
'Tis but the sign that meets the eye ;
The hidden deep reality
   In all its fulness still abides.
Behold the bread of angels, sent
For pilgrims in their banishment,
The bread for God's true children meant,
   That may not unto dogs be given :
Oft in the olden types foreshowed ;
In Isaac on the altar bowed,
And in the ancient paschal food,
   And in the manna sent from heaven.
Come then, good Shepherd, bread divine,
Still show to us thy mercy sign ;
Oh, feed us still, still keep us thine ;
So may we see thy glories shine
   In fields of immortality :
O thou, the wisest, mightiest, best,
Our present food, our future rest,
Come, make us each thy chosen guest,
Co-heirs of thine, and comrades blest
   With saints whose dwelling is with thee.

J. D. Aylward.

Sacred Heart of Jesus.

Part One.

Auctor beate sæculi.

O CHRIST, the world's creator bright,
   Who didst mankind from sin redeem,
Light from the Father's glorious Light,
   True God of God, in bliss supreme.

Thy love compelled thee to assume
   A mortal body, man to save;
Reversing the old Adam's doom,
   Our ransom the New Adam gave.

That love which gloriously framed all—
   The earth, the stars and wondrous sea—
Took pity on our parents' fall,
   Broke all our bonds and set us free.

O Saviour, let thy potent love
   Flow ever from thy bounteous heart;
To nations that pure fount above
   The grace of pardon will impart.

His heart for this was opened wide,
   And wounded by the soldier's spear,
That freely from his sacred side
   ·Might flow the streams our souls to clear.

Glory to Father and to Son,
   And to the Holy Ghost the same,

To whom all power, when time is done,
And endless rule, in endless fame.

F. C. Husenbeth.

En, ut superba criminum.

Lo, how the savage crew
  Of our proud sins hath rent
The heart of our all-gracious God,
  That heart so innocent.

The soldier's quivering lance
  Our guilt it was that drave,
Our wicked deeds that to its point
  Such cruel sharpness gave.

O wounded heart, whence sprang
  The Church, the Saviour's bride;
Thou door of our salvation's ark
  Set in its mystic side.

Thou holy fount, whence flows
  The sacred seven-fold flood,
Where we our filthy robes may cleanse
  In the Lamb's saving blood:

By sorrowful relapse
  Thee will we rend no more;
But like thy flames, those types of love,
  Strive heaven-ward to soar.

Father and Son supreme
  And Spirit, hear our cry;
Whose is the kingdom, praise and power
  Through all eternity.

E. Caswall.

Cor, arca legem continens.

Jesus, behind thy temple's veil,
  Hid in an ark of gold,
On stones engraven, lay the law
  Thy finger wrote of old.

But in thy body's temple new,
  Thy life-blood's throbbing shrine,
Held, upon fleshly tables graved,
  The law of love divine.

And when that heart in death was stilled,
  Each temple's veil was riven:
And lo, within thy love's red shrine,
  To us to look was given.

There make us gaze, and see the love
  Which drew thee, for our sake,
O great high-priest, thyself to God
  A sacrifice to make.

Thou, Saviour, cause that every soul
  Which thou hast loved so well,
May will within thine opened heart
  In life and death to dwell.

Grant, O Father, only Son
  And Spirit, God of grace,
To whom all worship shall be done
  In every time and place.

Roman Breviary, 1873.

Part Two.

Quicumque certum quæritis.

Haste, all who 'mid life's thorny ways,
  Sure comfort seek and peace and rest;
Haste, all by burning care weighed down,
  By sharp and bitter pain opprest.

To Jesu haste, the spotless Lamb,
  The Lamb by love for sinners slain,
Haste to his meek and wounded heart,
  The solace sweet for every pain.

Oh, list those sweet and loving words,
    His mercy list, his ardent call :
'To me, poor weary wanderers, haste;
    Haste all opprest by sin's dark thrall.'

Oh, say what heart more sweet, more meek,
    Than his, who nailed unto the cross,
Doth for his murderers mercy beg,
    To ward away their souls' sad loss.

O heart, the joy of heavenly hosts,
    Of man the hope, the only stay,
Drawn by thy sweet and loving voice,
    To thee we haste and humbly pray.

Oh, free us from our sinful stains,
    And wash us in thy saving gore,
A new heart give to all who now
    With weeping hearts thy love implore.

T. J. Potter.

Summi Parentis Filio.

To Christ, the Prince of peace,
    And Son of God most high,
The Father of the world to come,
    Sing we with holy joy.

Deep in his heart for us
    The wound of love he bore;
That love, wherewith he still inflames
    The hearts that him adore.

O Jesu, victim blest,
    What else but love divine
Could thee constrain to open thus
    That sacred heart of thine?

O fount of endless life,
    O spring of waters clear,
O flame celestial, cleansing all
    Who unto thee draw near.

Hide me in thy dear heart,
For hither do I fly;
There seek thy grace through life, in death
Thine immortality.

Praise to the Father be,
And sole-begotten Son;
Praise, holy Paraclete, to thee,
While endless ages run.

E. Caswall.

Part Three.

Auctor beate sæculi.

Great Maker of the world's wide frame,
All hail, our souls' redeeming Lord,
The Father's bright eternal flame,
His sole, his uncreated Word.

Thy bright and burning love thee clad
In nature's weak and fragile clay,
That thou to nature mightst restore·
What the first Adam took away.

That same pure ardent love did form
The earth, the sea, the glowing stars;
Bewailing all our father's faults,
Thou healest all our sinful scars.

Oh, in thy sweet and loving heart,
Ne'er let this burning love decay;
But let this fountain still remain,
To wash our sinful stains away.

For this the lance thy heart did pierce,
For this upon the cross it bled,
That o'er our stains its mingled stream
It might in loving plenty shed.

To God the Father and the Son
   May brightest glory still remain ;
Whilst equal power and equal might
   The Holy Spirit e'er doth claim.

T. J. Potter.

En, ut superba criminum.

Of sin and love the Lord had died :
   Of sin, but not his own ;
Of love, self-sprung, that drew him down
   For sinners to atone.

And sin, when in the last strong cry
   Had passed his latest breath,
Still aimed the soldier's spear to pierce
   His pulseless heart in death.

Sin pierced him ; but his love called life
   Out of the streams sin wrung :
The Church, from out his heart of love,
   In blood and water sprung.

Where men would drown in sin, he set
   That Church o'er sin's black tide ;
An ark of safety, whose wide door
   Was opened in his side.

Love gave those streams from out his heart
   In seven-fold tide to flow,
Wherefrom our robes by faith and love
   May whiter rise than snow.

Oh, may we lay our sins aside,
   Those sins that pierced his heart ;
And pray of him new hearts of flesh,
   Hearts Christ-like, to impart.

Grant it, O Father, only Son
   And Spirit, God of grace,
To whom all worship shall be done
   In every time and place.

Roman Breviary, 1879.

Sacred Heart: Part Three.

Cor, arca legem continens.

O tender Heart, strong ark which doth enshrine
   The whole sweet law that rules the heart of man ;
   No longer held as slaves beneath a ban,
Grateful and free we live by love divine.

O Heart, O sanctuary undefiled,
   Of that new law of love unto us given ;
   O veil more precious than of old was riven ;
O temple holier than the ancients piled.

For love thou sufferest a gaping wound,
   A wound towards which our human sorrows turn;
   So we may feel thy love within us burn,
And worship thee with all our sores unbound.

Under love's symbol, sweet to us and dread,
   Mystic and human woes hath Christ endured —
   Our priest whose sacrifice our heaven secured,
Offering his blood and flesh as wine and bread.

What living heart is there that will not come
   At his redeeming call, that doth not sigh
   To give him love for love, and will not fly
Into his heart, our everlasting home ?

Honour be to the Father and the Son ;
   And to the Holy Spirit honour be ;
   All power, glory, sway is of the Three
Who through all ages live and love in One.

                                   Rosa Mulholland.

Transfiguration.

Part One.

Quicumque Christum quæritis.

O ye who seek the Lord,
  Lift up your eyes on high,
For there he doth the sign accord
  Of his bright majesty.

We see a dazzling sight
  That shall outlive all time,
Older than depth or starry height,
  Limitless and sublime.

'Tis he for Israel's fold
  And heathen tribes decreed,
The king to Abraham pledged of old
  And his unfailing seed.

Prophets foretold his birth,
  And witnessed when he came,
The Father speaks to all the earth
  To hear and own his name.

To Jesus, who displays
  To babes his beaming face,
Be, with the Father, endless praise,
  And with the Spirit of grace.

Cardinal Newman.

Quicumque Christum quæritis.

O ye, the truly wise,
Who in the Lord delight,

Unto the hills lift up your eyes,
  And see that glorious sight.

O form surpassing far
  All loveliness of earth,
More ancient than the morning-star,
  In thy mysterious birth.

Thou only art our head,
  'Tis thou whom we adore,
To faithful Abraham promisèd
  A king for evermore.

Beholding we rejoice,
  We hail the promised day,
And hearkening to the Father's voice,
  The only Son obey.

To lowly hearts revealed,
  Our Saviour we adore,
Like tribute to the Father yield,
  And Spirit evermore.
                            R. Campbell.

Lux alma, Jesu, mentium.

O Christ, when thy chaste light inspires,
Our tepid hearts with heavenly fires,
Thy love does such sweet flames excite,
Thy yoke grows sweet and burden light.
Co-heir of God's paternal throne,
Thou sovereign bliss, to sense unknown,
Thrice happy they, who filled with thee
Possess the saints' felicity.
O source of all, who from above
Descend'st in streams of light and love,
By these returning streams may we
Direct our course and end in thee.

Glory to Christ, whose light displays
To little ones his saving ways;
Whilst endless hymns of praise repeat,
The Father and the Paraclete.

Primer, 1706.

Part Two.

Quicumque Christum quæritis.

All you who seek the Lord of love,
Look to the clear bright sky above;
There may your faith descry those rays
Of glory bright which God displays.

Behold an object, grand, sublime,
That knows no bounds, no place, no time;
Immortal, glorious and high,
More old than chaos, or the sky.

Hail, mighty king, whose loving sway
The Gentile and the Jew obey;
To Abraham promised and decreed
While earth shall last to rule his seed.

The prophets thy dread name unfold,
And sing the truth by them foretold:
Thee God the Father from his throne
Commands the world to hear and own.

Glory to Jesus, who displays
To simple souls his saving ways;
To thee, O Father, we repeat
The same, and to the Paraclete.

T. J. Potter.

Lux alma, Jesu, mentium.

Light of the troubled heart,
   Jesus, thy suppliants cheer;
Bid thou the shades of sin depart,
   And shed thy brightness here.

O happy he, whose breast
    Thou makest thine abode—
Clear light that with the pure will rest,
    For they shall see their God.

Sweetness of God above,
    Immeasurable grace,
Within our hearts impart thy love,
    And make thy dwelling-place.

To lowly minds revealed,
    Our Saviour we adore ;
Like tribute to the Father yield,
    And Spirit evermore.

R. *Campbell.*

Part Three.

Quicumque Christum quæritis.

All that desire with Christ to rise,
To Thabor's mount lift up your eyes ;
See there how Christ in glorious rays
The majesty of God displays.

Behold a sun more old than night,
A blaze of uncreated light ;
So high, so deep and vast of space,
It knows no bounds of time or place.

This is that king whose sovereign sway
The Gentiles and the Jews obey,
Promised to Abraham and decreed
To rule his numerous faithful seed.

The law and prophets him unfold,
And sign the truth by them foretold ;
Him God the Father from his throne
Commands the world to hear and own.

Glory to Christ whose light displays
To little ones his saving ways ;
To God the Father let's repeat
The same, and to the Paraclete.
Cento, 1706-1748-1763.

Quicumque Christum quæritis.

O you who truly seek your Lord,
    Look up and lift your hearts on high ;
Signs of his Deity adored
    There will your trembling view descry.

Illustrious, infinite, sublime,
    Unbounded in his high domains,
Our glorious God, unchanged by time,
    Older than heaven and chaos reigns.

He is the Gentiles' mighty king,
    The monarch of the Hebrew race,
To Abraham promised, forth to bring
    Him and his seed from sin's disgrace.

Prophets who marked his future way,
    Attest his splendid presence near ;
The Son refulgent on this day,
    The Eternal Father bids us hear.

Jesus, be glory given to thee,
    Thus to thy lowly ones displayed,
With God thy Father equally,
    And with the Holy Ghost arrayed.
F. C. Husenbeth.

Lux alma, Jesu, mentium.

Light of the anxious heart,
    Jesu, thou dost appear,
To bid the gloom of guilt depart,
    And shed thy sweetness here.

Joyous is he with whom,
　God's Word, thou dost abide ;
Sweet light of our eternal home,
　To fleshly sense denied.

Brightness of God above,
　Unfathomable grace,
Thy presence be a fount of love
　Within thy chosen place.

To thee, whom children see,
　The Father ever blest,
The Holy Spirit, One and Three,
　Be endless praise addrest.

Cardinal Newman.

Holy Redeemer.

Part One.

Creator alme siderum.

GREAT Maker of the glittering stars,
Our light amid the world's dark wars,
Jesu, our souls' redeeming praise,
Oh, hear the vows we humbly raise.

Thy burning love did bring thee down
From heaven above, thy happy throne,
Lest to destruction, hell's foul king,
A fainting world should quickly bring.

Who, that thou mightst our ransom pay,
And gladly wash our stains away,
The Virgin's spotless shrine didst leave,
And on the cross a victim bleed.

Whene'er thy great and awful name
The lips in trembling accents frame,
The powers of heaven and hell agree
To own its might on bended knee.

Great judge, at that last awful day,
Thy mercy sweet we humbly pray;
Thy heavenly grace in plenty send,
And from their foes thy own defend.

Jesu, to thee, the Virgin's Son,
Be everlasting homage done,

To God the Father we repeat
The same, and to the Paraclete.

T. J. Potter.

Jesu, dulcis memoria.
The memory of Jesus blest
Gives joy to be the bosom's guest;
But over honey-dew doth rest
His sweetest presence in the breast.

No fairer note can music sing,
No dearer sound from lip can spring,
No hidden thought such transport bring,
As Jesus, Son of God, our king.

O refuge of the contrite mind,
How prompt the sinner's wounds to bind;
To all who seek thee good and kind,
But what, oh what, to them that find?

Thou balm of hearts, in whom unite
The living fount, the Spirit's light;
And joy, surpassing far the might
Of all desire and all delight.

For what it is thy love to share
No pen can write, no tongue declare;
The heart alone can witness bear
That feels the love of Jesus there.

And I will seek thee in my cell,
My bosom's chamber guarded well;
And when abroad with men I dwell,
Still seek with love unquenchable.

And I will watch thy tomb beside,
With Mary at the morning-tide,
And there with plaintive cry abide,
My soul, and not mine eye the guide.

My tears thereon shall fall apace,
My lamentation fill the place,

Mine arms thy wounded feet enlace,
And hold them in a long embrace.

And I will in thy footstep press,
And tread thy path in faithfulness ;
Nor shall my heart its sighs repress
Till thou thyself its longing bless.

O Jesus, ever-wondrous king,
Great victor, nobly triumphing,
The all-desirable, the spring
Of sweets beyond imagining :

When thou inhabitest the heart,
Then does the truth its light impart ;
The vanities of earth depart,
And all but love's enkindled dart.

Then Jesus one and all proclaim ;
Implore his love and bless his name ;
To seek him be your fervent aim,
Till in the search ye grow aflame.

Thee, Jesus, may our tongues adore,
Our lives in thine example soar,
Our hearts to thee their homage pour,
And love thee now and evermore.

J. O'Hagan.

Part Two.
Creator alme siderum.

Creator of the stars above,
Eternal source of light and love,
Jesus, Redeemer, hear our prayer,
May all thy free redemption share.

When man, by Satan's wiles deceived,
His promise, fraught with death, believed,
The world thus lost, to gain and save
Thy love a rich redemption gave.

To free a world enslaved in guilt,
Thy pure atoning blood is spilt,
Unsullied from the Virgin's womb,
A victim to the cross and tomb.

When far resounds thy glorious fame,
And heard is thine immortal name,
O Jesus, Saviour, God, to thee
Heaven, earth and hell shall bow the knee.

We deprecate thy dreadful ire,
Thou that wilt judge the world by fire;
Defend us by the arms of grace;
Assist us every foe to chase.

May honour, glory, praise be given
To God, the eternal king in heaven;
The Father, his co-equal Son,
And Holy Ghost, in essence one.

F. C. Husenbeth.

Jesu, dulcis memoria.

Jesus, the only thought of thee
   With sweetness fills my breast;
But sweeter still it is to see,
   And on thy beauty feast.
No theme so soft, nor sound so gay
   Can art of music frame;
No words, nor even thought can say,
   Thy most mellifluous name.

Sole hope, when we our sins repent,
   So bounteous of thy grace;
If thus thou'rt good while we lament,
   Oh, what when face to face?
Jesus, that name inspires my mind
   With springs of life and light;
More than I ask in thee I find,
   And lavish in delight.

No eloquence, nor art can reach
    The joys of those above ;
The blest can only know, not reach
    What they in Jesus prove.
Thee then I'll seek retired apart,
    From world and business free ;
When noise invades I'll shut my heart,
    And keep it all for thee.

An early pilgrim thus I'll come,
    With Magdalen, to find
In sighs and tears my Saviour's tomb,
    And there refresh my mind.
My tears upon his grave shall flow,
    My sighs the garden fill ;
Then at his feet myself I'll throw,
    And there I'll seek his will.

Jesus, in thy blest steps I'll tread,
    And haunt thee through thy ways ;
I'll mourn, and never cease to plead
    'Till I'm restored to grace.
Great conqueror of death, thy fire
    Does such sweet flames excite,
That first it raises the desire,
    Then fills it with delight.

Thy quickening presence shines so clear
    Through every sense and way,
That souls, who once have seen thee near,
    See all things else decay.
Come then, dear Lord, possess my heart,
    And chase the shades of night ;
Come, pierce it with thy flaming dart,
    And ever-shining light.

Then, I'll for ever Jesus sing,
    And with the blest rejoice ;

Then all the vaulted towers shall ring,
And echoing hearts and voices sing,
  And still repeat, 'Rejoice.'
                              Primer, 1706.

Part Three.
Creator alme siderum.

Creator of the starry pole,
  Saviour of all who live,
And light of every faithful soul,
  Jesu, these prayers receive.

Who, sooner than our foe malign
  Should triumph, from above
Didst come, to be the medicine
  Of a sick world, in love;

And the deep wounds to cleanse and cure
  Of a whole race, didst go,
Pure Victim, from a Virgin pure,
  The bitter cross unto.

Who hast a name, and hast a power,
  The height and depth to sway,
And angels bow, and devils cower,
  In transport or dismay;

Thou too shalt be our judge at length;
  Lord, in thy grace bestow
Thy weapons of celestial strength,
  And snatch us from the foe.

Honour and glory, power and praise,
  To Father and to Son
And Holy Ghost, be paid always,
  The eternal Three in One.
                    Cardinal Newman.

Jesu, dulcis memoria.

Jesus, how sweet the thought of thee,
Joy heartfelt, true serenity;

But more than all and honey-sweet
Our Saviour face to face to meet.
No song can be so sweet to hear,
No sound so well the heart can cheer,
The mind no thought so glad can frame
As Jesus Christ's most holy name.

O Jesus, hope of sinners' fears,
How kind thou art to suppliant prayers;
To those who seek for thee, how kind;
But what art thou to those who find?
No tongue can make the hearer guess,
Nor writing say how thou dost bless;
Those only who have tried can tell
What 'tis to love their Jesus well.

Jesus, our only bliss be thou,
Who wilt all future joy bestow;
Oh, may our love and glory be
For endless ages drawn from thee.
Jesus, our king, admired, revered,
The conqueror of all that's feared;
True sweetness all—thou dost impart
Far more than asks the trembling heart.

When thou dost seek the mourner's breast,
Truth smiles anew with promise blest,
No longer earth and sin defiles,
Love warms the soul and hope beguiles.
Jesus, in thee each heart delights,
Thou living fountain, light of lights,
Exceeding every dearest bliss,
And every dream of happiness.

Oh, haste to Jesus, hasten all,
May love your every wish enthral:
Oh, seek your Jesus and adore,
And seeking, love him more and more.

Holy Redeemer: Part Three.

Oh, may our hymns repeat thy name,
And may our lives our love proclaim;
May we for ever Jesus love,
And endless years our love improve.

Whom thou most favourest, more will crave;
Who have thee most, far more would have :
Still must the heart that loves thee want,
Still—still for Jesus must it pant.
O Jesus, whom my soul desires,
To whom most fondly it aspires ;
For whom calm tears bedew mine eyes ;
To whom mine inward spirit sighs ;

Oh, stay with us, dear Jesus, stay,
Illume us with thy saving ray;
All darkness from our minds remove,
And fill the world with light and love.
Jesus, the Virgin's only Son,
May every heart thy sweetness own,
May honour, blessings, praise and fame
For ever hail thy holy name.

J. R. Beste.

Festivals of the Holy Cross.

Part One.

INVENTION OF THE CROSS.

Vexilla regis prodeunt.

THE great King's banner shines above,
The glorious mystery of his love,
The cross, where Life himself would die,
Our life thus dying to supply.

The spear's sharp point laid open wide
That source of grace, his sacred side,
When forth with water streamed his blood
To wash our souls, a saving flood.

Then was fulfilled what David's tongue
To nations erst prophetic sung;
That God in after-ages should
Reign monarch from the cross' wood.

O beauteous tree, thy branches shine,
Empurpled by our king divine,
Preferred his sacred limbs to bear,
Such honour worthiest deemed to share.

Blest cross, to grateful souls endeared,
Our ransom on thine arms was reared,
And when thy balance proved its worth,
It snatched from hell the sons of earth.

Holy Cross: Part One.

O cross, with hope the Christian prays,
Rejoicing in these paschal days,
Grace for the guilty and the just,
Through Christ, our sole resource and trust.

Blest Trinity, salvation's spring,
Thy praise may every spirit sing;
And where the cross' triumphs glow,
The cross' glorious crown bestow.

F. C. Husenbeth.

Ita suos fortiores.

Thus its votaries it assureth,
For them victory procureth,
Weakness and diseases cureth,
    Keeps at bay demoniac force;
Satan's captives liberating,
Life to sinners renovating,
All in glory reinstating
    Jesus' all-resplendent cross.
Tree, triumphal might possessing,
Earth's salvation, crown and blessing,
Every other pretergressing
    Both in bloom and bud and flower.
Medicine of the Christian spirit
Aid as with thy saving merit,
Thou dost might for works inherit
    Overpassing human power.

A. D. Wackerbarth.

Patris sapientiæ, veritas divina.

'Twas at the solemn Matins'-hour, when by the traitor's sign
The Father's Wisdom, God and Man, the source of truth divine,
Was sold, betrayed, delivered up, abandoned by his own,
And left amidst his enemies, afflicted and alone:

Lord Jesu, let each spirit bring
　　The homage of his praise to thee;
And rule o'er us who love to sing
　　The cross, the cross that made us free.

Our Lord was led to Pilate at the dawning hour of Prime,
And charged by false accusers with many a feigned crime;
They smote him, bound his sacred hands, and spat upon that face
Which shone so bright with tender light of heaven's gentle grace:
　　Lord Jesu, let each spirit bring, etc.

At Terce he wears the purple robe, when like a tempest loud
The cry of 'Crucify him,' swells from all that angry crowd;
His sacred head all bleeding sore, a thorny garland wears,
And meekly to the place of death the heavy cross he bears:
　　Lord Jesu, let each spirit bring, etc.

At Sext they nail his hands and feet fast to the cruel wood,
Which midway 'twixt the gibbet of the dying robbers stood;
He thirsts; and his desiring lips they drench with bitter gall—
Sad mockery to the dying Lamb, who shed his blood for all:
　　Lord Jesu, let each spirit bring, etc.

At None he cries 'Eli, Eli;' and as his torment ends,
Into his Father's hands his meek and patient soul commends;

Deep in his side the soldier rude did thrust the
    guilty spear;
Earth to her inmost centre shook; the sun shrank
    back for fear:
        Lord Jesu, let each spirit bring, etc.

Down from the cross they take him as the Vespers'-
    hour draws on;
But all his glorious might is with his conquering
    spirit gone;
Thus he, the balsam of our life, a bitter death hath
    found;
And thus, alas, is glory's crown cast down upon the
    ground:
        Lord Jesu, let each spirit bring, etc.

The corpse of him, our life's sole hope, they at the
    Compline-hour
Embalm with precious sweets, and lay in its sepul-
    chral bower;
Thus duly was accomplished what an ancient scrip-
    ture saith,
Oh, let our memories love to dwell upon his bitter
    death:
        Lord Jesu, let each spirit bring
            The homage of his praise to thee;
        And rule o'er us who love to sing
            The cross, the cross that made us free.

    These prayers rehearsed in order due
    To thee I consecrate anew,
    And beg for tender charity
    That thou, dear God, who diedst for me,
    Wouldst thy celestial comforts shed
    All gently round my dying bed.
                        J. D. Aylward.

Part Two.

RHYTHMICAL HYMN
IN PRAISE OF THE HOLY CROSS.

Laudes crucis attollamus

Come, let us with glad music
  Extol the holy cross ;
With special exultation
  We glory in the cross :
For by the cross we triumph,
  Our foemen we destroy ;
Its standard is our signal
  For victory and joy.

Now let our hymns most tuneful
  Trill far into the skies,
The wood that's sweetest merits
  The sweetest harmonies ;
Nor be our life in discord
  With what our voices sing,
These may not clash together
  True symphony to bring.

All ye, the cross' servants,
  Be in its praises rife;
Without the cross ye perish—
  The fountain of your life :
'Hail, all the world's salvation,'
  Your salutation be,
In loudest proclamation,
  Of this all-healing tree.

How blest, how bright this altar,
  Wherefrom salvation beams ;
Pours down the Lamb upon it
  His blood in ruddy streams—

Holy Cross: Part Two.

The Lamb that hath no blemish,
  From their primeval crime
Hath purified all ages
  Until the end of time.

Lo, here the sinner's ladder
  Where Christ, from heavenly throne,
Hath to himself drawn all things,
  And made each step his own :
See, with the cross' banner
  The truth itself unfurled,
Its four points comprehending
  The confines of the world.

New sacraments are dawning,
  But still in types, that so
The cross' bright religion
  May blaze with tempered glow :
Wood cast in it by Moses
  Makes Mara's water sweet ;
Obeying wood, the flint-stone
  Pours water at his feet.

The master hath no safety
  For his doomed house, before
The cross upon the lintel
  Hath fortified the door:
This sign what man soever
  Hath set his faith upon,
The sword hath lost its power—
  He saves alive his son.

The widow of Sarephtha
  Gained from her gathered wood
The sweet hope of salvation,
  When near the prophet stood ;
Of wood the mystic virtue
  Where is no faith to feel,

The cruse of oil avails not,
    Nor handful yet of meal.

What sense beneath such figures
    Lay hid in holy writ,
Is now revealed to Christians,
    The cross' benefit :
Kings yield belief, and foemen
    Bow to the cross alone—
Where Christ himself is captain,
    A thousand flee from one.

The cross makes strength the stronger;
    It conquers without fail ;
It heals the sick and feeble ;
    It makes the demons quail ;
It gives to captives freedom,
    With new life it indues ;
The dignity of all things
    The cross again renews.

Hail cross, thou tree triumphal,
    Salvation's only shrine,
Nor stem, nor leaf, nor flower
    Hath other tree like thine :
The health art thou of Christians,
    Their medicine when ill ;
When human help is helpless,
    Be our protection still.

Hear all thy cross' praises
    Thou hallower of the cross,
Nor let thy cross' servants
    Hereafter suffer loss ;
But in the heavenly mansions,
    Departed hence, appear,
Where God himself their light is
    And dried is every tear.

If thou allot us torture,
  Let torture not be felt;
But in thine hour of anger,
  Be mercy to us dealt:
To thee, against the oppressor,
  Confirm our last appeal,
And quickly let us enter
  Our everlasting weal.
                    H. W. Lloyd.

Part Three.

EXALTATION OF THE CROSS.

Vexilla regis prodeunt.

See, see the royal banners fly,
Now beams the cross' mystery,
For life was still within the tomb
When death by life was overcome.

Where smote the spear with direst blow,
Thence blood and water did o'erflow;
These all our guilty stains efface,
And wash our souls with saving grace.

Fulfilled are now the things foretold
By David's faithful song of old;
He said to all, in mystic strain,
'From off a tree the God did reign.'

O noble tree, thy branches fair
The royal purple colours wear;
Well chosen from an honoured sort,
Such holy members to support.

O blessed tree, whose arms can show
The ransom of a world from woe;
His limbs the only weight could tell
What price might ransom man from hell.

O cross, our only hope sublime,
Whose triumph cheers this glorious time;
Let grace renewed the just repay,
And wash the sinner's guilt away.

Hail, Trinity, the song of praise
Redeemed mankind should ever raise;
May those, who now in patience bear
The cross on earth, thy guerdon share.

J. R. Beste.

Salve crux sancta.

All hail, O cross divine,
Around thy stem entwine
All honour, hope and joy. In thee we find
Peace amid deadly strife;
Thou art the tree of life
That yields the living fruit to all mankind.

Lost through one fatal tree
We were redeemed through thee;
Life-giving cross, sole glory of this earth,
We praise thee and adore;
For we were slaves before,
But now are free men through thy sovereign worth.

O Christ, who through the cross
Repaird'st our ancient loss;
Our souls' most secret stains wash clean away;
Thy pity cannot fail
The wanderers poor and frail,
Who own their steps have greatly gone astray.

Oh, hold us by thy side,
Saved, blest and sanctified,
Sealed with the cross as with a heavenly sign;
Let not disease, nor sin,
Nor danger entrance win,
To bosoms guarded by the cross divine.

From the dear cross whereon
Died the eternal Son,
Be glory given to the eternal Sire,
And to the Holy Ghost,
While the celestial host
With ransomed souls to sing the cross conspire.
J. D. Aylward.

Patris sapientiæ, veritas divina.

As night departing brings the day,
True God and Man, truth's rising ray,
To Jews betrayed is captive led;
With night his loved disciples fled,
And left their master sold to foes,
Distressed with grief and whelmed with woes.

Now Prime the purple morn begins,
When falsely Christ accused of sins
At Pilate's curst tribunal stands,
Profaned with blows and impious hands,
Whilst Jews blaspheme the God of grace
By spitting in their maker's face.

At the third hour they raise their cry,
And all demand their God should die;
Then crowned with thorns in purple vest,
The King of kings, the people's jest,
Was forced to bear that fatal cross
Where conquering death he paid our loss.

At the sixth hour, the noon of day,
Christ's sacred arms extended lay
Nailed to the cross amidst the thieves,
Whilst gall his sacred thirst relieves;
Thus God they with derision pay
The Lamb that takes their sins away.

At None, the fatal hour of three,
All nature shook, amazed to see
How Christ, the God of nature, died;
His parting sighs and wounded side—
The sun's eclipsed, the rocks relent—
And all but man his pains resent.

The sable evening mourns its loss,
Whilst Christ is taking from the cross;
Thus God and man by mortal strife
Paid down the ransom of our life;
And thus the crown of glory lay
Trodden and mixt with common clay.

The Compline-hour concludes our praise,
And Christ in his sepulchre lays;
With him embalmed is treasured up
The sacred pledge of future hope;
And scriptures are fulfilled: may we,
O Christ, preserve thy memory.

Accept, O Christ, these humble vows,
And to the last our cause espouse;
That we may find support in thee
In death's deplorèd agony.

Primer, 1706.

Index of First Lines.

Part I.

HYMNS FROM THE SACRED OFFICES.

NO.		PAGE
27.	A Boy is born in Bethlehem,	27
42.	A Child for us is born this day,	40
5.	A heavenly voice and early ray,	6
9.	A thrilling voice rings clear and high,	10
95.	A wondrous mystery this day,	82
190.	Above the starry spheres,	162
201.	Again the slowly circling year,	172
82.	Again the time appointed see,	73
253.	All hail, O cross divine,	226
134.	All tender lights, all hues divine,	116
239.	All that desire with Christ to rise,	207
237.	All you who seek the Lord of love,	206
64.	Alleluia, sweetest lay,	57
109.	Already thirty years have shed,	97
79.	Angels, look down and weep,	70
135.	As at morn's golden ray,	117
254.	As night departing brings the day,	227
164.	At the Lamb's high feast we sing,	138
154.	Aurora spreads her cheerful rays,	129
106.	BANNERS of our King are streaming,	94
69.	Behold our God upon the rood,	61
97.	Behold the appointed time to win,	83
210.	Behold the fiery sun recede,	179
203.	Behold, the radiant sun departs,	175
114.	Behold, the royal banners fly,	101
110.	Behold the royal ensigns fly,	98
86.	Benignant Maker, here at last,	76

Index of First Lines.

NO.		PAGE
47.	Bethlehem, of noblest cities,	44
25.	Blest day, when from the Saviour flowed,	26
207.	Blest Light, eternal Trinity,	177
124.	Blest Maker of the radiant light,	110
211.	Blest Three in One and One in Three,	179
1.	Bright Maker of the starry poles,	3
167.	Bring, all ye dear-bought nations, bring.	141
105.	By the cross of expiation,	93
103.	By the cross, on which suspended,	89
138.	CHRIST, the glory of the sky,	119
73.	Christ's peerless crown is pictured in,	64
176.	Christians, your voices raise,	149
4.	Clear rings a voice; it chides the world,	5
198.	Come, Holy Ghost, send down those beams,	169
195.	Come, Holy Ghost, to us send down,	166
146.	Come, Holy Ghost, who ever One,	123
251.	Come, let us with glad music,	222
38.	Come, O faithful, with sweet voices,	36
192.	Come, O Spirit, Lord of grace,	164
160.	Come to the regal feast displayed,	134
193.	Creating-Spirit, come, possess,	165
80.	Creator, bounteous and benign,	71
127.	Creator, God immense and wise,	112
246.	Creator of the starry pole,	215
244.	Creator of the stars above,	212
189.	Creator-Spirit, all divine,	161
196.	Creator-Spirit, from thy throne,	167
199.	Creator-Spirit, Lord of grace,	170
50.	Crown of the angels, thy sweet name,	46
67.	DAUGHTER of Sion, cease thy bitter tears,	59
6.	Day of wrath, that day whose knelling,	7
11.	Day of wrath, the heart dismaying,	11
157.	ETERNAL King, whose equal reign,	132
149.	FATHER of lights, by whom each day,	124
140.	Father of mercies infinite,	120
182.	Fearful thought of endless doom,	155
26.	From every part o'er which the sun,	26
84.	From heaven's own school's mysterious ways,	74
41.	From the far-blazing gate of morn,	39
113.	Full thirty years were freely spent,	100

Index of First Lines. 231

NO.		PAGE
89.	GLORY and praise to thee, Redeemer blest,	78
71.	Go forth, ye Sion's daughters, now,	63
62.	God needeth not the cleansing wave,	55
242.	Great Maker of the glittering stars,	210
231.	Great Maker of the world's wide frame,	201
92.	HAIL, holy nails ; hail, blessed spear,	79
102.	Hail, holy wounds of Jesus, hail,	87
216.	Hail, the body bright and glorious,	185
194.	Hail, this joyful day's return,	166
186.	Hail thou, who man's Redeemer art,	158
21.	Hark, a joyful voice is thrilling,	20
15.	Hark, an awful voice is sounding,	15
55.	Hark, in the wilderness	50
229.	Haste, all who 'mid life's thorny ways,	199
33.	Hasten, ye faithful, glad, joyful and holy,	32
101.	He who once, in righteous vengeance,	86
173.	Heavenly choirs with anthems sweet,	146
220.	Hidden God, devoutly I adore thee,	189
162.	High heaven's eternal Lord,	136
37.	Holy Babe, our great salvation,	36
119.	Holy cross, blest tree, outvying,	105
202.	Holy Spirit, come and shine,	173
174.	How sweet those words of soothing were,	148
28.	IN triumph, joy and holy fear,	28
152.	JERUSALEM, thy song be new,	127
96.	Jesu, as though thyself wert here,	82
53.	Jesu, highest heaven's completeness,	48
52.	Jesu, king o'er all adored,	48
184.	Jesu, our ransom from above,	157
23.	Jesu, our soul's redeeming Lord,	24
183.	Jesu, slain for earth's release,	156
166.	Jesu, the earth's Redeemer thou,	140
228.	Jesus, behind thy temple's veil,	198
247.	Jesus, how sweet the thought of thee,	215
34.	Jesus, Redeemer, ere the light,	33
245.	Jesus, the only thought of thee,	215
39.	Jesus, the Ransomer of man,	37
94.	Jesus, when on thy fatal day,	81
175.	Jesus, who didst redeem mankind,	149
180.	Jesus, who man's Redeemer art,	153
29.	LAMB, whose blood for all men streamed,	29

Index of First Lines.

NO.		PAGE
213.	Let old things pass away,	181
63.	Let other cities strive, which most,	56
143.	Let us arise and watch by night,	122
241.	Light of the anxious heart,	208
238.	Light of the troubled heart,	206
87.	Like faithful Abraham's holy child,	76
227.	Lo, how the savage crew,	198
123.	MAKER of the earth and sky,	109
12.	Maker of the starry sphere,	13
139.	Man's sovereign God, to whom we owe,	119
137.	May the dread Three in One, who sways,	118
141.	Morning shines with Eastern light,	121
35.	Now ancient shadows flee,	34
200.	Now Christ had pierced the skies to claim,	171
197.	Now, far above the starry plain,	168
24.	Now signs of mourning disappear,	25
150.	Now that the daylight dies away,	125
168.	Now to the Lamb's high festival,	141
117.	Now, when full thirty annual suns,	103
75.	Now with the slow-revolving year,	66
179.	O CHRIST, the source of our delight,	152
88.	O Christ, the true and endless Day,	77
226.	O Christ, the world's creator bright,	197
236.	O Christ, when thy chaste light inspires,	205
253.	O cross, our only hope sublime,	226
187.	O day, so dear to man once lost,	159
111.	O faithful cross, O noblest tree,	99
115.	O faithful cross, O peerless tree,	102
107.	O faithful cross, of trees the fairest,	95
204.	O God, by whose command is swayed,	175
128.	O God from God, and Light from Light,	112
148.	O God, unchangeable and true,	124
147.	O God, who canst not change nor fail,	124
130.	O God who, when at nature's birth,	113
136.	O God, whose watery stores supply,	117
74.	O gracious Lord, Creator dear,	66
77.	O gracious Lord, incline thine ears,	68
83.	O gracious Maker, bend thine ears,	73
49.	O Jesu, Lord, most mighty king,	46
188.	O Jesu, our redemption,	160
155.	O maids and striplings, hear love's story,	129

NO.		PAGE
31.	O night of nights, supreme delights,	31
185.	O Saviour Christ, O God most high,	157
32.	O Saviour of the world forlorn,	32
133.	O source of light, whose glorious ray,	115
76.	O sovereign Sun, diffuse thy light,	68
233.	O tender heart, strong ark which doth enshrine,	203
178.	O thou eternal King most high,	151
153.	O thou, the heaven's eternal King,	128
17.	O thou, the maker of each star,	17
206.	O thou, who dost all nature sway,	176
8.	O thou, who thine own Father's breast,	9
99.	O thou, who though high-priest, art victim made,	84
235.	O ye, the truly wise,	204
234.	O ye, who seek the Lord,	204
240.	O you, who truly seek your Lord,	208
70.	O'erwhelmed in depths of woe,	62
232.	Of sin and love the Lord hath died,	202
222.	Of the glorious body bleeding,	191
43.	Oh come, all ye faithful,	40
108.	Oh, sing my tongue, God's glory sing,	96
93.	Oh, turn those blessed points, all-bathed,	80
91.	On Calvary with what a mystery gleams,	79

144.	PALER have grown the shades of night,	122
18.	Predestinate of God most high,	18
221.	Proceeding forth, the Word supernal,	190

177.	SAVIOUR of men, who dost impart,	151
252.	See, see the royal banners fly,	225
65.	See the eternal Word descending,	58
36.	Sent from his heavenly throne on high,	35
151.	Sing, for the dark Red Sea is past,	126
225.	Sing forth, O Sion, sweetly sing,	194
116.	Sing loud the conflict, O my tongue,	102
212.	Sing, my joyful tongue, the mystery,	180
219.	Sing, my tongue, the body glorious,	188
120.	Sing, my tongue, with glowing accents,	105
112.	Sing, O my tongue, devoutly sing,	99
125.	Sleep has refreshed our limbs, we spring,	110
98.	Slow and mournful be our tone,	84
121.	Soon the sweetest blossom wasting,	106
126.	Splendour of the Father's glory,	111
2.	Supernal Word, proceeding from,	4

Index of First Lines.

NO.		PAGE
13.	Supernal Word, who didst proceed,	13
132.	Swift as shadows of the night,	115
22.	THAT day of wrath and grief and shame,	21
16.	That day of wrath, that dreadful day,	15
20.	The advent of our God at hand,	20
170.	The angel's gracious message came,	143
59.	The beauteous star that beams on high,	53
61.	The bright and morning-star arose,	55
3.	The coming of our God,	4
85.	The darkness fleets, and joyful earth,	75
158.	The dawn was purpling o'er the sky,	133
217.	The eternal God, by human birth,	186
78.	The fast that, in the ancient law,	69
142.	The fiery sun now rolls away,	121
205.	The fiery sun now rolls away,	176
248.	The great King's banner shines above,	218
129.	The herald of the morn,	113
159.	The holy paschal work is wrought,	133
118.	The King of kings his banner rears,	104
243.	The memory of Jesus blest,	211
48.	The memory sweet of Jesus' name,	45
165.	The morn had spread her crimson rays,	139
19.	The period is come; and lo, to-day,	19
56.	The princely city passing by,	50
156.	The Red Sea now is passed, and now,	131
172.	The Red Sea's dangers now are past,	145
191.	The rolling year pursues its way,	163
161.	The ruddy light now newly born,	135
145.	The star of morn to night succeeds,	123
214.	The Word supernal, from the heavens descending,	182
218.	Thee prostrate I adore, the Deity that lies,	187
7.	Thou builder of the starry skies,	8
66.	Thou, Creator, art possest,	59
72.	Thou didst not need creation's aid,	64
46.	Thou from the cradle to the grave,	43
209.	Thou great mysterious Three and One,	178
249.	Thus its votaries it assureth,	219
230.	To Christ, the Prince of peace,	200
122.	To-day the blessed Three in One,	108
40.	To earthly kings fresh names accrue,	38
90.	To thee, O Christ, be glory, praises loud,	78
181.	Thy sacred race, O Lord, is run,	154
51.	Thy sweet remembrance, Lord, imparts,	47

Index of First Lines.

NO.		PAGE
250.	'Twas at the solemn Matins-hour, when by the traitor's sign,	219
104.	WEEPING sore, the Mother stood,	91
223.	Welcome with jubilee,	192
45.	What beauteous sun-surpassing star,	42
54.	What makes thee, cruel Herod, shake,	49
14.	What sound doth Jordan's streams appal,	14
10.	When clouds of darkness veil the sky,	10
208.	Whilst fades the glowing sun away,	178
100.	With glad and joyous strains now let each street resound,	85
68.	With sorrow deep opprest, now let us sadly wail,	60
81.	Who hath heard what God hath wrought?	72
131.	Who madest all and dost control,	114
58.	Word of God, eternal Son,	53
224.	Word of God to earth descending,	193
57.	Why, cruel Herod, dost thou fear?	52
60.	Why, cruel Herod, dost thou fear?	54
44.	Why, ruthless Herod, why should fear?	42
169.	YE choirs of New Jerusalem,	142
30.	Ye people, cease from tears,	30
171.	Ye sons and daughters of the Lord,	144
163.	Young men and maids, rejoice and sing,	137
215.	ZION, thy Redeemer praising,	183

ANNUS SANCTUS.
PART II.

ANNUS SANCTUS.

PART II.

Contents.

MODERN, ORIGINAL AND OTHER HYMNS.

First and Second Advent.

NO.   PAGE

1. GREATER Antiphons for Advent. *O Wisdom, that proceedest from.* From the Sentence of Kaïres and other Poems.
    Rev. Henry Nutcombe Oxenham, 1854–1867.   3

2. Ancient of Days. *Ancient of days, thy throne on high.*
    Robert Campbell, of Skerrington, 1849–1850.   4

3. Dies Finalis. *Rise, O Lord, in all thy glory.* From the Passion of Jesus; and Hymns of the Heart. *Matthew Bridges*, 1848–1852.   6

4. Fragment of 'Dies Iræ.' *Dread and strange the trumpet's tone.*
    Very Rev. Prior James A. Dominic Aylward, Order of Preachers, 1843–1850.   7

5. German Advent Hymn. *Clouds of heaven, shower the Just One.* *John Charles Earle*, 1883.   8

6. Song of the Seraphs. *Crown him with many crowns.* *Matthew Bridges*.   9

7. Fragment of 'Dies Iræ.' *Oh, how great shall be the fear.* *Robert Campbell*.   11

8. The red Robe. *The winepress, the winepress.*
    Matthew Bridges.   12

NO.		PAGE
9.	Imitation of 'Dies Iræ.' *Woe is the day of ire.* From Poems, 1883. *Richard Dalton Williams,* 'Shamrock,' 1843.	13
10.	Pilgrims of the Night. *Hark, hark, my soul, angelic songs are swelling.* From Oratory Hymns. *Very Rev. Father Frederick William Faber, London Oratory,* 1848–1861.	16

Nativity of our Lord.

11.	Christmas Carol. *Primeval night had repossessed.* From May Carols, 1870. *Aubrey de Vere,* 1855–1870.	18
12.	The Child Jesus: a Cornish Carol. *Welcome that star in Judah's sky.* From Ecclesia. *Robert Stephen Hawker,* 1840.	19
13.	Verbo Caro factum est. *Dry your tears, ye silent mourners.* *Lady Catherine Petre,* 1854–1875.	19
14.	Christmas Eve and Morn. *I gaze out on the moonlit earth.* *E. Louisa Lee,* 1864–1874.	20
15.	Birth of Jesus. *In a silence deep at midnight.* From Foregleams of the Desired, 1881. *Very Rev. Henry A. Rawes, Oblate of St. Charles,* 1864.	21
16.	The Infant Jesus. *Dear Little One, how sweet thou art.* *Father Faber.*	23
17.	Midnight Mass of the Nativity. *Alleluia, Lord most holy.* *Rev. H. N. Oxenham.*	24
18.	Carol for Christmas Night. *Once to Bethlehem's lowly shepherds.* *E. Louisa Lee.*	25
19.	The Hour of silent Midnight. *At hour of silent midnight.* *Rev. Francis Stanfield,* 1858–1860.	26
20.	Shepherds at the Manger. *Stars of glory, shine more brightly.* From Lyra Messianica. *Very Rev. Provost F. C. Husenbeth,* 1862.	27
21.	The Christmas Moon. *The moon that now is shining.* From a Chaplet of Verses. *Adelaide A. Procter,* 1863.	28

Contents.

Epiphany and Holy Name.

NO.   PAGE

22. The Infant King. *They leave the land of gems and gold.* From the Sisters, Inisfaïl and other Poems, 1861.   *Aubrey de Vere.*   31

23. Magian Gifts. *Oh, for the light of that fair star.*
    T. E. B.   31

24. Dormi, Fili, dormi. *Sleep, my Child, the Mother singeth.*   *Denis Florence MacCarthy,* 1872.   33

25. To the ever-precious Name. *Hail, to the ever-precious Name.*   *Lady Catherine Petre.*   34

26. Epiphany of Jesus. *King of Israel, Word incarnate.*   *Father Rawes.*   35

27. Jesus, my God and my All. *O Jesus, Jesus, dearest Lord.*   *Father Faber.*   36

28. Transfiguration of our Lord. *Oh, it is good for me to dwell in sweetness.* *Lady Catherine Petre.*   37

29. Vidimus Stellam ejus. *Hushed is the starry night.*
   Emily Bowles, 1871.   38

30. A Carol of the Kings: an Armenian Myth. *Three ancient men in Bethlehem's cave.*
   R. S. Hawker.   40

31. Thabor, Calvary and Olivet. *Dear Saviour, when thy chosen three.* Lyra Messianica, 1864.
   Provost Husenbeth.   41

32. Beside the Manger. *There in the narrow manger, cold and bleak.*   *S. J.,* 1871.   42

33. Song of Praise to the Name of Jesus. *Jesus is the sweetest name.*   *J. C. Earle,* 1881.   43

34. Puer natus est nobis. *I caused those infant-tears to flow.* From Hymns for the Use of Churches, 1882.   *F. A. J.,* 1834.   44

35. Stabat Mater speciosa. *By the crib wherein reposing.*   *D. F. MacCarthy,* 1871.   45

Lent and the Precious Blood.

NO.   PAGE

36. Jesus, our Love, is crucified. *Oh, come and mourn with me awhile.*   *Father Faber.*   48

37. In Passione Domini. *In the Lord's atoning grief.* From Devotions on the Passion.
    Very Rev. Canon Frederick Oakeley, 1842.   49

38. Gethsemani. *The olive-garden of Gethsemani.*
    Father Rawes.   49

39. Lent by Mary's side. *The purple shroud is stretched upon our altar.*   *Lady Catherine Petre.*   50

40. Ash-Wednesday Evening. *Behold and bless the solemn day.*   *Robert Campbell.*   52

41. To the holy Spear and Nails. *What tongue shall give thee thanks, in fitting strains repeat?* From the Catholic Psalmist.
    Rev. Professor T. J. Potter, All-Hallows College, Dublin, 1857–1858.   52

42. Christum ducem, qui per crucem. *To Christ, whose cross repaired our loss.*   *Canon Oakeley.*   53

43, 44, 45. Hymns from the Daily Procession of the Franciscan Friars at Jerusalem. (At the Altar of Flagellation.) *Come, let us tell of him whose woes.* (At the Chapel of Imprisonment.) *Thou, O my Jesus, thou wast pleased.* (At the Chapel of Coronation.) *Go forth, ye children of our God.* From the Order of Compline, 1880.
    Anonymous, 54, 55, 56

46. Personal agencies in the Passion of Jesus. *My Jesus, say, what wretch has dared.* From the Sacred Poetry of St. Alphonso Maria Liguori.
    Anonymous, 1863.   57

47. Road to Calvary. *Steep is the hill and weary is the road.*   *Lady Catherine Petre.*   58

48. Sacred Wounds of Christ. *All hail, ye wounds of Christ.*   Σ. 1868.   59

Contents.

NO. | PAGE
49. The Reproaches. *What, O my people, have I done to thee?* From Lyra Liturgica.
Canon Oakeley, 1865. 61

50. Oh, hearken when we cry. *Now are the days of humblest prayer.* *Father Faber.* 62

51. The Heavenly Stranger. *A Stranger in the pale moon-light.* *Rev. H. N. Oxenham.* 63

52. The Washing of the Altar. *Pour forth the wine-floods rich and dark.* From Poems, 1851.
Aubrey de Vere. 64

53. God-forsaken. *Thousands have felt thy healing power.* From Lyra Messianica, 1864.
Cecilia M. Caddell, 1862. 65

54, 55. Last Words from the Cross. (The Fifth Word.) *Hard is the painful wood, his bed of death.* (The Last Word.) *Bow down, my soul, for he hath bowed his head.* *Lady Catherine Petre.* 65, 66

56. The Precious Blood. *Hail, Jesus, hail, who for my sake.* *Father Faber.* 67

57. Ave, Jesu, qui mactaris. *Hail, Jesus, hail; who while they slay.* From Poems, 1882.
Father H. I. D. Ryder, Birmingham Oratory,
1880. 68

58. To the Instruments of the Passion of Jesus. *O, ruthless scourges, with what pain you tear.* From St. Alphonsus. *Anonymous*, 1863. 69

59. Sign of the Cross. *O Christians, ever bear in mind.*
Robert Campbell. 70

60. Self-sacrifice. *When Christ let fall that sanguine shower.* *Aubrey de Vere.* 70

61, 62. Hymn to Christ. I. *Laud we Jesus, who did ease us.* II. *Who untiedst, when thou diedst.* From Lyra Ecclesiastica.
Rev. Athanasius Diedrich Wackerbarth, 1842-1843. 71, 72

63. The Five Wounds. *Ye priestly hands, which on the cruel cross.* *Rev. G. F. L. Bampfield*, 1864. 73

viii *Contents.*

NO. PAGE
64. Agony in the Garden. *Jesus, O my Lord and God.* *J. C. Earle,* 1881. 75
65. Invitation to the Sinner. *O come to the merciful Saviour that calls you.* *Father Faber.* 75

Evening, Vespers and Compline Hymns.

EVENING HYMNS.

66. Even-song. *Starry hosts are gleaming.*
E. Louisa Lee. 77
67. Hymn from the Paris Breviary. *In the light all light excelling.* *Rev. H. N. Oxenham.* 78
68. Respice stellam, voca Mariam. *Drear is the nightfall.* From Catholic Hymns.
Rev. Francis Stanfield, 1858-1860. 79
69. Angels' Visits. *In that cold cave with spices sweet.*
Aubrey de Vere. 80
70. Evening Hymn at the Oratory. *Sweet Saviour, bless us ere we go.* *Father Faber.* 81
71. Return of the Dove. *Finding no place of rest. S.* 81
72, 73. Evening Hymn to Jesus and Mary. *I. Hear thy children, gentle Jesus. II. Hear thy children, gentlest Mother. Rev. Francis Stanfield.* 82
74. Night Hymn from the Breviary. *O Christ, thou brightness of the day.* *Prior Aylward.* 84

VESPERS HYMNS.

75, 76, 77, 78. Lucis Creator optime.
I. Maker, by whose unuttered word.
Rev. H. N. Oxenham. 84
II. Eternal source of light's clear stream.
Robert Campbell. 85
III. Maker of light, most holy king. From Church Hymns, 1849.
J. Richard Beste, 1839. 85
IV. O blest Creator of the light.
Charles Kent, 1883. 86

Contents.

NO.
79, 80, 81. Jam sol recedet igneus.
 I. The blazing sun is well-nigh gone. From
  Catholic Christian Manual, 1847.
      Ambrose Lisle Phillipps. 87
 II. Now lowly sinks the fiery sun.
      J. Richard Beste. 87
 III. While now the flaming sun declines.
      Charles Kent, 1883. 87

COMPLINE HYMNS.

82, 83, 84, 85. Te lucis ante terminum.
 I. Before the closing of the day. From the
  Complete Office of the Holy Week, 1670.
      W. K. Blount. 88
 II. Thee, God, before the close of light.
      Charles Kent, 1883. 88
 III. Before the day's last moments fly.
      Robert Campbell. 89
 IV. Before the closing of the day.
      Rev. H. N. Oxenham. 89

Resurrection and Ascension.

86. Resurrection of Jesus. *Bringing life and peace and gladness.* *Father Rawes.* 90
87. The risen King. *Hail, mighty King, in risen strength victorious.* *Rev. Francis Stanfield.* 91
88. The Ascension. *Why is thy face so lit with smiles?*   *Father Faber.* 92
89. Attollite portas, Principes, vestras. *Lift up, ye princes of the sky.* *Prior Aylward.* 93
90. Triumph of the Conqueror. *Rise, glorious Conqueror, rise.* *Matthew Bridges.* 94
91, 92. Hymns from the Daily Procession of the Franciscan Friars at Jerusalem. (At the Altar of St. Mary Magdalen.) *Jesus, thy love was pleased to all.* (In the Church of the Apparition.) *Mother of God and Mother mine.* From the Order of Compline, 1880. *Anonymous.* 95, 96

x   *Contents.*

NO.		PAGE
93.	Jesus risen. *All hail, dear Conqueror, all hail.* *Father Faber.*	96
94.	Mount Olivet. *Lo, on Mount Olivet's fair height.* *Rev. Francis Stanfield.*	97
95.	Pone luctum, Magdalena. *Woeful Mary, cease from sighing.* *Anonymous,* 1875.	98
96.	German Easter Hymn. *The Saviour is arisen.* *J. C. Earle,* 1883.	99
97.	O Rex gloriæ. *O Christ, our glorious king.* *Prior Aylward.*	100
98.	Ascension of Jesus. *In the brightness of the sunshine.* *Father Rawes.*	101

Pentecost and Trinity Sunday.

99.	Trinity Sunday. *God of life and light and motion.* From Lyra Liturgica. *Canon Oakeley,* 1865.	102
100.	Descent of the Holy Ghost. *O mighty Mother, why that light?* *Father Faber.*	102
101.	Hours from the Little Office of the Holy Ghost. *Oh, may the Paraclete divine his grace to us impart.* *Prior Aylward.*	104
102.	To the Holy Spirit. *The wind rang out from depths of woods.* *Aubrey de Vere.*	106
103.	The Fountain of Love. *Fountain of Love, thyself true God.* *Father Faber.*	106
104.	Canticle to the Holy Ghost. *Thou Paraclete, whom Jesus sent to me.* *Father Rawes.*	107
105.	The Most Holy Trinity. *Have mercy on us, God most high.* *Father Faber.*	109
106.	Ever-blessed Trinity. *God the Father, whose relation.* *Canon Oakeley.*	110
107.	The Eternal Spirit. *Eternal Spirit, God supreme.* *Robert Campbell.*	111
108.	Fragment of 'Beata nobis gaudia.' *A fire from heaven all-trembling came.* *Prior Aylward.*	111

Contents. xi

NO.		PAGE
109.	To the Holy Ghost. *Holy Ghost, come down upon thy children.* Father Faber.	112

The Sacred Humanity.

110. Cor Jesu, Cor purissimum. *O heart of Jesus, purest heart.* From Madonna : Verses on our Lady and the Saints.
  Father Matthew Russell, S. J. 1869–1880. 114
111. Fount of Divine Love. *O heart of Jesus, heart of God.* Lady Georgiana Fullerton, 1876. 115
112. The true Shepherd. *I was wandering and weary.* Father Faber. 116
113. Haven of Rest. *Sweet Jesus, thou a haven art.* Rev. Francis Stanfield. 117
114. Sinner's cry to Jesus. *Jesu, meek and lowly.* Father Henry Collins, Cistercian Order, 1860. 118
115. The Sacred Heart. *What wouldst thou have, O soul.* Adelaide A. Procter, 1862. 119
116. Jesus our Rest. *Night falls apace; the shades grow long.* From Lyrics of Life and Light, 1875. E. Louisa Lee. 121
117. Latus Salvatoris. *There is an everlasting home.* Matthew Bridges. 123
118. The riven Heart. *For this the wound, for this thy heart is riven.* Lady Catherine Petre. 124
119. Jesus is God. *Jesus is God; the solid earth.* Father Faber. 124
120. Dreams of Time. *I arise from dreams of time.* From Hymns for the Ecclesiastical Year. Robert Monteith, 1878. 125
121. On the Sacred Heart of Jesus. *I dwell a captive in this heart.* From St. Alphonsus. Anonymous, 1863. 128
122. Jesus, my Lord, I thee adore. *Jesus, my Lord, my God, my all.* Father H. Collins. 128
123. Our Home. *O sacred Heart, our home lies deep in thee.* Rev. Francis Stanfield. 129

NO.		PAGE
124. Come to Jesus. *Souls of men, why will ye scatter?* *Father Faber.*		130
125. Piercing of the Sacred Heart. *Love, thou dost all excell.* *Lady Catherine Petre.*		131
126. Two Messages. *A Message from the sacred Heart. From Emmanuel: a Book of Eucharistic Verses.* *Father Matthew Russell, S. J.*		132
127. Cento from Little Office of the Sacred Heart. *O heaven's glorious king.* *Anonymous*, 1765.		132
128. We come to thee, sweet Saviour. *We come to thee, sweet Saviour.* *Father Faber.*		133
129. Rest in the Sacred Heart. *O sacred Heart, all blissful light of heaven.* *Rev. Francis Stanfield.*		134
130. The Soul to her Beloved. *Jesu, end of my desires.* *J. C. Earle*, 1881.		135
131. Confido et Conquiesco. *Fret not, poor soul, while doubt and fear.* *Adelaide A. Procter*, 1863.		136

PART II.
MODERN, ORIGINAL AND OTHER HYMNS.

First and Second Advent.

Greater Antiphons for Advent.

(*O Sapientia.*)

O WISDOM, that proceedest from
　The mouth of the Most High,
And through illimitable space
　Extendest mightily;
Thou, that in sweetest harmony
　Disposest all creation,
Come, guide our souls along the path
　Of prudent contemplation.

(*O Adonai.*)

O Adonai, Israel's ruler thou,
　To Moses in the flame-girt bush revealed,
Who gavst to him the law on Sinai's brow,
　Come, lift thine outstretched arm our souls to shield.

(*O Radix Jesse.*)

Root of Jesse, ensign thou
　Set forth to every nation,
Unto thee all kings shall bow
　In speechless adoration.
Thine aid the Gentiles shall implore;
Come and redeem us; tarry now no more.

(*O Clavis David.*)

Key of David, and sceptre of Israel's race,
Who openest and closest the portals of grace.
　When thou openest, none close,
　When thou shuttest, none ope:
　Come, lead from their bondage
　　The 'prisoners of hope;'

Make speed, O Redeemer, the captives to save,
Who in darkness abide, and the gloom of the grave.

(O Oriens.)

O Day-spring, brightness of eternal light,
    O sun of righteousness;
Come thou, the dwellers in dark shades of night
  And in death's valley with thy rising beams to bless.

(O Rex Gentium.)

O King, desire of every nation,
  O corner-stone that both to one dost mould,
Come thou, accomplish man's salvation,
  Man, whom thou formedst from the clay of old.

(O Emmanuel.)

O Law-giver and king, Emmanuel, come:
  Come thou, the Gentiles tarry for thy birth,
Predestined Saviour; from sin's righteous doom,
  Come, save, O Lord our God, the tribes of earth.

H. N. Oxenham.

Ancient of Days.

Ancient of days, thy throne on high,
Who like the Son of Man draws nigh?
Ye everlasting gates unfold;
The king, the Lord of Hosts behold.

He comes arrayed in garments red,
Captivity his captive led;
Before the mercy seat to show
His blood poured forth for all below.

His blood that ever vocal flows,
But calls not vengeance on his foes;
Things better far than Abel's pleads,
And for his murderers intercedes.

And with his heavenly offering one,
From east to west beneath the sun

First and Second Advent.

The pure oblation see arise,
The great, mysterious Sacrifice.

Though o'er the waterflood his seat,
And all things placed beneath his feet,
For human woe he still can feel,
And sends his balm our wounds to heal.

In every want, in every fear,
We know that he to us is near;
The mother from her babe may part,
But we are graven in his heart.

Though hid from us a little while,
We hear his voice, we see his smile;
Our brother, Saviour and our friend,
He loved and loves us to the end.

Lord, from the deep to thee we call,
To thee who art our all in all;
O Lord, remember all thy pain,
Nor let it prove for us in vain.
R. Campbell.

Dies Finalis.

Rise, O Lord, in all thy glory,
  On the last and dreadful day;
Lo, the lofty hills are hoary
    Trembling ere they melt away:
      Come to judgment, come to judgment,
      Let thy wheels no longer stay.

Crash on crash of distant thunder
  Peals aloud from pole to pole;
As in wrath they burst asunder,
    And the skies together roll,
      Clothed in sackcloth, clothed in sackcloth,
      Withering like a parchment scroll.

Now the universe in motion
    Sinks upon her funeral pyre—
Earth dissolving—and the ocean
    Vanishing in final fire :
        Hark the trumpet, hark the trumpet,
        Loud proclaims the hour of ire.

Graves have yawned in countless numbers ;
    From the dust the dead arise ;
Legions, out of silent slumbers,
    Wake in overwhelmed surprise,
        Where all nature, where all nature,
        Wrecked and torn in ruin lies.

See the judge our nature wearing,
    Pure, ineffable, divine ;
See the great archangel bearing
    High in heaven the mystic sign ;
        Cross of glory, cross of glory,
        Christ be in that moment mine.

Lo, that last long separation
    As the cleaving crowds divide ;
And one dread adjudication
    Sends each soul to either side :
        Lord of mercy, Lord of mercy,
        How shall I that day abide ?

Sign of safety, see it lightening,
    Once the cross of crimson shame,
And with heavenly lustre brightening
    Those who suffered in its name—
        Mighty millions, mighty millions,
        Radiant with their wings of flame.

Rise, O Lord, in all thy glory
    On thine amaranthine throne,
Thousand thousand worlds adore thee
    From the centre to the zone ;

First and Second Advent.

Hail Emmanuel, hail Emmanuel,
  Let our hearts be all thine own.
Oh, may thine own Bride and Spirit
  Then avert a fearful doom ;
And me summon to inherit
  An eternal blissful home :
    Ah, come quickly, ah, come quickly ;
    Let thy Second Advent come.
M. Bridges.

Fragment of 'Dies Iræ.'

Dread and strange the trumpet's tone,
Loud through death's dominion blown,
All shall gather round the throne.

Death and nature in surprise,
Shall behold the dead arise,
Summoned to that last assize.

When the judge assumes his throne,
Sins unpunished shall be none,
Every secret shall be known.

King of dreadful majesty,
Saving whom thou savest free,
Fount of pity, save thou me.

Think, good Jesus, think, I pray,
Thou for me didst tread life's way ;
Spare me in the dreadful day.

Me thy wearied love still sought,
On the cross my ransom bought ;
Shall such toils be counted nought ?

Much I mourn the guilt which thou
Readest on my crimson brow ;
Spare, good Lord, thy suppliant now.

Annus Sanctus.

Fix, at thy right hand, my place
With thy sheep, the sons of grace,
Severed from the goats' foul race.

Here I pray, low bending down—
My crushed heart like ashes grown—
Dying, take me to thine own.

Day of wrath and bitter weeping,
When men rise from death's dark sleeping,
Called to meet the judge divine,
Save this soul and make it thine:
Unto all, O Saviour blest,
Grant the saints' eternal rest.

J. D. Aylward.

German Advent Hymn.

Clouds of heaven, shower the Just One,
  Rain him on the earth like dew,
Thus through that long night of ages
  Faithful souls more fervent grew :
Neath the curse of God confounded,
Satan reigned and death abounded,
And salvation's heir must wait
Still before the fast-closed gate.

Yet the Father moved in mercy
  To effect a vast design,
And the Son of God consenting
  Closed with this decree divine,
Gabriel brought the news astounding
And the response, heaven-ward bounding,
' Lo, the Handmaid of the Lord,
To fulfil his gracious word.'

Nought but thine obedience saved me,
  Carrying out the wondrous plan
Of the Holy Ghost's o'ershadowing
  And the Word made flesh for man ;

First and Second Advent.

In the dust, ye men, adore him;
Hell and hell-craft, bow before him;
Well to those of Adam's race,
For the Saviour comes and grace.

Hark, I hear a call resounding,
   Brother, wake, from sleep arise,
For assured salvation nears us,
   And the red dawn fills the skies;
Every hated idol breaking,
Every well-tried weapon taking,
March, disown the deeds of night,
March, ye children of the light.

Let us walk as in the day-time
   Not in gluttony and wine,
Not in aught that human passion
   Wills against the law divine;
Let us make our sole election
Jesus, type of all perfection,
Who will come in many ways
For our weal and to his praise.

Glory to the world's Redeemer:
   He is coming; let us wait,
Earnest, prayerful and expectant
   Till our thirst he satiate
With himself; and grant our spirit
Christ to know and Christ inherit,
Christ to cherish and to feel,
Christ the future Christ reveal.
J. C. Earle.

Song of the Seraphs.

Crown him with many crowns,
   The Lamb upon his throne;
Hark how the heavenly anthem drowns
   All music but its own:

Awake my soul, and sing
    Of him who died for thee ;
And hail him as thy matchless king
    Through all eternity.

Crown him the Virgin's Son,
    The God incarnate born ;
Whose arm those crimson trophies won
    Which now his brow adorn :
Fruit of the mystic rose,
    As of that rose the stem ;
The root, whence mercy ever flows,
    The Babe of Bethlehem.

Crown him the Lord of love :
    Behold his hands and side,
Rich wounds, yet visible above,
    In beauty glorified :
No angel in the sky
    Can fully bear that sight,
But downward bends his burning eye
    At mysteries so bright.

Crown him the Lord of peace,
    Whose power a sceptre sways
From pole to pole, that wars may cease
    Absorbed in prayer and praise ;
His reign shall know no end,
    And round his pierced feet
Fair flowers of Paradise extend
    Their fragrance ever sweet.

Crown him the Lord of years,
    The potentate of time,
Creator of the rolling spheres,
    Ineffably sublime :
Glazed in a sea of light,
    Whose everlasting waves

First and Second Advent.

Reflect his form, the Infinite,
  Who lives and loves and saves.
Crown him the Lord of heaven,
  One with the Father known,
And the blest Spirit through him given
  From yonder triune throne:
All hail, Redeemer, hail,
  For thou hast died for me;
Thy praise shall never, never fail
  Throughout eternity.
M. Bridges.

Fragment of 'Dies Iræ.'

Oh, how great shall be the fear,
When on clouds the judge draws near,
All to try with search severe.

Hear the trumpet's awful tone—
Opening graves the summons own,
Quick and dead surround the throne.

To the judge's piercing eye
Undiscovered nought can lie,
Nought shall pass unheeded by.

Jesus, think—my debt to pay
Thou didst tread the mournful way;
Lose me not in thy dread day.

Thou wast wearied seeking me,
And didst buy me on the tree;
Let not vain thy labour be.

Righteous judge, before the day
When too late for grace to pray,
Cancel what I ne'er can pay.

Let me with thy sheep find grace;
Severed from the guilty race,
On the right appoint my place.

Suppliant, Lord, to thee I bend ;
From the dust my groans ascend;
Leave me not at my last end.

Day that shall awake the dead,
Day of weeping, day of dread,
Who thy terrors shall abide ?
Mercy, O our God, provide :
Jesu, Saviour, of thy love,
Call us to the bliss above.

R. Campbell.

The red Robe.

The winepress, the winepress,
    The voice is from God ;
The floor of his fury
    Is now to be trod ;
The sins of all nations
    Are full to o'erflowing,
And the blast of his anger
    From heaven is blowing.

The thunder, the thunder,
    A firmament burns ;
All nature in wonder
    To trembling turns ;
Forked flashes of lightning
    Illumine the skies,
As the universe brightening
    In agony dies.

The angels, the angels,
    They ride on the storm,
And their maker's commandments
    Prepare to perform ;
To punish the guilty,
    To utter the ban,
And empty their vials
    Of vengeance on man.

First and Second Advent.

The victim, the victim,
    Behold he is here ;
He looks on the tempest,
    Its clouds disappear ;
In the red robe of scourging
    Triumphant he stands,
And blots out the sentence
    With blood on his hands.

Roll backward, roll backward,
    Thou ocean of ire ;
Ye bolts of bright vengeance
    In silence expire ;
One drop of this purple
    Which Jesus has spilt,
Has ransomed his people
    And paid for their guilt.

M. Bridges.

Imitation of 'Dies Iræ.'

Woe is the day of ire,
Shrouding the earth in fire—
Sibyls' and David's lyre
    Dimly foretold it :
Strictly the guilty land
By the avenger scanned,
Smitten aghast, shall stand
    Still to behold it.

Start from your trance profound ;
Through the rent graves around,
Hark, the last trumpet-sound—
    Dolorous clangour ;
Death sees in mute surprise
Ashes to doom arise—
Dust unto God replies,
    God in his anger.

Bring forth the judgment-roll,
Blazon aloud the whole
Guilt of each trembling soul—
    Justice hath bidden:
Then shall all hearts be known,
Sin's abyss open thrown,
Vengeance shall have her own—
    Nought shall be hidden.

Oh, on that dreadful day
What shall the sinner say,
When scarce the just shall stay
    Judgment securely?
Save me, tremendous king,
Who the saved soul dost bring
Under thy mercy's wing,
    Through thy grace purely.

Jesus, remember I
Caused thee to toil and die;
Sin brought thee from the sky—
    I am a sinner:
Break my soul's bitter chain;
Thou for her love wast slain;
Gushed thy heart's blood in vain,
    Saviour, to win her?

Just judge and strong, we pray,
Ere the accusing day,
From every stain of clay
    Grant us remission:
Guilty and sore in fear
I, clad in shame, appear—
Yet, for thy mercy hear,
    Lord, my petition.

Who madest Mary pure,
And the good thief secure,

First and Second Advent.

Gav̈est me also sure
   Hope of salvation :
Though to my shrinking gaze,
Hell's everlasting blaze
Glares through the judgment-day's
   Dire desolation.

Lamb for the ransom slain,
Then 'mid thy snowy train
At thy right hand to reign
   Place me for ever :
While at thy dread command,
Those at thy left who stand
Far from the chosen band,
   Lightnings shall sever.

Rings the last thunder-shock—
Earth's broken pillars rock—
Down the accursed flock—
   Numberless falling :
Down to the fiery doom,
Gulphed in hell's hopeless tomb,
Shriek through the ghastly gloom
   Horrors appalling.

Contrite in pale dismay,
Lord, hear a sinner pray—
On that tremendous day
   Spread thy shield o'er him :
Day of great anguish, when
God from the dust again
Summons us guilty men,
   Wailing before him.

Clement thou art as just—
Mercy, O God, on dust—
In thee alone we trust,
   Shelter and save us :

When on the day of dole
Death-bells of nations toll,
Spare the immortal soul
Thy Spirit gave us.

R. D. Williams.

Pilgrims of the Night.

Hark, hark, my soul, angelic songs are swelling
  O'er earth's green fields and ocean's wave-beat shore;
How sweet the truth those blessed strains are telling
  Of that new life where sin shall be no more.
    Angels of Jesus; angels of light,
    Singing to welcome the pilgrims of the night.

Darker than night life's shadows fall around us,
  And like benighted men we miss our mark;
God hides himself, and grace hath scarcely found us,
  Ere death finds out his victims in the dark.
    Angels of Jesus; angels of light,
    Singing to welcome the pilgrims of the night.

Onward we go, for still we hear them singing,
  'Come, weary souls, for Jesus bids you come';
And through the dark, its echoes sweetly ringing,
  The music of the gospel leads us home.
    Angels of Jesus; angels of light,
    Singing to welcome the pilgrims of the night.

Far, far away, like bells at evening pealing,
  The voice of Jesus sounds o'er land and sea;
And laden souls, by thousands meekly stealing,
  Kind Shepherd, turn their weary steps to thee.
    Angels of Jesus; angels of light,
    Singing to welcome the pilgrims of the night.

First and Second Advent.

Rest comes at length : though life be long and dreary,
  The day must dawn, and darksome night be past;
All journeys end in welcomes to the weary,
  And heaven, the heart's true home, will come at last.
    Angels of Jesus ; angels of light,
    Singing to welcome the pilgrims of the night.

Angels, sing on, your faithful watches keeping,
  Sing us sweet fragments of the songs above;
While we toil on, and soothe ourselves with weeping,
  'Till life's long night shall break in endless love.
    Angels of Jesus ; angels of light,
    Singing to welcome the pilgrims of the night.
F. W. Faber.

Nativity of our Lord.

Christmas Carol.

PRIMEVAL night had repossessed
   Her empire in the fields of space;
Calm lay the kine on earth's dark breast;
   The earth lay calm in heaven's embrace.

That hour, where shepherds kept their flocks,
   From God a glory sudden fell;
The splendour smote the trees and rocks,
   And lay like dew along the dell.

God's angel close beside them stood;
   'Fear nought,' that angel said; and then,
'Behold, I bring you tidings good;
   The Saviour Christ is born to men.'

And straightway round him myriads sang
   Loud song, again and yet again,
Till all the hollow valley rang,
   'Glory to God, and peace to men.'

The shepherds went, and wondering, eyed
   In Bethlehem born, the heavenly stranger:
Mary and Joseph knelt beside;
   The Babe was cradled in the manger.

Thus in the violet-scented grove,
   The May breeze murmuring softly by them,
The children sang. Who Mary love
   The long year through have Christmas nigh them.

A. de Vere.

Nativity of our Lord.

The Child Jesus: a Cornish Carol.

Welcome, that star in Judah's sky,
  That voice o'er Bethlehem's palmy glen,
The lamp far sages hailed on high,
  The tones that thrilled the shepherd-men:
'Glory to God in loftiest heaven;'
  Thus angels smote the echoing chord—
'Glad tidings unto man forgiven;
  Peace, from the presence of the Lord.'

The shepherds sought that birth divine;
  The Wise-men traced their guided way;
There, by strange light and mystic sign,
  The God they came to worship lay:
A human Babe in beauty smiled,
  Where lowing oxen round him trod;
A Maiden clasped her awful Child,
  Pure offspring of the Breath of God.

Those voices from on high are mute;
  The star the Wise-men saw is dim;
But hope still guides the wanderer's foot,
  And faith renews the angel-hymn:
'Glory to God in loftiest heaven;'
  Touch with glad hand the ancient chord—
'Good tidings unto man forgiven;
  Peace, from the presence of the Lord.'

R. S. Hawker.

Verbum Caro factum est.

Dry your tears, ye silent mourners;
  Fling the sorrow from your breast;
See the dawn of happy Christmas—
    'Verbum caro factum est.'
Christ hath come to dwell among us,
  He hath come to give us rest;
He hath come our foes to vanquish—
    'Verbum caro factum est.'

Angels sing their joyous carol,
  Angels in the snowy vest,
Bowing down in adoration—
    ' Verbum caro factum est.'

Welcome him with loving worship ;
  Welcome him our precious guest ;
Bless him now and bless him ever—
    ' Verbum caro factum est.'

Oh, the jubilee in heaven ;
  Oh, the raptures of the blest ;
Unto us a Child is given—
    ' Verbum caro factum est.'

Ring the bells and swing the censers ;
  Let our gladness be expressed
In each outward act and token—
    ' Verbum caro factum est.'

Grateful words will give him pleasure,
  But our grateful deeds are best ;
Let them all be for his honour—
    ' Verbum caro factum est.'

Lady C. Petre.

Christmas Eve and Morn.

I gaze out on the moon-lit earth,
  Hushed, still and solemn all around ;
The frosty air is cold and keen,
  The crisp snow glitters on the ground.

So cold and sharp ; and yet, I know
  On such a winter night of old
He came, the holy Child, and lay
  In manger-cradle, rude and cold.

The angels' song rang out to tell
  Of Jesus on his Mother's breast ;
For there, as weary souls do now,
  He found a shelter safe and rest.

Nativity of our Lord.

She worshipped, while his tender cries
  Spake to her soul of mysteries deep ;
Strange visions passed of tears and blood,
  Of cruel cross and death's calm sleep.

Yes, spotless Mother, he has come
  A Saviour to a ruined race ;
That swathèd form, so tender framed,
  Is crucified to win us grace.

O wondrous joy, O living truth,
  Which guides us as we journey on ;
God came in time with us to dwell,
  The Word made flesh, sweet Mary's Son.

*   *   *

Peace falls apace from angel-hands,
  Peace for poor earth this Christmas morn ;
The bells ring out ; the altar gleams ;
  For us a Saviour-king is born.

Then, let us gather where the choir
  At midnight sings a joyous strain,
To join and worship Bethlehem's Babe
  Till Christmas-tide comes round again.

E. Louisa Lee.

Birth of Jesus.

In a silence deep at midnight,
  When the hills were white with snow,
Jesus, the Desired of nations,
  Came into this world of woe.
Then he came, an infant Saviour,
  To our Lady's sweet embrace,
As she waited for his coming,
  Longing to behold his face.

In his strength he came, that evil
  May be driven far away,

'Till to all the scattered kingdoms
    Reacheth his resistless sway.
He had kept one chosen Virgin
    Safe from every stain of sin ;
Graciously, in her redemption,
    First-fruits of his cross to win.

Swathing-bands were wrapt about him
    In the manger he was laid ;
There adored three Hebrew shepherds,
    Joseph and the Mother-maid.
God made man, the Word incarnate,
    Mary watched him sleeping there ;
Never had that child-like Mother
    Looked upon a sight so fair.

There the ox and ass were standing,
    Knee-deep in the fragrant hay,
Gazing with a solemn wonder
    At the crib where Jesus lay.
Angels came to David's city,
    Met their Lord with hymns of praise,
Sang their joyous songs of triumph,
    Worshipping in glad amaze :

' Unto us a Son is given ;
    Unto us a Child is born ;
Glory to the first-begotten ;
    He has come this Christmas morn.
He has come, the Lord almighty,
    In a pure and painless birth ;
Glory be to God in heaven,
    Peace be given to men on earth.'

Thus the angels, peace-proclaiming,
    To the Word made flesh drew nigh ;
Far and near their voice of welcome
    Rang through all the listening sky :

Thus our Lord, the long-expected,
  Came the healer of all woe,
When the shepherds knelt before him
  In the stable white with snow.

H. A. Rawes.

The Infant Jesus.

Dear Little One, how sweet thou art,
  Thine eyes how bright they shine,
So bright, they almost seem to speak
  When Mary's look meets thine.

How faint and feeble is thy cry,
  Like plaint of harmless dove,
When thou dost murmur in thy sleep
  Of sorrow and of love.

When Mary bids thee sleep thou sleep'st;
  Thou wakest when she calls;
Thou art content upon her lap,
  Or in the rugged stalls.

Simplest of babes, with what a grace
  Thou dost thy Mother's will;
Thine infant fashions well betray
  The Godhead's hidden skill.

When Joseph takes thee in his arms,
  And smoothes thy little cheek,
Thou lookest up into his face
  So helpless and so meek.

Yes, thou art what thou seem'st to be,
  A thing of smiles and tears;
Yet thou art God, and heaven and earth
  Adore thee with their fears.

Yes, dearest Babe, those tiny hands,
  That play with Mary's hair,
The weight of all the mighty world
  This very moment bear.

Art thou, weak Babe, my very God?
 Oh, I must love thee then,
Love thee, and yearn to spread thy love
 Among forgetful men.
F. W. Faber.

Midnight Mass of the Nativity.

Alleluia, Lord most holy,
 In thy manger-throne we hail thee;
Alleluia, meek and lowly,
 Never shall our worship fail thee.

Alleluia, choirs of angels
 Sing at midnight-hour thy glory,
To the watchful shepherds telling
 From the skies thy natal story.

Alleluia, Child of Mary,
 Low the shepherds bend before thee;
Alleluia, Eastern monarchs
 With their costliest gifts adore thee.

Alleluia, still unending
 Rings the angel-note above;
From our shrines in praise ascending
 Echoes earth's response of love.

Alleluia, shine the tapers,
 Gleams the holly's burnished spray;
Alleluia, chant the Credo,
 Christ, we welcome thee to-day.

Alleluia, Lord most mighty,
 Come upon our shrines to dwell;
Alleluia, Word incarnate;
 Hark, it sounds—the sanctus-bell.

Nativity of our Lord.

Down in adoration falling,
   Hail, sweet Sacrament divine;
Hail, to thee our souls are calling,
   Thou art ours and we are thine.
H. N. Oxenham.

Carol for Christmas Night.
Once to Bethlehem's lowly shepherds
   Came a strain of heavenly mirth,
Angel-lips in chorus singing,
   Peace proclaiming o'er the earth:
'Glory in the highest, glory;
   Praise to God, who reigns on high,
And to men of good-will mercy—
   God to sinners draweth nigh.

'He is born, great prince and Saviour,
   Offspring of the Mother-maid,
As an Infant ye shall find him,
   Swathed and in a manger laid.'
Such the glad and wondrous story
   Which the rapturous angels tell;
Sons of earth, with hearts exulting,
   Let your voice their chorus swell.

God and man for ever bonded,
   Jacob's ladder firmly set,
Gates of paradise re-opened,
   Peace and justice sweetly met:
Jesus, shelter in the desert,
   Where the weary may abide;
Jesus, healer of the leprous
   By a fountain open wide.

Seek him then, or young or hoary,
   Whilst he may be surely found;
Come ye to the mystic manger,
   With the shepherds worship round;

See, a Babe, divine and human,
    Mary holds him forth to view ;
Now upon his earthly altars
    He is present still for you.
Meekly then, in adoration
    Worship where the lights are lit ;
Glory in the highest, glory;
    God with man once more is knit ;
Christmas joys for high and lowly,
    Jesus Christ brings peace divine ;
Up above, when years are ended,
    May his face upon us shine.
E. Louisa Lee.

The Hour of silent Midnight.

At hour of silent midnight,
    Oh, mystery of love,
Earth's longed and sighed-for Saviour,
    Descended from above :
Awake, awake, creation;
    Arise, for light is come ;
Lo, earth is changed to heaven,
    For earth is Jesus' home.
Glory to God on high ; praise to our new-born king :
Peace unto men on earth, sweet Infant-Jesus bring.

Amid the star-lit heavens
    There shines a glorious light,
And hosts of gleaming angels
    Illume the lonely night ;
They leave their thrones of glory,
    To seek their new-born king,
And ranged in countless armies
    Glad hymns of triumph sing.
        Glory to God on high ; etc.

The praises of the angels
    Were wafted from above,

Nativity of our Lord.

And shepherds left their night watch
    To seek the God of Love ;
They longed to gaze on Jesus,
    To see the new-born Child ;
They found the God of heaven,
    An Infant meek and mild.
        Glory to God on high ; etc.

And there the Mother kneeling,
    Bends fondly o'er her Son,
Watching with blest St. Joseph,
    Her cherished Little One :
See Jesus in the manger,
    How still and meek he lies;
Now smiles play on his features ;
    Now tears are in his eyes.
        Glory to God on high ; etc.

Christians redeemed, oh, hasten
    To Bethlehem's sacred shrine,
And gather around Jesus,
    To kiss his lips divine :
Oh, bless our new-born Saviour,
    Our Infant-God adore,
Till love shall sweetly lead us
    Home to the eternal shore.
Glory to God on high ; praise to our new-born king :
Peace unto men on earth, sweet Infant-Jesus bring.
                            F. Stanfield.

Shepherds at the Manger.

Stars of glory, shine more brightly,
    Purer be the moon-light's beam,
Glide ye hours and moments lightly,
    Swiftly down time's deepening stream :
Bring the hour that banished sadness,
    Brought redemption down to earth,

When the shepherds heard with gladness
Tidings of a Saviour's birth.

See a beauteous angel soaring
  In the bright celestial blaze,
On the shepherds low adoring
  Rest his mild, effulgent rays:
'Fear not'—cries the heavenly stranger—
  'Him whom ancient seers foretold,
Weeping in a lowly manger,
  Shepherds, haste ye to behold.'

See the shepherds quickly rising,
  Hastening to the humble stall,
And the new-born Infant prizing,
  As the mighty Lord of all;
Lowly now they bend before him,
  In his helpless infant state,
Firmly faithful they adore him
  And his greatness celebrate.

Hark the swell of heavenly voices
  Peals along the vaulted sky;
Angels sing, while earth rejoices—
  'Glory to our God on high;
Glory in the highest heaven,
  Peace to humble men on earth;
Joy to these and bliss is given,
  In the great Redeemer's birth.'

F. C. Husenbeth.

The Christmas Moon.

The moon that now is shining
  In skies so blue and bright,
Shone ages since on shepherds
  Who watched their flocks by night:

Nativity of our Lord.

There was no sound upon the earth,
   The azure air was still,
The sheep in quiet clusters lay
   Upon the grassy hill.

When lo, a white-winged angel
   The watchers stood before,
And told how Christ was born on earth
   For mortals to adore;
He bade the trembling shepherds
   Listen, nor be afraid,
And told how in a manger
   The glorious Child was laid.

When suddenly in the heavens
   Appeared an angel band—
The while in reverent wonder
   The Syrian shepherds stand—
And all the bright host chanted
   Words that shall never cease:
'Glory to God in the highest,
   On earth goodwill and peace.'

The vision in the heavens
   Faded and all was still,
And the wondering shepherds left their flocks
   To feed upon the hill;
Towards the blessed city
   Quickly their course they held,
And in a lowly stable
   Virgin and Child beheld.

Beside a humble manger
   Was the Maiden-mother mild,
And in her arms her Son divine,
   A new-born Infant smiled:
No shade of future sorrow
   From Calvary then was cast;

Only the glory was revealed,
  The suffering was not past.

The Eastern kings before him knelt,
  And rarest offerings brought ;
The shepherds worshipped and adored
  The wonders God had wrought ;
They saw the crown for Israel's king,
  The future's glorious part—
But all these things the Mother kept
  And pondered in her heart.

Now we that Maiden-mother
  The Queen of heaven call ;
And the Child we call our Jesus,
  Saviour and judge of all—
But the star that shone in Bethlehem
  Shines still, and shall not cease ;
And we listen still to the tidings
  Of glory and of peace.

Adelaide A. Procter.

Epiphany and Holy Name.

The infant King.

THEY leave the land of gems and gold,
  The shining portals of the East;
For him, the Woman's Seed foretold,
  They leave the revel and the feast.

To earth their sceptres they have cast,
  And crowns by kings ancestral worn;
They track the lonely Syrian waste;
  They kneel before the Babe new-born.

O happy eyes, that saw him first;
  O happy lips, that kissed his feet;
Earth slakes at last her ancient thirst;
  With Eden's joy her pulses beat.

True kings are those who thus forsake
  Their kingdoms for the eternal King;
Serpent, her foot is on thy neck;
  Herod, thou writh'st, but canst not sting.

He, he is King and he alone,
  Who lifts that infant hand to bless;
Who makes his Mother's knee his throne,
  Yet rules the starry wilderness.

A. de Vere.

Magian Gifts.

Oh, for the light of that fair star
Which led the Magians from afar,
  Their Infant-God to greet;

Oh, for the wisdom of the kings,
Who chose those mystic offerings,
    To lay before his feet.

Ah, had we but their faith and love,
It would our sluggish spirits move
    To raptures almost wild,
To see that scene of wondrous grace,
To gaze on Mary's sinless face,
    And worship Mary's Child.

And yet, when Jesus calls his own
To worship round his altar-throne,
    His majesty concealed;
What need have we to find our Lord
Of other star than God's own word,
    To holy Church revealed?

For nestling there on Mary's breast,
The Babe, to those three kings of East,
    No holier gladness lent,
Than now to faith-illumined hearts
The beauty of his love imparts
    In this sweet sacrament.

And though his Mother's arms no more
Supply the throne where we adore,
    Yet well her children feel
That still her smiles of welcome fall
With blessings from her Son, on all
    Who in his presence kneel.

Oh then, with loyal hearts and wise
Bring we our gifts, in lowly guise
    Prostrating human pride;
For gold and frankincense and myrrh
Bring purest love and fragrant prayer,
    And passion mortified.

T. E. B.

Epiphany and Holy Name.

Dormi, Fili, dormi.

Sleep, my Child, the Mother singeth;
  Sleep, my Babe, so sweet and young;
Sleep, in silver tones outringeth
  From his foster-father's tongue:
    Songs of praise to thee we raise
    Many a thousand thousand times.

Darling mine, thy couch renewing,
  See, I smooth thy simple bed;
Sleep, the soft sweet hay I'm strewing
  Will support thy infant head.

Sleep, the angel's hands receive thee;
  Take, as from thy heavenly home,
Milk, thy Mother's breast will give thee—
  Honey from the honey-comb.

Balm of honey, Baby, rest thee;
  Sugar-sweet, repose my Child;
Life of her whose arms have pressed thee,
  Offspring of the undefiled.

I will give thee what thou willest—
  Sleep, my darling, sleep, my dove;
Sleep, thy Mother's heart thou fillest
  With o'erflowing founts of love.

Heart and throne together blending,
  Sleep, my Child, divine and dear;
Like a strain from heaven descending,
  Falls thy breathing on my ear.

Sun-flower of the golden city,
  Fold thy leaves in balmy rest;
Sleep, thy father sings his ditty;
  Sleep, she sings thy Mother blest.

Be nought wanting, violets, roses,
  I the fragrant hay strew o'er;
Lilies, where thy cheek reposes,
  Hyacinths upon the floor.

Wouldst thou music? I will bring thee
  Shepherds from the star-lit plains;
None can purer carols sing thee;
  None can play thee sweeter strains:
    Songs of praise to thee we raise
    Many a thousand thousand times.
D. F. MacCarthy.

The ever-precious Name.

Hail, to the ever-precious Name:
  Keep it within thy breast;
Hence mayst thou aid and strength reclaim
  To set thy soul at rest.

When peace from thee far off is driven,
  Thy cross too sharp appears;
Remember, that sweet name was given
  In suffering and tears.

Oh, doth not Jesus love us much?
  He burns with strong desire
Some piercing thorns at least to touch,
  Ere childhood's days expire.

He will not wait for manhood's prime;
  He seeks an earlier woe—
As though he thirsted for the time
  When all his blood should flow.

And thus the name we prize so well,
  With purest grace replete,
In loving souls its sounds shall tell
  Of sorrow, calm and sweet;

Of holy blood-drops shed for man,
  God's anger to appease—
Now let us follow, if we can,
  The road of selfish ease.

Sweet name of Jesus : thoughts of love
  Beam o'er our mortal strife ;
Thou art our watch-word from above,
  The solace of our life.

Let us but breathe thee to the last,
  'Till the dear voice shall call ;
O death, thy bitterness is past—
  Thou hast no sting at all.
Lady C. Petre.

Epiphany of Jesus.

King of Israel, Word incarnate,
  Now with joy we turn to thee,
In the brightness of thy rising,
  At thy first Epiphany :
Sleeping in the arms of Mary,
  Thou art God for ever blest ;
Thee thy servants love and worship
  In the sweetness of thy rest.

Taught of God, three Eastern sages
  Come to greet thee from afar ;
First-fruits of the Gentile-kingdoms,
  Guided by the promised star :
Soon they find thee with thy Mother,
  Soon their treasures they unfold,
Offerings for prophetic welcome,
  Incense, bitter myrrh and gold.

Infant Jesus, in thy mercy
  Thou art come to save the lost ;
Evermore a light of refuge
  Shining for the tempest-tost :

Thou, desired, art come, the Saviour
    Of a world by sin opprest,
Sent to heal the broken-hearted,
    Sent to succour the distrest.

Stands thy throne on high for ever,
    Welcome sight for weary eyes;
There the lilies cannot wither
    In the breath of paradise:
'Midst the golden-hearted lilies
    Blooming in the second spring,
All the chosen see thy glory,
    All rejoice in thee, O king.

What the rapture of thy presence,
    What its blessedness may be,
In thy Father and thy Spirit
    Evermore to gaze on thee,
Thought of man can never fathom,
    Tongue of man can never tell,
But thine angels and thy ransomed,
    Rapt, adoring, know it well.

King of Gentiles, Light of ages,
    Very gracious, Lord, art thou;
Save us by thy holy childhood,
    By the crowns upon thy brow:
Bring us to the heavenly Eden,
    Where the living live in thee,
Likened to thy changeless beauty
    In the great Epiphany.

H. A. Rawes.

Jesus, my God and my All.

O Jesus, Jesus, dearest Lord,
    Forgive me if I say
For very love thy sacred name
    A thousand times a day.

I love thee so, I know not how
  My transports to control ;
Thy love is like a burning fire
  Within my very soul.

Oh wonderful, that thou shouldst let
  So vile a heart as mine
Love thee with such a love as this,
  And make so free with thine.

For thou to me art all in all,
  My honour and my wealth,
My heart's desire, my body's strength,
  My soul's eternal health.

What limit is there to thee, love?
  Thy flight where wilt thou stay?
On, on, our Lord is sweeter far
  To-day than yesterday.

O love of Jesus, blessed love,
  So will it ever be ;
Time cannot hold thy wondrous growth,
  No, nor eternity.
                              F. W. Faber.

Transfiguration of our Lord.

Oh, it is good for me to dwell in sweetness ;
Lord, I will pitch my tent on Thabor's mount,
And taste of holy joys in their completeness
      From heaven's pure fount.

Nay, nay, my soul, thirst not for delectation ;
It is not good to dwell in rapturous joy ;
Earth is not meant for constant jubilation,
      Without alloy.

Despair not, though thy path of prayer be lonely ;
Fret not, because thou seemest dull and cold ;
Trials like these receive as blessings only,
      Precious as gold.

Oh, 'tis a glorious thing to serve God purely,
Making this end alone our recompense,
To serve him daily, steadily and surely
    In penitence.

Shall I be perfected through consolation,
When I such coward-heart to Jesus bring?
When he was perfected, for our salvation
    Through suffering?

The holy saints sought out profound abjection,
Nor asked from God the raptures that he sent;
But gave unto the cross their best affection—
    Be thou content.

The path of dryness may be safer for thee,
My soul, then bend thee not in sadness down;
A life of sweetness wins not future glory,
    Nor heavenly crown.

Courage, the flame of love may still be burning,
Although its genial heat thou dost not feel;
Courage, and to the holy fight returning
    Renew thy zeal.

Supremely bright, beyond what tongue can mention,
Is the reward for those that suffer here,
Who serve their master with a pure intention
    Through many a tear.

But ask not thou much recompense for sorrow;
Be generous; and at thy Lord's command
Strive on to-day—and calmly leave to-morrow
    Safe in his hand.
              Lady C. Petre.

Vidimus Stellam ejus.

    Hushed is the starry night,
      Orion rests in might,
Lo, where he beckons with his jewelled hand;

Epiphany and Holy Name.

    The world doth hold her breath,
    Above, around, beneath,
To see this wondrous three glide through the land.

    All crowned and robed they move,
    Their large eyes fixed in love,
In love which seeks in heaven the mystic sign;
    They tarry not for food,
    Reck nought of rock or flood,
And seek unknowing, David's kingly line.

    O royal-hearted men,
    Was it within your ken
To watch the far-strayed people's gathering tide—
    Gathering from sin and death,
    To light of your clear faith,
And flowing through the heavenly gate set wide?

    Was yours the opened ear,
    New litanies to hear
Of martyrs and apostles, virgins white;
    Of innocents gem-dyed,
    Their Lord's escape to hide,
And all the bands who bless the living Light?

    To your prophetic eye
    Was Christ's great kingdom nigh,
Unrolling myriad years in one brief day;
    Through all this wintry world,
    The Bridegroom's flag unfurled,
While nations rage and swell and pass away?

    That faith we scarce may scan,
    True faith which sight outran,
And drew them o'er the lonely star-lit wild;
    We see them kneeling low,
    And while they worship, know
The Mother and the Son—her God and Child.

They feel no sad amaze,
   The glamour of earth's ways
Betrays them not to fail and shrink in scorn;
   Safe in their heart abides
   That truth the world derides;
Their God is hid in flesh, in flesh is born.

   O star-crowned kings, behold,
   The world in waxing old
Waxed foolish, scorning Mary and her Child;
   Oh, help us then to rise,
   With swift feet and glad eyes
To seek the incarnate GOD in life's grey wild.
                                    Emily Bowles.

A Carol of the Kings: an Armenian Myth.

   Three ancient men in Bethlehem's cave
      With awful wonder stand;
   A voice that called them from their grave
      In some far Eastern land.

   They lived, they trod the former earth
      When the old waters swelled;
   The ark, that womb of second birth,
      Their house and lineage held.

   Pale Japhet bows the knee with gold;
      Bright Sem sweet incense brings;
   And Cham, the myrrh his finger holds—
      Lo, the three orient kings.

   Types of the total earth, they hailed
      The signal's starry frame;
   Shuddering with second life, they quailed
      At the Child-Jesus' name.

   Then slow the patriarchs turned and trod,
      And this their parting sigh:
   'Our eyes have seen the living God;
      And now—once more to die.'
                                    R. S. Hawker.

Thabor, Calvary and Olivet.

Dear Saviour, when thy chosen three
Ascended Thabor's mount with thee,
   And when thy glory threw
Around thy form resplendent rays,
It circled thee with heavenly blaze,
   Dazzling to mortal view.

Then did thy great apostle pray
On Thabor's radiant mount to stay,
   And make his dwelling there ;
Held by thy glory's potent spell,
There he proclaimed it good to dwell,
   That tranquil bliss to share.

Little did that apostle know
What toils awaited him below
   Ere bliss should crown his head :
Ah, little did thy favourite think
So deeply of thy cup to drink ;
   He knew not what he said.

When thou didst vanish from their sight,
From Olivet's majestic height,
   · To mount thy glorious throne,
Thy chosen ones gazed fondly there,
And watched thee till the bright cloud's glare
   Left them in grief alone.

They, as they gazed from Olivet,
Their charge too quickly could forget,
   They loved to linger there ;
Till angels warned them to retire,
For him who would return in fire
   With fervour to prepare.

From Calvary thy followers fled ;
Where thy redeeming blood was shed,
   None of thy twelve were found,

Save thy beloved John—who stood
Faithful beneath the saving wood,
 When numbers scoffed around.
With him, oh, let my station be ;
Dear Saviour, let me mourn with thee—
 Thy cross to me is sweet ;
Oh, be thy sorrowing path my way ;
Lord, it is good for me to stay
 And press thy sacred feet.
F. C. Husenbeth.

Beside the Manger.

There in the narrow manger, cold and bleak,
 My Lord, thou art;
And there within those hands, so soft and weak,
 I lay my heart.
Beneath those tiny feet I bow my head,
 O blessed Child,
And kiss the straw that forms thy chilly bed
 In winter wild.
Show me thy wondrous Babe, O Mother-maid,
 Foretold of yore ;
The treasure on thy virgin-bosom laid
 Let me adore.
That small hand place upon my prostrate brow,
 O Mother dear ;
For crouching in his infant-presence, now
 I quake with fear.
Upon thy fair and youthful face I read
 A look of love—
A look which bids me trust thee in my need,
 Spouse of the Dove.
Mother of God, commend me to thy Son
 As here I bend ;
And oh, commend me when my task is done,
 And life shall end.

A sinner kneeling at an Infant's cot,
    I call on thee ;
A sinner at the cross forget me not,
    But plead for me.
And thus in faith assured I leave my heart,
    Blest Child, with thee ;
A worthless gift with which thou wilt not part
    Eternally.
S. J.

Song of Praise to the Name of Jesus.

Jesus is the sweetest name
    Unto mortals ever spoken ;
High exalted above all blame,
    And of every virtue token ;
        Lovely name, spread far and wide,
        Like no lovely name beside.

Jesus sets the sinner free,
    To the whole world brings salvation ;
As a mighty champion, he
    Hurls the fiend from loftiest station ;
        Wheresoe'er his name is known,
        Powers of hell are overthrown.

Jesus, sweet and only source
    Of our life and health and vigour,
Helps to bear with special force
    Sufferings of unwonted rigour;
        Take thou Jesus in thine heart,
        Quickly ceases all its smart.

Jesus, fountain never dry,
    Souls with endless life supplying,
From the depths of yonder sky
    Light interior ne'er denying ;
        Wouldst thou glad and joyous be,
        Ask him to abide in thee.

Jesus is a vast abyss,
  Always full of untold treasure,
And a paradise of bliss,
  And a sea of sacred pleasure;
    Morn and eve his grace is new,
    Falling on the heart like dew.

Jesus is the loveliest name
  That in the ear of mortal ringeth;
In the vale by which we came
  Of the joys of heaven it singeth;
    Am I glad? None but the Lord
    Sober gladness can afford.

Jesus is the heavenly bread,
  Energy and content bestowing,
Raising even from the dead,
  And with life and health o'erflowing;
    To my lips what taste so sweet?
    To my wounds what balm so meet?

Jesus is the tree of life,
  Souls with fruit of virtue feeding;
Are the tares within you rife?
  To his grace, lo, all is ceding;
    Let his shadow only fall,
    Poisons, weeds, they vanish all.

Jesus is of all things good,
  Highest, best, in earth and heaven;
From his throne and from his rood
  Sadness-chasing grace is given;
    And his name alone shall be
    Dearest of all names to me.

J. C. Earle.

Puer natus est nobis.

I caused those infant-tears to flow;
  I chilled those sacred limbs;

I in the manger laid him low,
  Whose praise the seraph hymns.

I made that little bosom heave
  In sighs and bitter sobs ;
That tender heart I made to grieve :
  For me, for me it throbs.

I caused that infant-voice to moan,
  That shivering frame to ache :
The Prince of Peace, through love alone,
  Weeps, suffers for my sake.

For me he breathes, for me he sighs,
  To me his arms extend ;
On me he casts his loving eyes,
  He loves me to the end.

What can I do, my Jesus sweet,
  Thy great love to repay ?
If my heart be an offering meet,
  I give it from this day.
                              F. A. J.

Stabat Mater speciosa.

By the crib wherein reposing,
With his eyes in slumber closing,
  Lay serene her Infant-boy,
Stood the beauteous Mother feeling
Bliss that could not bear concealing,
  So her face o'erflowed with joy.

Oh, the rapture nought could smother
Of that most immaculate Mother
  Of the sole-begotten One ;
When with laughing heart exulting,
She beheld her hopes resulting
  In the great birth of her Son.

Who would not with gratulation
See the happy consolation
  Of Christ's Mother undefiled?
Who would not be glad surveying
Christ's dear Mother bending, praying,
  Playing with her heavenly Child?

For a sinful world's salvation,
Christ her Son's humiliation
  She beheld and brooded o'er;
Saw him weak, a Child, a stranger,
Yet before him in the manger
  Kings lie prostrate and adore.

O'er that lowly manger winging,
Joyful hosts from heaven were singing
  Canticles of holy praise;
While the old man and the Maiden,
Speaking nought, with hearts o'erladen,
  Pondered on God's wondrous ways.

Fount of love, for ever flowing,
With a burning ardour glowing,
  Make me, Mother, feel like thee;
Let my heart, with graces gifted,
All on fire, to Christ be lifted,
  And by him accepted be.

Holy Mother, deign to bless me,
With his sacred wounds impress me,
  Let them in my heart abide;
Since he came, thy Son, the Holy,
To a birth-place, ah, so lowly,
  All his pains with me divide.

Make me with true joy delighted,
To Child-Jesus be united
  While my days of life endure;

Epiphany and Holy Name.

While an exile here sojourning,
Make my heart like thine be burning
   With a love divine and pure ;
Spotless Maid and sinless Woman,
Make us feel a fire in common,
   Make my heart's long longing sure.

Virgin of all virgins highest,
Prayer to thee thou ne'er denyest,
   Let me bear thy sweet Child too ;
Let me bear him in my bosom,
Lord of life, and never lose him,
   Since his birth doth death subdue.

Let me show forth how immense is
The effect on all my senses
   Of an union so divine :
All who in the crib revere him,
Like the shepherds watching near him,
   Will attend him through the night.

By thy powerful prayers protected,
Grant, O Queen, that his elected
   May behold heaven's moving light :
Make me by his birth be guarded,
By God's holy word be warded,
   By his grace 'till all is done ;
When my body lies obstructed,
Make my soul to be conducted
   To the vision of thy Son.

D. F. MacCarthy.

Lent and the Precious Blood.

Jesus, our Love, is crucified.

OH, come and mourn with me awhile ;
See, Mary calls us to her side ;
Oh, come and let us mourn with her :
   Jesus, our Love, is crucified.

Have we no tears to shed for him,
While soldiers scoff and Jews deride ?
Ah, look how patiently he hangs :
   Jesus, our Love, is crucified.

What was thy crime, my dearest Lord ?
By earth, by heaven, thou hast been tried,
And guilty found of too much love :
   Jesus, our Love, is crucified.

Oh break, oh break, hard heart of mine,
Thy weak self-love and guilty pride
His Pilate and his Judas were :
   Jesus, our Love, is crucified.

Come, take thy stand beneath the cross,
And let the blood from out that side
Fall gently on thee drop by drop :
   Jesus, our Love, is crucified.

O love of God, O sin of man,
In this dread act your strength is tried ;
And victory remains with love—
   For he, our Love, is crucified.

F. W. Faber.

In Passione Domini.

In the Lord's atoning grief
Be our rest and sweet relief;
Store we deep in heart's recess
All the shame and bitterness.
    Thorns and cross and nails and lance,
Wounds our treasure that enhance,
Vinegar and gall and reed,
And the pang his soul that freed:
    May these all our spirits sate,
And with love inebriate;
In our souls plant virtue's root,
And mature its glorious fruit.
    Crucified, we thee adore,
Thee with all our hearts implore;
Us with saintly bands unite
In the realms of heavenly light.
    Christ, by coward hands betrayed,
Christ, for us a captive made,
Christ, upon the bitter tree
Slain for man, be praise to thee.
F. Oakeley.

Gethsemani.

The olive-garden of Gethsemani
  To Jesus, on the way of death, was dear;
  The might and hour of evil drawing near,
He knelt there, prayed there, in his agony.

Wrung from his veins by suffering without bound,
  Slow-trickling, drippeth a red rain of blood;
  In anguish, sweeping o'er him like a flood,
He lies in fear with face upon the ground.

The paschal moon looks down upon his pain—
  This sweat of blood through bitterness of grief;
  Afflicted, yet among ten thousand chief,
The paschal victim goeth to be slain.

No cost he counteth, in desire that we
    From evil saved may dwell with him in rest
    Foretold, the 'many mansions' of his blest
Abode, far-off, God-built, 'above and free.'

Thick storm-clouds gather on his way of gloom ;
    While he is led to darkness, not to light ;
    In weakness showeth he his hidden might,
Destroying hell and all the ancient doom.

Without one rest, or promise of repose
    He passeth onward from the garden-shade ;
    Upon the Man of Sorrows there is laid
Sin's weight, a dim oppressiveness of woes.

Soon thorns, sin-gathered, pierce his kingly head ;
    Soon scourges plough long furrows on his back
    The way of sorrow shows a crimson track,
Where drops of blood around his feet are shed.

Why cometh the Desired in guise like this ?
    Why is his raiment red ? In blood, why dyed ?
    His heart's distress far reaches, deep and wide,
To creatures' thought a fathomless abyss.

Thus falls on him our chastisement of peace ;
    He bears the heat and burden of the day ;
    With blood he washes all our sins away,
To break our chains and give us swift release.

In death he hangeth on a ruddy tree,
    A holocaust of mercy, God and Man ;
    The rain there endeth which for him began
Beneath the olives of Gethsemani.
                                      H. A. Rawes.

Lent by Mary's side.

The purple shroud is stretched upon our altar,
    And now we must not falter,
But leave for silence, penitence and prayer
    The world's cold pomp and glare,

Lent and the Precious Blood.

And follow step by step the Crucified,
    Close by dear Mary's side.

Oh, what deep calmness and what sweet repose
    This blessed season throws
O'er souls which long from earth's poor joys to turn,
    To watch and weep and mourn—
'Tis like soft moonlight with its cooling beam,
    After the sun's hot gleam.

O God, thou callest us in calm retreat
    To hide us at thy feet;
We linger not thy summons to obey:
    Too precious is the day,
Too dear the time to holy penance given,
    To train our souls for heaven.

Mother of him who bore without relief
    His heavy load of grief;
Mother most sorrowful, guide us, we pray,
    Along the thorny way
Where Christ hath walked, when his worn feet have bled,
    Where we should love to tread.

Oh, what a bliss with him, 'mid earthly strife,
    To lead the hidden life,
Outwardly struggling with a world of sin,
    But hearts all pure within;
For this, O Mother mild, thine aid we ask,
    This be our Lenten task.

Painful, perchance, may be each sacrifice,
    But oh, beyond all price
Is the bright joy, when all to God is given;
    'Tis the foretaste of heaven:
Let us work on—hereafter we shall rest
    For ever on his breast.

Lady C. Petre.

Ash-Wednesday Evening.

Behold and bless the solemn day
That calls to mourn the soul's decay;
And ere the fierce destruction sweep,
Before the throne of grace to weep.

Oh, let us strive, before too late,
To shun the sinner's awful fate;
To flee the flames that ever burn,
The prison dark whence no return.

Vain on the past to close the eyes,
For sin unpardoned never dies;
And painfully must be replaced
God's image in the soul defaced.

Oh, ponder well the eternal shame—
Eternal, evermore the same;
Nor deadly wounds of sin conceal
From those empowered on earth to heal.

So pardon will unloose the spell
That binds the guilty soul to hell;
Our Lord will shed his healing balm,
The soul regains a holy calm.

Such blessing, Lord, our prayers implore,
This evening and for evermore;
Hear us, O Father; hear, O Son;
And Holy Spirit—Three in One.
R. Campbell.

To the holy Spear and Nails.

What tongue shall give thee thanks, in fitting strains repeat
Thy praise, thrice blessed spear, in heaven or on earth?
Which opening Christ's blest side, that saving wound didst form,
    From whence the Church gained life and birth.

Lent and the Precious Blood.

When first the world was made, from Adam sunk in
    sleep,
By God's almighty hand was Eve his helpmate
    formed ;
From that co-mingled stream which from his side did
    flow,
    His Church the Second Adam formed.

Be equal praise to you, O high and blessed nails,
Which nailed our gentle Lord unto the bitter tree ;
For his all-saving blood our doom of death effaced,
    And routing hell, made all men free.

Oh, may thy saints, sweet Lord, with deepest joy e'er
    praise
That ever-burning love, which doth thy wounds retain
In that eternal clime, where with the Father, thou
    And Holy Ghost, dost ever reign.
                                     T. J. Potter.

Christum ducem, qui per crucem.

To Christ, whose cross repaired our loss,
    Be praise and glory given ;
Be he the song of our glad throng,
    Echoing the lauds of heaven.

May the strong throe of thy last woe
    Thy sacred blood outpoured,
Our hearts subdue thy grace to sue,
    Jesu, Redeemer, Lord.

By his all-glorious wounds victorious,
    Spitting, stripes and twisted cord,
Gifts ever new to us accrue,
    Christ's measureless reward.

Our hearts forlorn with grace to mourn,
    May thy blest wounds supply ;
May that rich stream our souls redeem,
    Kind framer of the sky.

Our hearts uplift with the pure gift
    Thy passion, Lord, secures ;
In pity deign for us to gain
    The bliss that aye endures.

Who by the power of that dark hour
    The bonds of sin didst burst in twain—
Lord, guide us sure to peace secure,
    Blest leader of the virgin-train.

The nauseous draught by thee was quaffed,
    Amid the stripes most bitterly,
All to efface sin's deadly trace,
    Eternal Lord, thou king most high.

To thine elect, who have respect
    To all thy pains for sinners borne,
Grant virtue's health and saving wealth,
    Redeemer of a world forlorn.

With streams of blood, a costly flood,
    The altar of thy cross is gory ;
Jesu divine, thou king benign,
    Partaker of the eternal glory.

The accuser-foe thou didst lay low,
    Blood of the Lord most innocent :
Oh, let us haste, to the glad feast
    Of Christ, the Lamb all provident.
                        F. Oakeley.

Hymns from the Daily Procession of the Franciscan Friars at Jerusalem.

(*At the Altar of Flagellation.*)

Come, let us tell of him whose woes
    Have made us sons of God ;
Come, let us tread with contrite hearts
    The paths that Jesus trod.

His paths who took away the sin
  Once wrought by Adam's hand,
And bleeding at this pillar dread,
  For us was pleased to stand.

Here, O my Jesus, thou wast pleased
  In all thy flesh to bear
The stripes that I have merited,
  And feel their sharpness there—

'Till joints and marrow, bones and flesh,
  In thee seemed like to part,
And 'mid thy bowels e'en as wax
  Melted the sacred heart.

Thus didst thou give thyself to them
  Who laid my stripes on thee,
The Father's wrath to quench for us,
  And open heaven for me.
            Order of Compline, 1880.

(*At the Chapel of Imprisonment.*)
Thou, O my Jesus, thou wast pleased
  To bear the cross for me,
To shed thine own most precious blood
  From sin to set me free.

Thou Lord of heaven and of earth,
  Amid thy creatures found,
Art with the wicked reckoned here,
  And with transgressors bound.

Thou, for the tree of knowledge robbed,
  Hast raised life's quickening tree ;
By death thou hast our death destroyed,
  And bound, the bound set free.

Thou unto whom the gates of brass
  In death's dark realm shall yield,

Amidst the living, in the gloom
  Of prisons art concealed.

Thou, light of men, the pledge of peace
  Made betwixt earth and heaven,
Amid the creatures of thine hands
  Here unto bonds art given.

But thou, like Samson blind and bound,
  Hast crushed thy foes at length ;
Thine own life thou hast sacrificed,
  And shown in death thy strength.

Thy bonds have made thy martyrs feel
  That bonds for thee are sweet,
Bright is the road to death that shines
  Marked by thy blessed feet.

Jesus, the very thought of thee
  With sweetness fills the breast—
His breast who is thy bonds-man here,
  Who waits in heaven thy rest.

Order of Compline, 1880.

(At the Chapel of Coronation.)

Go forth, ye children of our God,
  Go forth to greet your king,
Clad in his woeful robe of state,
  His people's offering.

Go forth, ye children of his love,
  The Man of Sorrows see,
The royal Son of David come
  Outcast of men to be.

Behold Isaiah's word fulfilled,
  See how he turneth there
His face to them that smite, his cheek
  To them that pluck the hair.

Lent and the Precious Blood. 57

On him whose mouth shall speak thy doom,
  My soul, thine eyes fix thou ;
From sole of foot to crown of head
  There is no soundness now.

The Lord in glory in the bush
  Moses beheld of old ;
Jesus, beneath his crown of thorns,
  With spittle fouled behold.

The mystic Isaac in the crown
  That here his brow adorns,
Stands like the ram Moriah saw
  Entangled in the thorns.

My God, let not the shameful robe
  That here in scorn wrapped thee,
Nor thorns, nor blows, nor rod have been
  Suffered in vain for me.
        Order of Compline, 1880.

Personal Agencies in the Passion of Jesus.

My Jesus, say, what wretch has dared
  Thy sacred hands to bind ?
And who has dared to buffet so
  Thy face so meek and kind ?
    'Tis I have thus ungrateful been,
      Yet, Jesus, pity take ;
    Oh, spare and pardon me, my Lord,
      For thy sweet mercy's sake.

My Jesus, who with spittle vile
  Profaned thy sacred brow ?
And whose unpitying scourge has made
  Thy precious blood to flow ?
    'Tis I have thus ungrateful been, etc.

My Jesus, whose the hands that wove
  That cruel thorny crown ?

Who made that hard and heavy cross
  Which weighs thy shoulders down?
    'Tis I have thus ungrateful been, etc.

My Jesus, who has mocked thy thirst
  With vinegar and gall?
Who held the nails that pierced thy hands,
  And made the hammer fall?
    'Tis I have thus ungrateful been, etc.

My Jesus, say who dared to nail
  Those tender feet of thine?
And whose the arm that raised the lance
  To pierce that heart divine?
    'Tis I have thus ungrateful been, etc.

And Mary, who has murdered thus
  Thy loved and only One?
Canst thou forgive the blood-stained hand
  That robbed thee of thy Son?
    'Tis I have thus ungrateful been,
      To Jesus and to thee;
    Forgive me for thy Jesus' sake,
      And pray to him for me.

From St. Alphonsus.

Road to Calvary.

Steep is the hill and weary is the road,
    Beneath that crushing load;
And he who treads it with a grace so meek,
    Is bruised and faint and weak;
His mighty love alone can aid him there
    That heavy cross to bear.

Oh, if we would in spirit, day by day,
    Follow this blood-stained way,
With loving sorrow, storing as a prize
    The contrite thoughts which rise,

For us the road to Calvary would be
   The road to sanctity.

Our crosses then would never more appal—
   They are so slight and small ;
And we might understand the saints' sweet cry,
   'To suffer or to die ; '
And learn to watch affliction's waves increase
   With all enduring peace.

Alas, the world's bright fields have ever been
   So gay and fair a scene,
That our good angels have hard work to do
   To keep us brave and true ;
To turn our wandering feet with constant care
   To the calm paths of prayer.

And yet, those shady paths how sweet they are ;
   Their perfume from afar
Would draw us on, if we were not engrossed
   By earth's alluring host—
Those fading pleasures, ever false and vain
   And marked with many a stain.

Let us henceforth with our own hearts be stern,
   That they may quickly learn
The rules of daily self-denying strife,
   While dangers are so rife :
Oh, let us urge them on with mighty sway,
   Nor linger on the way.
                              Lady C. Petre.

Sacred Wounds of Christ.

All hail, ye wounds of Christ,
   Of boundless love the token,
From which the crimson blood
   Still flows in stream unbroken.

In sheen ye pass the stars;
  The rose, the balm in savour;
In price, the Indian gem;
  The honeycomb in flavour.

In you our souls possess
  A refuge free from danger,
Where safe we may defy
  The cruel foeman's anger.

In Pilate's hall what blows
  My Jesus' flesh are crushing;
What countless drops of gore
  From his torn limbs are gushing.

His beauteous brow, alas,
  A thorny crown has riven;
While blunted nails amain
  Through hands and feet are driven.

And when, with his full will,
  His life of love is ended,
They pierce his heart, and lo,
  Bursts forth a streamlet blended.

My ransom-cup to fill,
  His heart my Jesus straineth;
Nor for himself one drop
  Of life-blood he retaineth.

Then come, whoe'er by sin
  Your chrisome-robe have stainèd;
By laving in this bath
  Its whiteness is regainèd.

Then praise to him, who still
  Throned by his Sire abideth,
Who saved us by his blood,
  And by his Spirit guideth.
                              Σ.

The Reproaches.

What, O my people, have I done to thee?
What have I done? how wronged thee? answer me:
From Egypt's land I led and rescued thee,
And thou hast wrought a bitter cross for me.

Holy God, holy and strong, holy and immortal,
       Have mercy on us.

Full forty years along the desert sand
I led thee with a father's gentle hand;
And gave thee for thy meat the angels' food,
And brought thee to a fertile land and good:
Was it for this, which I have done for thee,
That thou preparedst this bitter cross for me?
  Holy God, holy and strong, etc.

What could I do, and have not done for mine?
I planted thee a fair and fruitful vine,
And thou hast served me bitterly enough,
And with thine acrid juices, crude and rough,
My parched and fevered lips hast rudely plied,
And plunged a javelin in thy Saviour's side.
  Holy God, holy and strong, etc.

Egypt and her firstborn I scourged for thee;
And thou hast scourged and basely dealt with me.
  What, O my people, have I done to thee?

I led thee forth from Egypt, and for thee
Drowned Pharaoh and his host in the Red Sea;
And thou, for paltry gain, hast bartered me.
  What, O my people, have I done to thee?

For thee I cleft apart the billowy tide;
And thou hast plunged a javelin in my side.
  What, O my people, have I done to thee?

In sheen ye pass the stars ;
  The rose, the balm in savour ;
In price, the Indian gem ;
  The honeycomb in flavour.

In you our souls possess
  A refuge free from danger,
Where safe we may defy
  The cruel foeman's anger.

In Pilate's hall what blows
  My Jesus' flesh are crushing ;
What countless drops of gore
  From his torn limbs are gushing.

His beauteous brow, alas,
  A thorny crown has riven ;
While blunted nails amain
  Through hands and feet are driven.

And when, with his full will,
  His life of love is ended,
They pierce his heart, and lo,
  Bursts forth a streamlet blended.

My ransom-cup to fill,
  His heart my Jesus straineth ;
Nor for himself one drop
  Of life-blood he retaineth.

Then come, whoe'er by sin
  Your chrisome-robe have stainèd ;
By laving in this bath
  Its whiteness is regainèd.

Then praise to him, who still
  Throned by his Sire abideth,
Who saved us by his blood,
  And by his Spirit guideth.
                                Σ.

The Reproaches.

What, O my people, have I done to thee?
What have I done? how wronged thee? answer me:
From Egypt's land I led and rescued thee,
And thou hast wrought a bitter cross for me.

Holy God, holy and strong, holy and immortal,
                    Have mercy on us.

Full forty years along the desert sand
I led thee with a father's gentle hand;
And gave thee for thy meat the angels' food,
And brought thee to a fertile land and good:
Was it for this, which I have done for thee,
That thou preparedst this bitter cross for me?
      Holy God, holy and strong, etc.

What could I do, and have not done for mine?
I planted thee a fair and fruitful vine,
And thou hast served me bitterly enough,
And with thine acrid juices, crude and rough,
My parched and fevered lips hast rudely plied,
And plunged a javelin in thy Saviour's side.
      Holy God, holy and strong, etc.

Egypt and her firstborn I scourged for thee;
And thou hast scourged and basely dealt with me.
      What, O my people, have I done to thee?

I led thee forth from Egypt, and for thee
Drowned Pharaoh and his host in the Red Sea;
And thou, for paltry gain, hast bartered me.
      What, O my people, have I done to thee?

For thee I cleft apart the billowy tide;
And thou hast plunged a javelin in my side.
      What, O my people, have I done to thee?

The livelong night that torch burnt on,
  Yet all was dark within.

A Stranger in the morning light,
  Still at the door he stood;
His locks are drenched with dews of night,
  His raiment stained with blood.
                                H. N. Oxenham.

The Washing of the Altar.

Pour forth the wine-floods rich and dark,
  Over the altar-stone:
The time is short; the yew-trees, hark,
  How mournfully they moan:
    It is the sacred blood of Christ,
      By angels poured o'er earth;
    While sable turns to amethyst,
      And death to the new birth.

O'er all the altar pour the wine,
  With joyful strength amain;
The streams alone from God's great vine
  Can clear that altar's stain:
    It is the Saviour's wondrous blood:
      The insanguined planet now
    Ascends from this baptismal flood,
      As bright as Christ's own brow.

The flood that cleanses on and in,
  Roll, sacred brethren, roll;
But thou whose sufferings purged our sin,
  Oh, wash each sinful soul:
    It is the atoning blood of him
      By whom all worlds are shriven;
    Who lights with love our midnight dim,
      And changes earth to heaven.
                                A. de Vere.

God-forsaken.

Thousands have felt thy healing power,
  Thousands from thee their lives have taken,
And can it be that in thine hour
  Of utmost need thou art forsaken?

Forsaken; oh, what grief and love
  That word expresses on thy tongue:
Thou, in thy Godhead bright above
  And thus on earth by sorrow wrung.

Infinite God and finite Man,
  So high thy state, thy state so low,
No human thought can sound or span
  The boundless deeps of such a woe.

Yet, at that cry of sore distress,
  Our hearts to some dim knowledge waken;
And 'mid the gloom we faintly guess
  What God has felt when God-forsaken.

Cecilia M. Caddell.

Last Words from the Cross.

(The Fifth Word.)

Hard is the painful wood, his bed of death;
  And with his failing breath
He speaks again: and as he looks around,
  The crowd upon the ground
Are ready with their hate to do their worst;
  And then he says, 'I thirst.'

His tongue is parched—his fevered lips are burnt;
  And yet, we have not learnt
That thirst to quench—that fever to allay;
  We will not yet obey,

Nor give him that he asks and longs to gain—
   Oh, must he thirst in vain?

Shall we continue thus his soul to steep
   In woes that make him weep?
Shall we refuse the hearts he thirsts to win,
   And yield them yet to sin?
The day will come, our memories will be curst
   With those sad words, 'I thirst.'

Sweet Jesus, thou hast thirsted for each soul
   That pants in sin's control;
Oh, break our fetters, that we may be free
   To give ourselves to thee;
The world has held us; but its bonds we break,
   And spurn it for thy sake.
                              Lady C. Petre.

(*The Last Word.*)

Bow down, my soul, for he hath bowed his head;
Adore and weep and pray—thy Lord is dead:
His soul into his Father's hands commended;
His tears, his woes—yea, everything is ended.

Oh, for the gift of tears, that I might weep;
Oh, for the gift of prayer, that I might keep
Beneath the cross, in spirit, night and day,
And never from its shade be torn away.

The earth is darkened—rent the temple's veil;
Now do the hearts of men with terror fail;
Rend thou my heart, O God, in this dread hour;
Break it with sweet contrition's holy power.

Into thy hands my spirit I commend,
That thou mayst keep it safe unto the end;
Keep it, lest earth and sin should tear away
The grace my Saviour won for me this day.
                              Lady C. Petre.

The Precious Blood.

Hail, Jesus, hail, who for my sake
Sweet blood from Mary's veins didst take,
   And shed it all for me ;
Oh, blessed be my Saviour's blood,
My life, my light, my only good,
   To all eternity.

To endless ages let us praise
The precious blood, whose price could raise
   The world from wrath and sin ;
Whose streams our inward thirst appease,
And heal the sinner's worst disease,
   If he but bathe therein.

O sweetest blood, that can implore
Pardon of God, and heaven restore,
   The heaven which sin had lost :
While Abel's blood for vengeance pleads,
What Jesus shed still intercedes
   For those who wrong him most.

Oh, to be sprinkled from the wells
Of Christ's own sacred blood, excels
   Earth's best and highest bliss :
The ministers of wrath divine
Hurt not the happy hearts that shine
   With those red drops of his.

Ah, there is joy amid the saints,
And hell's despairing courage faints
   When this sweet song we raise :
Oh, louder then, and louder still,
Earth with one mighty chorus fill,
   The precious blood to praise.
F. W. Faber.

Ave, Jesu, qui mactaris.

Hail, Jesus, hail; who while they slay
Dost freely for thy murderers pray
   Pardon for that they owe :
Oh, make us easy to forgive,
Not seeking vengeance while we live,
   In thought, or word, or blow.

Hail, Jesus, hail; who to the thief
Repenting him, of goods the chief
   Dost promise to restore :
Oh, with contrition such as his,
Both now and when our death-hour is,
   Endow us we implore.

Hail, Jesus, hail; who 'neath the rood
The while thy Mother weeping stood
   Commendest her to John :
With a like care for us provide,
That we may steadfastly abide
   When dangers hurry on.

Hail, Jesus, hail; by that sad way
Thou dost unto thy Father say,
   'Thou hast forsaken me ;'
Forsake me not, but bid me stand,
Secure by thy supporting hand
   In mine extremity.

Hail, Jesus, hail; who criest, 'I thirst,'
And with a sponge in gall immersed
   Wast drenched, yet feedest all ;
Oh, make us thirst for joys above,
Nor waste below a foolish love
   On joys that fade and fall.

Hail, Jesus, hail; who dost fulfil
Wholly, for us, thy Father's will ;
   For us thy merits stand ;

Lent and the Precious Blood. 69

'"Tis finished;' may what we intend
Beginning well still better end,
　The fruit of thy command.

Hail, Jesus, hail; ere death could close
Thy loving speech and dying throes,
　Delivering up thy soul
Unto thy Father; grant that we
Live cleansed and justified in thee,
　And dying, win the goal.
　　　　　　　　　　H. I. D. Ryder.

To the Instruments of the Passion of Jesus.

O ruthless scourges, with what pain you tear
My Saviour's flesh, so innocent and fair—
Oh, cease to rend that flesh divine;
　My loving Lord torment no more;
Wound, rather wound this heart of mine,
　The guilty cause of all he bore.

Ye cruel thorns, in mocking wreath entwined
My Saviour's brow in agony to bind—
Oh, cease to rend that flesh divine;
　My loving Lord torment no more;
Wound rather, wound this heart of mine,
　The guilty cause of all he bore.

Unpitying nails, whose points with anguish fierce
The hands and feet of my Redeemer pierce—
Oh, cease to rend that flesh divine;
　My loving Lord torment no more;
Wound rather, wound this heart of mine,
　The guilty cause of all he bore.

Unfeeling lance, that dar'st to open wide
The sacred temple of my Saviour's side—
Oh, cease to wound that flesh divine;
　My loving Lord insult no more;

Pierce rather, pierce this heart of mine,
The guilty cause of all he bore.
From St. Alphonsus.

Sign of the Cross.

O Christians, ever bear in mind
The cross upon the forehead signed ;
And oft as ye the sign re-trace,
Oh, let your hearts the cross embrace.
   Then though temptations hard assail,
Against them all shall ye prevail ;
The soul that on the cross relies,
Unmoved, the powers of hell defies.
   Away, ye terrors of the night ;
Away, ye thoughts of fond delight ;
Flee, serpent, 'tis the fatal sign
To thee, and thy accursed line.
   O Christ, when all is dark around
Be thou within our bosoms found ;
Though slumbers deep the eyelids seal,
Thy presence to the soul reveal.
   All praise to God the Father sing ;
All praise to Christ, our heavenly king ;
All praise, O Holy Ghost, to thee,
For ever and for ever be.
R. Campbell.

Self-sacrifice.

When Christ let fall that sanguine shower
   Amid the garden-dew,
Oh say, what amaranthine flower
   In that red rain upgrew ?
If yet below the blossom grow,
   Then earth is holy yet ;
But if it bloom forgotten, woe
   To those who dare forget.

No flower so healing and so sweet
  Expands beneath the skies ;
Unknown in Eden—there unmeet :
  Its name? Self-sacrifice.
The very name we scarce can frame,
  And yet that flower's dark root
The monsters of the wild might tame,
  And heaven is in its fruit.

Alas, what murmur spreads around?
  'The news thereof hath been ;
But now no more the man is found
  Whose eye that flower hath seen ':
Then nobles all, leave court and hall,
  And search the wide world o'er ;
For whoso finds this Sangreal
  Stands crowned for evermore.
A. de Vere.

Hymn to Christ.

I.

Laud we Jesus, who did ease us
  From foes on the accursèd tree,
Joyous raising voice of praising,
  Exult the heavens with praises free.

May thy dying sorrows trying,
  And spilling of thy precious blood,
Our desiring to inquiring
  For thee, our sole redemption-goad.

By his blessèd wounds impressèd,
  The spittle, scourges, agony,
Be conceded, e'en as needed,
  Christ's endless gifts of charity.

Swell our grieving, on perceiving
  The blood that pours from out thy scars,

Wherein mergèd, be we purgèd,
  O mild Creator of the stars.
Saviour precious, oh, refresh us
  With those good gifts thy passion bought,
In whose power thou wouldst shower
  Blessed joys with heavenly glories fraught.

II.

Who untiedst, when thou diedst
  The bonds of sin and Satan's thrall,
Gently tend us, quiet send us,
  O Jesus, Virgin's coronal.
Scourges tearing cruel bearing,
  Thou drank'st thy bitter cup of gall,
For transgression our commission,
  Thou everlasting king of all.
While we ponder, full of wonder,
  The torments of thy death our theme,
Virtue send us, safety lend us,
  O Christ, who all men didst redeem.
Down the cross' altar courses
  Thy blood in agonising streams,
Christ divinest, king benignest,
  Bright partner of thy Father's beams.
Christ's blood purest, that procurest
  Our fiendish persecutor's fall,
Oh, concede us thirst, and lead us
  Unto the Lamb's high festival.
                    A. D. Wackerbarth.

The Five Wounds.

Ye priestly hands, which on the cruel cross
  Were stretched so wide to welcome all our race,
Lift up your wounds before your Father's eyes,
  That I one day may feel your dear embrace:

Ah, sinless Saviour, wounded all for me
  With thorns and lashes of my grievous sin,
  Wound thou my heart with wound of deep remorse,
    But close sin's wounds and make me whole within.

Ye weary feet, way-worn and pierced for me,
  Which sorrowing Mary bathed with tearful grief,
Oh, let me lie, like her, beneath your wounds,
  And find for sin's disease a sure relief :
    Ah, sinless Saviour, etc.

And thou, thou wounded heart of pity deep,
  Through which my way lies to thy Father's throne,
Teach me the love which rent that crimson path,
  Gave us thy life, but made our pains thine own :
    Ah, sinless Saviour, etc.

Windows of heaven, which once on sin-struck earth
  Poured forth the deluge of your bleeding tide,
Pour yet on me the grace for guilt to mourn,
  And bring me wounded to that wounded side :
    Ah, sinless Saviour, wounded all for me
      With thorns and lashes of my grievous sin,
      Wound thou my heart with wound of deep remorse,
        But close sin's wounds and make me whole within.

G. F. L. Bampfield.

Agony in the Garden.

Jesus, O my Lord and God,
  What, then, is befalling,
That thou liest on the sod
  Unto heaven calling—
That thy blood of crimson dye
O'er thy face is springing,

And an angel standeth by,
   Solace to thee bringing?

Ah, thou seest the mighty pain,
   Pain itself outriding,
Soul and body, nerve and vein,
   Tearing and dividing:
Seest the sins of all mankind—
   Sins that I was sharing—
Laid on thee, O Lord most kind,
   With their weight unsparing.

Ah, thy tender heart perforce
   Shuddered, quaked and trembled,
Feeling even then the course
   Of thy pangs assembled;
All the burden of offence
   On thy spirit pressing—
Who can tell what anguish hence
   Every sense possessing?

Ah, my Saviour, could I yet
   Mitigate that sorrow,
Wipe away the sanguine sweat,
   And thy burden borrow?
Could I, Lamb of God, by thee
   Stand when thou art weeping—
Stem in part the raging sea
   O'er the bridegroom sweeping?

Dearest Lord, thou for my sake
   Life and death fulfillest;
That thy very heart should break
   For my need thou willest;
In unheard-of want and ill
   Without murmur pinest—
Thy will to the Father's will
   Perfectly resignest.

Lent and the Precious Blood.

O my Lord and God, then save
  This my soul distressèd,
When it trembles by the grave
  And the foe oppressèd ;
When thou biddest me depart
  From this vale of sighing,
Let thine agony impart
  Comfort to my dying.
             J. C. Earle.

Invitation to the Sinner.

Oh, come to the merciful Saviour that calls you,
  Oh, come to the Lord who forgives and forgets ;
Though dark be the fortune on earth that befals you,
  There's a bright home above, where the sun never sets.

Oh come, then, to Jesus whose arms are extended
  To fold his dear children in closest embrace :
Oh come, for your exile will shortly be ended,
  And Jesus will show you his beautiful face.

Then come to the Saviour, whose mercy grows brighter
  The longer you look at the depth of his love ;
And fear not, 'tis Jesus, and life's cares grow lighter
  As you think of the home and the glory above.

Have you sinned as none else in the world have before you ?
  Are you blacker than all other creatures in guilt?
Oh fear not, oh fear not, the mother that bore you
  Loves you less than the Saviour whose blood you have spilt.

Oh come, then, to Jesus and say how you love him,
  And swear at his feet you will keep in his grace ;
For one tear that is shed by a sinner can move him,
  And your sins will drop off in his tender embrace.

Then come to his feet, and lay open your story
  Of suffering and sorrow, of guilt and of shame;
For the pardon of sin is the crown of his glory,
  And the joy of our Lord to be true to his name.

F. W. Faber.

Evening, Vespers and Compline Hymns.

EVENING HYMNS.

Even-song.

STARRY hosts are gleaming,
    Solemn night draws on,
Calm the moon's soft beaming,
    Toilsome day is done.
Vespers'-bells outringing
    Clear from tower and spire,
Voices sweetly singing
    In the lustrous choir.
Prayer and praises blending,
    Hearts in homage bowed,
Mary's song ascending
    With the incense cloud.
Rest and pardon needing,
    Prostrate 'neath the rood,
Sinful souls are pleading
    Wounds and cross and blood.
Hear our plaint, sweet Jesus,
    We are tired of sin;
From our bonds release us,
    Give us peace within.
Now we seek a city
    Where our feet may rest;
Bring us, in thy pity,
    To those mansions blest.

Light, 'mid darkness, send us
    Till our tramp be o'er ;
Angel-guards attend us
    To the palace-door.
Then a welcome meet us—
    Words of grace and love ;
Joyful voices greet us
    In the home above.
E. Louisa Lee.

Hymn from the Paris Breviary.

In the light all light excelling,
    Light that darkens mortal eye,
Thou, Supreme, hast fixed thy dwelling,
    Everlasting Trinity.
Angels veil their radiant faces ;
    Saints are trembling in thy sight ;
We the while, in earth's dark places,
    Watch the slowly waning night,
Watch 'till night is turned to morning,
    Morning of the eternal day ;
Suns our earthly heaven adorning
    Fade like starlight from its ray.
Yet we gaze and see no token ;
    Weary is it waiting here
Till the bonds of flesh are broken,
    And the promised day appear.
Then upon the cloudless vision
    Shall the ransomed spirit gaze ;
Endless love in God's fruition,
    Endless music in his praise.
Grant that here thy gifts receiving,
    We may there thy glory see,
Gazing then, no more believing,
    Trinity in Unity.
H. N. Oxenham.

Evening, Vespers and Compline Hymns.

Respice stellam, voca Mariam.

Drear is the night-fall,
   Lonely we roam,
Wandering exiles,
   Far from our home;
Borne on the billows
   Of life's stormy sea,
Bright Star of Heaven,
   Our trust is in thee:
When night falls drearily, when life flows wearily,
   Respice stellam, voca Mariam.

Winds of affliction
   Raise their rude blast,
Ruffling the ocean
   Whereon we're cast;
Waves of temptation
   Mountain-like roll,
'Neath their dark billows
   Sinking the soul:
Fear not, but gaze afar on the soft shining star;
   Respice stellam, voca Mariam.

When shall lone spirits
   Sorrow no more?
When shall our aching eyes
   Gaze on the shore?
Oh, for the twilight
   To break through the gloom;
Oh, for the rest
   Of our only true home:
Stay, mourner, stay thy fears; joy shall dry up thy tears;
   Respice stellam, voca Mariam.

Gentle and beautiful,
   Beaming above,
Shines out all-brightly
   The fair star of love;

> Rest of the weary,
>   Hope 'mid the night
> Guiding the lonely
>   In its soft light :
> Yes, 'mid the darkest night that star still shineth bright;
> Respice stellam, voca Mariam.
>
> *F. Stanfield.*

Angels' Vigils.

> In that cold cave with spices sweet,
>   When Christ, our Lord, lay dead,
> An angel sat beside his feet,
>   An angel by his head.
>
> All night their eyes to heaven they raised,
>   Their wings around him spread;
> All day on those dark eye-lids gazed,
>   But not a word they said.
>
> And when the morn sabbatical
>   Its paschal light had spread
> A chrysome robe o'er earth's dark ball,
>   To heaven those angels sped.
>
> Keep, holy Angels, keep, oh, keep
>   Such vigil by our bed;
> Calm visions from the urns of sleep,
>   O'er us calm visions shed.
>
> But when we wake to morning life
>   And night's pure calm is fled,
> Stay near us in our daily strife,
>   Or we are worse than dead.
>
> *A. de Vere.*

Evening Hymn at the Oratory.

> Sweet Saviour, bless us ere we go;
>   Thy word into our minds instil;
> And make our lukewarm hearts to glow
>   With lowly love and fervent will.

Evening, Vespers and Compline Hymns.

Through life's long day and death's dark night,
    O gentle Jesus, be our light.
The day is done ; its hours have run ;
    And thou hast taken count of all—
The scanty triumphs grace hath won,
    The broken vow, the frequent fall.
Through life's long day and death's dark night,
    O gentle Jesus, be our light.
Grant us, dear Lord, from evil ways
    True absolution and release ;
And bless us more than in past days
    With purity and inward peace.
Through life's long day and death's dark night,
    O gentle Jesus, be our light.
Sweet Saviour, bless us ; night is come,
    Mary and Philip near us be ;
Good angels watch about our home ;
    And we are one day nearer thee.
Through life's long day and death's dark night,
    O gentle Jesus, be our light.

F. W. Faber.

Return of the Dove.

Finding no place of rest
Above the swelling tide,
The dove resought her nest
    At even-tide :
Cleaving the welkin dark
With eager fluttering wing,
Steadfast to gain the ark
    Ere sun-setting.

* * *

From fruitless, earthly quest
And hopes, by love betrayed,
Seeking like her the rest
    From which I've strayed,

Father, I homeward fly,
Longing thy face to see,
And lose, without a sigh,
Myself in thee.
S.

Evening Hymn to Jesus and Mary.

Hear thy children, gentle Jesus,
   While we breathe our evening prayer,
Save us from all harm and danger,
   Take us 'neath thy sheltering care.

Save us from the wiles of Satan,
   'Mid the lone and sleepful night;
Sweetly may bright guardian angels
   Keep us 'neath their watchful sight.

Gentle Jesus, look in pity
   From thy great white throne above;
All the night thy heart is wakeful
   In thy sacrament of love.

Shades of even fast are falling,
   Day is fading into gloom—
When the shades of death fall round us,
   Lead thine exiled children home.

* * *

Hear thy children, gentlest Mother,
   Prayerful hearts to thee arise;
Hear us while our evening Ave
   Soars beyond the starry skies.

Darkling shadows fall around us,
   Restful stars their watches keep;
Hush the heart oppressed by sorrow,
   Dry the tears of those that weep.

Hear, sweet Mother, hear the weary,
   Borne upon life's troubled sea;

Gentle guiding Star of Ocean,
  Lead thy children home to thee.
Still watch o'er us, dearest Mother,
  From thy beauteous throne above ;
Guard us from all harm and danger,
  'Neath the sheltering wings of love.
F. Stanfield.

Night Hymn from the Breviary.

O Christ, thou brightness of the day
That chaseth night's dull shades away,
Thou splendour of thy Father's light
That show'st his glories to our sight :
  We meekly pray thee, holy Lord,
    Defend us through the nightly hours ;
  Thou canst a holy rest accord,
    Grant that such holy rest be ours.

Drive far the heavy sleep of sin
Lest the untiring foe steal in ;
And with his foul and deadly guile
The weak consenting flesh defile :
  Grant while our eyes are closed in sleep
    Our hearts may ever watch to thee,
  And let thine arm securely keep
    Each one of thy dear family.

Our sole defence, watch o'er us still
To guard from all the powers of ill ;
Rule thou o'er us, O King of heaven,
For whom thy blood was freely given :
  Be mindful of us, Lord, while we
    This dull and fleshly burden bear,
  And let our souls still find in thee,
    A sweet defence for ever near.

Mother of love and mercy mild,
Mother of graces undefiled,

Drive back the foe, and to thy Son
Conduct our souls when life is done:
  Glory to thee, our Saviour sweet,
    Born of a spotless Mother-maid;
  To Father and to Paraclete
    Like glory be for ever paid.
J. D. Aylward.

VESPERS HYMNS.
Lucis Creator optime.
I.
Maker, by whose unuttered Word
In depths of heaven the light was stored,
What time the first-created ray
O'er worlds new-born shed primal day;

Who sweetly blending morn with eve
Bad'st them the name of day receive;
The gloom of night again is nigh,
Our sins forgive, our needs supply.

Let not our souls, with guilt opprest,
While nought of heaven inspires the breast,
From this world's life in sin be driven,
Outcasts from earth, unmeet for heaven.

Grant us to knock at heaven's high gate,
For life's eternal prize to wait,
'Till, purged from sin's corroding stain,
Our souls may there sweet entrance gain.

Father of heaven, co-equal Son,
Consoler-Spirit, Three in One,
Most merciful, accept our cry;
Save us, most awful Trinity.
H. N. Oxenham.

II.
Eternal source of light's clear stream,
  Creator of the sun,

Who didst command the day to beam,
  And straightway it was done.
The morning and the evening-tide,
  Alike thy gifts we hail ;
And thou with us wilt still abide
  When shades of night prevail.
Remove our past transgression's load,
  From future ill protect,
And in the straight and narrow road,
  Our wandering feet direct.
So knocking at the heavenly door,
  And striving for the prize,
We may above temptation soar,
  And earthly joy despise.
These blessings of thy love confer,
  Father, co-equal Son,
And Holy Ghost the Comforter,
  Eternal Three in One.
                              R. Campbell.

III.

Maker of light, most holy king,
Who dost returning daylight bring ;
Thou, who at first didst form the light ;
Ere rose the world in freshness dight ;

Who didst the morn and evening blend
And call it day—great God, attend
And grant our prayers, ere night enfold
Creation as it did of old.

Oh, let no slumbering mortal die
While sins upon his conscience lie,
While, heedless of eternal years,
Vain sin allures and folly cheers.

No ; let him seek the gates of heaven,
And may the living prize be given ;

Let him avoid all deed of blame,
And here blot out whate'er might shame.

Be not our prayers, kind Lord, in vain ;
And thou, the Son, who e'er dost reign
With the great Spirit pure adored,
Hear, grant our prayer—oh, grant it, Lord.

J. R. Beste.

IV.

O blest Creator of the light,
   Who brought'st the first grand gleam of day,
That with primordial glory bright
   Shed on earth's germ its kindling ray ;

Who on the span 'twixt morn and eve
   Didst first the name of day bestow,
Ere night like chaos round us weave,
   See, hear, the suppliant tears that flow.

No soul, weighed down with crimes, deny
   The saving recompense of life,
While hours unheeded swiftly fly
   End not, 'mid sins unwept, earth's strife.

At heaven's gate beat with sounding prayers
   Eternal palm and crown to win ;
Fly noxious thoughts and worldly cares
   While purging from thy soul her sin.

Almighty Father, hear our sighs ;
   And thou of glory as complete,
Who reignest in the eternal skies
   One God, with Spirit-Paraclete.

C. Kent.

Jam sol recedit igneus.

I.

The blazing sun is well-nigh gone,
But thou, O undivided One,

Art light unwaning ; blessed Trine,
Shed in our hearts thy ray benign.

Thee in our lauds at break of day,
Thee, Lord, at eve we meekly pray,
That thou vouchsafe us, deeply awed,
'Mid saints and angels, thee to laud.

At once to Father and to Son,
As from the first hath aye been done,
And, O Holy Ghost, to thee,
Through endless ages glory be.
A. L. Phillipps.

II.

Now lowly sinks the fiery sun ;
But thou, eternal light—thou one
United Trinity—impart
Thy light of love to every heart.

To thee at morn our voices swell ;
At even our hearts on thee shall dwell ;
And may our praise hereafter rise
And blend with heaven's own symphonies.

To God the Father and the Son
And Holy Spirit, Three in One,
May holiest praises still ascend
Through coming years, and never end.
J. R. Beste.

III.

While now the flaming sun declines,
Thou only sovereign-light that shines,
Perennial in the courts above,
Oh, fill our lowly hearts with love.

Thou whom we praised when morning rose,
We deprecate at evening's close ;
Vouchsafe, O Lord, our suppliant cries
May blend with hymnings in the skies.

Alike to Father and to Son
And Holy Spirit, Three in One,
Who hath been, art, will ever be,
All glory through eternity.
C. Kent.

COMPLINE HYMNS.
Te lucis ante terminum.

I.

Before the closing of the day,
Creator, thee we humbly pray,
That, for thy wonted mercy's sake,
Thou us into protection take.

May nothing in our minds excite
Vain dreams and phantoms of the night;
Our enemy repress, that so
Our bodies no uncleanness know.

To Jesus, from a Virgin sprung,
Be glory given and praises sung ;
The like to God the Father be,
And Holy Ghost eternally.
W. K. Blount, 1670.

II.

Thee, God, before the close of light,
   Thy clemency and care we pray,
That through the darkness of the night
   Our hellish foes be scared away.

Hence evil dreams that torture sleep,
   Hence fancies with voluptuous guile,
Our souls in deadening sloth to steep,
   Our forms with visioned sins defile.

My suppliant voice, O Father, hear ;
   O Son, my wants, my wishes see ;
O Paraclete, now grant the prayer
   My heart adoring lifts to thee.
C. Kent.

III.

Before the day's last moments fly,
Maker of all, to thee we cry ;
Beneath thy kind protection take,
And shield us for thy mercy's sake.

Let no ill dreams our souls alarm,
No powers of night approach to harm ;
Defend us from the tempter's art,
And keep us ever pure in heart.

Father of mercies, hear our cry ;
Oh hear, co-equal Son most high;
Whom with the Spirit we adore,
One only God for evermore.
R. Campbell.

IV.

Before the closing of the day,
Creator of the world, we pray
That for thy wonted clemency
Thou wouldst our guide and guardian be.

Let no ill dream disturb our rest,
No phantom-sprite our souls molest ;
Do thou our ghostly foe restrain,
And keep our bodies pure from stain.

O Father, hear thy children's prayer ;
O Son of God, thy people spare ;
Eternal Spirit, hear our cry ;
Hear us, most holy Trinity.
H. N. Oxenham.

Resurrection and Ascension.

Resurrection of Jesus.

BRINGING life and peace and gladness
    To his people from the grave,
Jesus rose at break of morning
    Mighty in his strength to save.

Having rested from his labour,
    Waking from his sleep by night,
Morn brought back the Well-belovèd,
    Crowned with many crowns of light.

When the world was wrapt in slumber
    On the threshold of the day,
Then the Warrior-king, from Bosra,
    Passed on his triumphal way.

Treading down the powers of darkness
    In his anger, he arose
With redemption for his faithful,
    With destruction for his foes.

On the heights his feet, once-piercèd,
    Shone with brightness like a flame;
While there hung around his footsteps
    Heavenly splendours as he came.

He, the Warrior strong from Edom,
    Smote the battlements of hell,
Rode in chariots of salvation,
    When the ancient mountains fell.

He, the king in all his beauty,
   Whom the prison could not hold,
Rose with glittering spear and helmet
   Gleaming in the sun like gold.

Oh, the rest and deep rejoicing
   After warfare, after toil ;
Rest for those who reap the harvest,
   Joy for those who take the spoil.

Risen Jesus, long the nations
   Waited with desire for thee ;
Now the dragon thou hast smitten,
   Now hast made thy people free.

Glorious one, in dyed apparel,
   Conqueror by a fearful strife,
Thou didst cover heaven with triumph,
   Bringing gladness, peace and life.
H. A. Rawes.

The risen King.

Hail, mighty King, in risen strength victorious,
   Hail, orient Light of heaven's eternal day,
Flushed with the glow of five bright wounds all-glorious,
   Shedding their beams o'er life's benighted way.

'Wake, happy souls, awake to songs of gladness,
   'Till the strain swell to heaven's sunlit shore ;
Lift up your hearts, nor know one thought of sadness,
   Jesus your love is happy evermore.

Oh, with what joy enraptured hearts are swelling,
   E'en though earth's sorrows fall so thick and fast,
Not of their own, but joys of Jesus telling :
   Throned 'mid the light of endless bliss at last.

Mother of life, in sympathy we greet thee ;
   Hushed is thy plaint, and banished all thy fears ;

Lo, Love comes forth arrayed in light to meet thee ;
  Jesus' sweet smiles dispel the Mother's tears.

Angels from heaven, in glittering throngs descending,
  Herald the joyous victor on his way ;
Myriads of saints, with ranks of angels blending,
  Change Limbo's night to dawn of blissful day.

Now happy souls from earth to heaven soaring,
  While Alleluias fill the joyous air ;
'Mid the glad choirs of angel-hosts adoring,
  Breathe forth in suppliant love their earnest prayer,

Listen, sweet Jesus, to our spirit's yearning,
  Hear from thy throne, beyond all earthly skies ;
Soon may the blissful day of thy returning
  Dawn on our homeward path to paradise.
F. Stanfield.

The Ascension.

Why is thy face so lit with smiles,
  Mother of Jesus, why ?
And wherefore is thy beaming look
  So fixed upon the sky ?

From out thine overflowing eyes
  Bright lights of gladness part,
As though some gushing fount of joy
  Had broken in thy heart.

Mother, how canst thou smile to-day ?
  How can thine eyes be bright,
When he thy life, thy love, thine all,
  Hath vanished from thy sight ?

His rising form on Olivet
  A summer's shadow cast ;
The branches of the hoary trees
  Drooped as the shadow passed.

And as he rose with all his train
  Of righteous souls around,
His blessing fell into thine heart,
  Like dew into the ground.

Yes, he hath left thee, Mother dear;
  His throne is far above;
How canst thou be so full of joy
  When thou hast lost thy love?

Why do not thy sweet hands detain
  His feet upon their way?
Oh, why doth not the Mother speak
  And bid her Son to stay?

Ah no, thy love is rightful love,
  From all self-seeking free;
The change that is such gain to him
  Can be no loss to thee.
                    F. W. Faber.

Attollite portas, Principes, vestras.
  Lift up, ye princes of the sky,
  Lift up your portals, lift them high;
  And you, ye everlasting gates,
      Back on your golden hinges fly:
  For lo, the King of glory waits,
And he shall enter in with shouts of victory.

    Who is this King of glory? Tell
  Ye who can sing his triumph-song so well.

    The Lord of strength and matchless might,
    The Lord all-conquering in the fight:
    Lift, lift your portals, lift them high,
    Ye princes of the conquered sky;
    And you, ye everlasting gates,
        Back on your golden hinges fly:
    For lo, the King of glory waits,

And he with shout and choral song
Shall enter in, leading his train along.

Who is this King of glory ? Tell
Ye who can sing his triumph song so well.

The Lord of mighty hosts, the Lord most high,
He is the glorious King, king of the conquered sky.
J. D. Aylward.

Triumph of the Conqueror.

Rise, glorious Conqueror, rise
Into thy native skies—
   Assume thy right :
And where in many a fold
The clouds are backward rolled,
Pass through those gates of gold
   And reign in light.

Victor o'er death and hell,
Cherubic legions swell
   The radiant train :
Praises all heaven inspire ;
Each angel sweeps his lyre,
And claps his plumes of fire—
   Thou Lamb once slain.

Enter, incarnate God ;
No feet but thine have trod
   The serpent down :
Blow the full trumpets, blow ;
Wider yon portals throw ;
Saviour, triumphant, go
   And take thy crown.

Lion of Judah, hail,
And let thy name prevail
   From age to age :

Resurrection and Ascension.

Lord of the rolling years,
Claim for thine own the spheres,
For thou hast bought with tears
    Thy heritage.

Yet, who are these behind
In numbers more than mind
    Can count or say;
Clothed in immortal stoles,
Illumining the poles,
A galaxy of souls
    In white array?

And then was heard afar,
Star answering to star:
    'Lo, these have come,
Followers of him who gave
His life, their lives to save;
And now their palms they wave,
    Brought safely home.'

O Lord, ascend thy throne;
For thou shalt rule alone
    Beside thy Sire,
With the great Paraclete,
The Three in One complete—
Before whose awful feet
    All foes expire.
M. Bridges.

Hymns from the Daily Procession of the Franciscan Friars at Jerusalem.

(*At the Altar of St. Mary Magdalen.*)
Jesus, thy love was pleased to all
    Thy risen life to show,
But they who erst have loved thee best
    Are first that love to know.

The dew of spring's thrice-blessed morn
  Still on the garden lay,
When she whose love thy pardon won
  Hither hath found her way.
She who hath stood beside thy cross
  Seeks thee among the dead ;
The watch that guards thee scares her not ;
  Love hath disarmed her dread.
The same again to do she seeks
  Who twice thy feet annealed—
But lo, the Gardener 'mid his flowers—
  And Jesus is revealed.
             Order of Compline, 1880.

(*In the Church of the Apparition.*)
Mother of God and Mother mine,
  God willed that thou shouldst see
Thy Son, the victim of my sins,
  Hang dead upon the tree ;
But now, behold, the morning star
  Shines in the brightening sky,
And he, the light of death's black night,
  Thy Son again is nigh.
He that was dead is raised again,
  Alive for evermore,
And heaven and earth and sky and sea
  Their glad thanksgivings pour.
Glory and praise to him we raise
  Who reigns above the sky ;
May he be pleased that we may reach
  The marriage-feast on high.
             Order of Compline, 1880.

Jesus risen.
All hail, dear Conqueror, all hail ;
  Oh, what a victory is thine,

Resurrection and Ascension.

How beautiful thy strength appears,
  Thy crimson wounds how bright they shine.

Thou camest at the dawn of day ;
  Armies of souls around thee were,
Blest spirits thronging to adore
  Thy flesh, so marvellous, so fair.

The everlasting Godhead lay
  Shrouded within those limbs divine,
Nor left untenanted one hour
  That sacred human heart of thine.

They worshipped thee, those ransomed souls,
  With the fresh strength of love set free ;
They worshipped joyously, and thought
  Of Mary while they looked on thee.

They worshipped, while the beauteous soul
  Paused by the body's wounded side :
Bright flashed the cave—before them stood
  The living Jesus glorified.

Down, down, all lofty things on earth,
  And worship him with joyous dread ;
O sin, thou art undone by love ;
  O death, thou art discomfited.
                              F. W. Faber.

Mount Olivet.

Lo, on Mount Olivet's fair height,
  Lit in the noon-tide glow,
The glories of a vision bright
  Their golden radiance throw ;
And circling round their dear triumphant king,
A chosen band love's farewell tribute bring.

There, too, the Virgin-mother stands,
  Gazing with loving eyes,

Raising her gentle spotless hands
 Towards the illumined skies,
Where Jesus, welcomed with triumphant song,
Ascends on high amid the angelic throng.

When now the last bright lingering rays
 Fade on their trancèd sight,
They see, as still they gaze and gaze,
 Two angels clad in white :
' Ye men of Galilee gaze not in vain,
Hereafter Jesus so will come again.'

Thus spake the angels—so should we
 Work while 'tis yet called day ;
Jesus and Mary patiently
 Have toiled through life's rough way :
Though on temptation's troubled sea thou'rt cast,
Hope's star shines soft, and night will soon be past.

Then trustful still toil bravely on,
 Though life be full of cares ;
Soon shall unfading wreaths be won—
 Jesus our throne prepares :
Soon shall the joys of endless spring-time come,
And toil-worn spirits soon shall reach their home.
F. Stanfield.

Pone luctum, Magdalena.

Woeful Mary, cease from sighing,
 This is not a time for gloom ;
No more sorrow, no more crying,
 As in Simon's supper-room ;
'Tis a time for voices raising
Shouts of triumph and of praising ;
 Let the Alleluias ring.

Mary, smile in thankful gladness,
 Let thy brow be sweet and bright ;
Ended is the time of sadness,
 Shine a new and radiant light ;

Resurrection and Ascension.

Death is vanquished, Christ has spoken,
And the chains of men are broken;
　　Let the Alleluias ring.
Triumph, Mary; from the prison
　Of the grave in which he lay,
Comes the victor newly risen—
　Pain and anguish gone for aye;
Dying thou didst once bewail him,
Now in Easter glory hail him;
　　Let the Alleluias ring.
Mary, take thy fill of gazing,
　See how bright the look he wears;
See he liveth—joy amazing—
　See the five dear wounds he bears,
Jewels meet for his adorning
On this new and glorious morning;
　　Let the Alleluias ring.
Happy Mary, rapture burning,
　Thrills thy pulses in this hour;
Seeing thus thy light returning,
　Knowing death has lost his power;
No more grief and sad complaining,
Love and joy for ever reigning;
　　Let the Alleluias ring.
　　　　　　　　　Anonymous.

German Easter Hymn.

　　The Saviour is arisen,
　　　Set free from death's dark prison—
He who as a true paschal Lamb
To die and suffer for me came.
　　Now is mankind dispained,
　　　Now Satan is enchained,
And death has lost his sting; the stone
Is rolled away, the tomb left lone;

  The conqueror leads the train,
  That long has captive lain,
Into his Father's realm—the coast
For me and you by Adam lost.
  The wounds he bore for me,
  How radiant now they be;
And hark, the angels' choral breath
To him, the strong, who vanquished death.
  My faith should waver nought—
  Oh, comfort in the thought—
Through his arising I shall rise,
And from my grave shall reach the skies.
  The night that overtakes
  Me 'till the angel wakes
Is short; and then, my Saviour calls
Me to himself, in deathless halls.
  O sea of blessing deep,
  A place for me to keep—
Lo, my Redeemer soars above;
I follow on the wings of love.
  My soul once more alive
  Shall home-ward, heaven-ward, strive,
Where with thy Father throned thou livest,
And tenfold for each good deed givest.
  In judgment I shall stand
  And gaze on thy right hand;
The bleeding Lamb shall wash me white,
And to his bridal feast invite.
As thou, Lord, hast from death arisen,
Let us arise and burst our prison.

J. C. Earle.

O Rex gloriæ.

  O Christ, our glorious king,
  And Lord of all the armies of the sky,

Riding on glory's wing,
With conquering pomp thou goest up on high,
Far o'er the heaven of heavens, beyond where
thoughts can fly.
Ah, leave us not alone,
Unfriended here and parentless to pine;
But from thy beaming throne
Send us the Father's promised gift and thine,
The Spirit of truth and love, our Comforter divine.
J. D. Aylward.

Ascension of Jesus.

In the brightness of the sunshine
   Thou didst go from earth to heaven ;
When our Lady stood beside thee
   With the sorrowful eleven :
Then they gazed upon thee rising
   To the cloud that veiled the sky,
In the hour of thine ascension
   To thy Father's house on high.

Lifting up thy hands in blessing
   Thou wast parted from their sight,
When the golden doors stood open
   To the splendour of thy might :
Then the angels sang before thee,
   As thou wentest on thy way,
To thy throne of strength, predestined,
   In the city of the day.

As the fount of living water
   Thou dost dwell within the veil ;
Giving help to those who wander,
   Giving life to those who fail :
As the storehouse of all mercy
   Thou dost dwell in light above ;
Evermore our intercessor,
   Evermore our kingly love.
H. A. Rawes.

Pentecost and Trinity Sunday.

Trinity Sunday.

God of life and light and motion,
    Cause and centre, fount and home;
Limitless and tideless ocean;
    Past and present and to come:
Unbeginning, as unending;
    Uncontrolled by time or space;
Undefined, yet unextending;
    Boundless, yet in every place:
Self-existent, uncreated,
    Underived, evolved of none;
In sublimest peace instated,
    Perfect in thyself alone:
With unclouded vision seeing,
    Spread o'er one eternal page;
All the mysteries of being
    Traversing the course of age:
Every art of man detecting,
    Sketched in form or shaped in fact;
All his cherished plans inspecting,
    Locked in heart or bared in act:
Loving all, and all befriending
    With a love as deep as wide;
And to meanest creatures bending
    Low as if were none beside

F. Oakeley.

Descent of the Holy Ghost.

O mighty Mother, why that light
In thine uplifted eye?

Pentecost and Trinity Sunday. 103

Why that resplendent look of more
   Than queen-like majesty?
She sat; beneath her shadow were
   The chosen of her Son:
Within each heart and on each face
   Her power and spirit shone.

Queen of the Church, around thee shines
   The purest light of heaven,
And all created things to thee
   For thy domain are given.

Why waitest thou then, so abashed,
   Wrapt in ecstatic fear,
Speechless with adoration, hushed—
   Hushed as though God were near?

She is a creature; see, she bows,
   She trembles though so great—
Created majesty o'erwhelmed
   Before the Increate.

He comes, he comes, that mighty Breath
   From heaven's eternal shores;
His uncreated freshness fills
   His Bride as she adores.

One moment—and the Spirit hung
   O'er her with dread desire;
Then broke upon the heads of all
   In cloven tongues of fire.

Who knows in what a sea of love
   Our Lady's heart he drowned?
Or what new gifts he gave her then?
   What ancient gifts he crowned?

What gifts he gave those chosen men,
   Past ages can display;
Nay more, their vigour still inspires
   The weakness of to-day.

Oh, let us fall and worship him,
The love of Sire and Son,
The consubstantial Breath of God,
The co-eternal One.

F. W. Faber.

Hours from the Little Office of the Holy Ghost.

Oh, may the Paraclete divine his grace to us impart,
Who like a lucid shade o'erspread our Lady's gentle heart,
When the bright angel came to her his gracious news to tell,
And in her pure and chosen womb the Word began to dwell.

Lo, God's anointed Son is born—child of the Maiden-womb;
And now he suffers, now he dies, now lies within the tomb;
Now gloriously rising, behold him clearly given
To faithful eyes; and now he mounts above the clouds of heaven.

On Pentecost's expectant morn, God from his triune throne,
To comfort the apostles' hearts the Paraclete sends down;
Lo, how the tongues of parted flame fall sweetly on each head;
'I will not leave you orphans,' his sacred lips had said.

Then like a shower of fire divine, they felt the seven-fold grace,
And spake with fluent lips the tongues of every tribe and race :

They spread themselves o'er land and sea, and preached
  through every clime
The faith divine of holy Church, with its mysteries
  sublime.

His names are but the varied names of love, all-
  heavenly sweet—
The gift of God, the spring of life, the Spirit-Paraclete,
The gracious unction of the soul, the great eternal
  love,
The mystic flame, the seven-fold grace, the gift all
  gifts above.

May he, the strength of God's right-hand, our soul's
  unfailing stay,
Still keep us in his care and chase the evil-one away ;
Beneath the shadow of his wings protect and feed us
  still,
And guard us from our demon-foe and all the powers
  of ill.

Come then, O Comforter divine, lend us thy guiding
  light ;
And ever help us at our need, and lead our steps
  aright ;
That when the Lord to judgment comes upon the
  great white throne,
He bid us stand at his right hand, and count us for
  his own.

> These words breathed forth with love profound,
> And framed in sweetly ordered round,
> We consecrate with reverence meet
> To thee, our gracious Paraclete :
> Oh, grant us here thy needful grace,
> And when we end our earthly race,
> The glories of thy dwelling-place.
> *J. D. Aylward.*

To the Holy Spirit.

The wind rang out from depths of woods,
    And pealed through valleys bent
Among the echoing hills, like tubes
    Of some vast instrument :
Its sound we heard ; but knew not whence
    It came, nor whither went.

The wind upon our forehead blows
    In gleams of lambent flame ;
The sunbeams flash from wave and leaf :
    The hour is now the same
As when to Christ's anointed twelve
    That promised Spirit came.

The sound as of a rushing wind
    Before his wings he flung ;
And leaped on those uplifted brows
    In many a flaming tongue :
Oh, breathe on us thy seven-fold powers;
    Oh, dwell our hearts among.

Live thou in Christ's mysterious vine,
    Until her branches spread
Among the stars, to them as flowers
    'Mid locks of one new-wed ;
And clasp, in their descending arch,
    The earth's wide bridal-bed.
                        A. de Vere.

The Fountain of Love.

Fountain of Love, thyself true God,
    Who through eternal days
From Father and from Son hast flowed
    In uncreated ways.

O majesty unspeakable,
    O person all divine,

Pentecost and Trinity Sunday.

How in the threefold majesty
  Doth thy procession shine.

Proceeding, yet of equal age
  With those whose love thou art ;
Proceeding, yet distinct, from those
  From whom thou seem'st to part :

An undivided nature, shared
  With Father and with Son ;
A person by thyself ; with them
  Thy simple essence One.

I dread thee, unbegotten Love,
  True God, sole fount of grace ;
And now before thy blessed throne
  My sinful self abase.

That art a God of fire, that doth
  Create while he consumes ;
A God of light, whose rays on earth
  Darken where he illumes.

O Spirit, beautiful and dread,
  My heart is fit to break
With love of all thy tenderness
  For us poor sinners' sake.

Thy love of Jesus I adore ;
  My comfort this shall be,
That when I serve my dearest Lord
  That service worships thee.
F. W. Faber.

Canticle to the Holy Ghost.

Thou Paraclete, whom Jesus sent to me,
Who, one with him, didst give thyself to me,
Thou love of God most high, who lovest me,
Thou king and Lord, who sanctifiest me—
For love of the Desired I come to thee.

From Father and from Son proceedest thou ;
Of Father and of Son the love art thou ;
Their kiss of everlasting peace art thou ;
The bond unbroken of their rest art thou ;
One God with Father and with Son art thou.

My soul is faint, nay hopeless, without thee ;
My heart is weak, nay withered, without thee ;
My life is burnt, like stubble, without thee ;
I cannot say 'My Jesus' without thee—
Thou loved One, pour thy light of grace on me.

I come to thee, almighty, living One,
In poverty of soul, thou living One,
In sinfulness and death, thou living One ;
Make all my spirit thine, thou living One,
'Till thou art ever mine, thou living One.

For sorrow for my sins, I come to thee ;
For confidence in God, I come to thee ;
For faithfulness to grace, I come to thee—
To keep, O love, my promises to thee,
To walk in white with Jesus and with thee.

A wind rain-laden from the south art thou ;
The dew that falleth in the light art thou ;
A fountain in a desert-land art thou ;
A flame-girt temple on the hills art thou ;
The fiery-furnace of God's love art thou.

O Spirit of my Lord, who lightest me,
Thou, who didst come at Pentecost for me,
Thou Love, who seekest thirstingly for me—
Destroy all evil and all death in me,
Making my soul a holiness to thee.

Dear gift of Jesus crucified, O Love—
Send down thy showers upon thy fields, O Love ;
Fill all the valleys with thy corn, O Love ;
The mountains girdle with thy joy, O Love—
Thou first and last, thou uncreated Love.

Pentecost and Trinity Sunday.

Thou stoopest in eternal love to me ;
Thou crownest all the years with grace for me ;
Thou fillest all the stores of God for me ;
O Spirit bountiful, I cling to thee,
To love and bless and praise and worship thee.

My Jesus gave himself in death by thee,
A spotless sacrifice to God by thee ;
Thy gifts and fruits be perfected in me,
That in thy glory I may dwell with thee,
White-robed, palm-bearing, evermore with thee.
H. A. Rawes.

The Most Holy Trinity.

Have mercy on us, God most high,
    Who lift our hearts to thee ;
Have mercy on us worms of earth,
    Most holy Trinity.

When heaven and earth were yet unmade,
    When time was yet unknown,
Thou in thy bliss and majesty
    Didst live and love alone.

How wonderful creation is,
    The work that thou didst bless ;
And oh, what then must thou be like,
    Eternal loveliness.

O majesty most beautiful,
    Most holy Trinity,
On Mary's throne we climb to get
    A far-off sight of thee.

Oh listen, then, most pitiful,
    To thy poor creature's heart :
It blesses thee that thou art God,
    That thou art what thou art.

Most ancient of all mysteries,
    Before thy throne we lie ;

Have mercy now, most merciful,
Most holy Trinity.

      F. W. Faber.

Ever-blessed Trinity.

I.

God the Father, whose relation
 With the sole-begotten Son,
By a mystic generation,
 Stood ere time had learned to run :
God the Son, by tie supernal
 Ever with the Father bound ;
In the glorious folds eternal
 Of one single nature wound :
God the Spirit, stream vivific,
 Ceaselessly by both outpoured,
And in union beatific
 Equally with both adored :
God the Father, Son and Spirit,
 Three in One and One in Three,
Thine united glories merit
 Thanks and praise continually.

II.

Praise to thee and adoration
 On thy festival be done,
For the blessed incarnation
 Of the co-eternal Son :
For the coming of the Spirit ;
 For the grace of Mary's life ;
For the joys that saints inherit
 When they cease from earthly strife :
More than all, be praise unending
 Paid throughout the Church to thee,
For the majesty transcending
 Of thy triune Deity ;

Sun of splendour never waning,
  Fount of sweetness never dry,
Staff of comfort all-sustaining
  Ever-blessed Trinity.
                                    F. Oakeley.

The Eternal Spirit.

Eternal Spirit, God supreme,
Our friend in evil's worst extreme,
Descend, and let thy breast o'erflow
In streams of grace to all below.

The light that shone at thy command
Is hasting to another land;
Within our hearts, O Light divine,
O uncreated brightness, shine.

Companion of the heart's recess,
Repose in labour and distress;
By thee the sinful bosom bleeds,
By thee the smile of joy succeeds.

O fountain of all grace, to thee
From our frail hearts for aid we flee,
That we may conquer in the strife
And win the prize of endless life.

Oh, let thy fire our spirits burn,
And hymns of praise the flame return;
Praise to the Father and the Son,
And thee, O Spirit, Three in One.
                                    R. Campbell.

Fragment of 'Beata nobis gaudia.'

A fire from heaven all-trembling came,
Which shone like parted tongues of flame—
A sign that from their lips should roll
The accents of love's burning soul.

The Gentile crowds in wonder hung
To hear them speak the varied tongue ;
But frantic deemed with new-pressed wine,
Those men so filled with love divine.
In mystery deep these things were done,
For now the paschal-time had run,
And brought the morn when man awoke
To freedom from the legal yoke.
O God, with humbleness profound
And faces bending to the ground,
We pray that unto us be given
The Spirit's gift poured forth from heaven.
To Sire and Son be praises meet,
And to the holy Paraclete ;
May Christ the Spirit's gift send down
Soft-streaming from the mercy-throne.
J. D. Aylward.

To the Holy Ghost.

Holy Ghost, come down upon thy children,
   Give us grace and make us thine ;
Thy tender fires within us kindle,
   Blessed Spirit, Dove divine.

For all within us good and holy
   Is from thee, thy precious gift ;
In all our joys, in all our sorrows,
   Wistful hearts to thee we lift.
      Holy Ghost, etc.

For thou to us art more than father,
   More than sister, in thy love,
So gentle, patient and forbearing,
   Holy Spirit, heavenly Dove.
      Holy Ghost, etc.

Oh, we have grieved thee, gracious Spirit,
   Wayward, wanton, cold are we ;

Pentecost and Trinity Sunday.

And still our sins, new every morning,
  Never yet have wearied thee.
    Holy Ghost, etc.

Dear Paraclete, how hast thou waited
  While our hearts were slowly turned ;
How often hath thy love been slighted,
  While for us it grieved and burned.
    Holy Ghost, etc.

Now, if our hearts do not deceive us,
  We would take thee for our Lord ;
O dearest Spirit, make us faithful
  To thy least and lightest word.
    Holy Ghost, come down upon thy children,
      Give us grace and make us thine ;
    Thy tender fires within us kindle,
      Blessed Spirit, Dove divine.

F. W. Faber.

The Sacred Humanity.

Cor Jesu, Cor purissimum.

O HEART of Jesus, purest heart,
Altar of holiness thou art,
Cleanse thou my heart, so sordid, cold,
And stained by sins so manifold.

Take from me, Lord, this tepid will
Which doth thy heart with loathing fill ;
And then infuse a spirit new—
A fervent spirit, deep and true.

Most humble heart of all that beat,
Heart full of goodness, meek and sweet,
Give me a heart more like to thine,
And light the flame of love in mine.

But, ah, were e'en my heart on fire
With all the seraphim's desire,
Till love a conflagration proved,
Not yet wouldst thou enough be loved.

That therefore thou mayst worthily
Be loved, O loving Lord, by me,
That love which in thy heart doth burn
Give me to love thee in return.

May this thy love's most fiery dart
Strike deep and set on fire my heart,
And in that burning may it be
Dissolved and all-consumed in thee.

Death to be sought with yearnings high,
Thus from love's violence to die :
Ah, may my heart love's victim prove
For the Redeemer's heart of love.

So let me die for love of thee,
O Heart, all full of love for me,
That with a new heart's virgin-hoard
I may begin to love thee, Lord.

M. Russell.

Fount of Divine Love.

O Heart of Jesus, heart of God,
  O source of boundless love,
By angels praised, by saints adored,
  From their bright thrones above.

The poorest, saddest heart on earth
  May claim thee for its own ;
O burning, throbbing Heart of Christ,
  Too late, too little known.

The very sound of those sweet words,
  ' The sacred Heart ' can give,
To the most lone and burthened soul,
  Strength to endure and live.

A mother may forget her child,
  A father prove untrue ;
A brother or a sister turn
  Unkind and thankless too.

The hearts of men are often hard
  And full of selfish care ;
But in the sacred heart we find
  A refuge from despair.

To thee, my Jesus, then I come,
  A poor and helpless child ;
And on thine own words, ' Come to me,'
  My only hope I build.

The world is cold, and life is sad,
    I crave the blessèd rest
Of those who lay their weary heads
    Upon thy sacred breast.

For love is stronger far than death,
    And who can love like thee,
My Saviour, whose appealing heart
    Broke on the cross for me?

The purest, deepest earthly love,
    What is it, Lord, to thine?
A single drop from a great fount,
    Eternal and divine.

Lady G. Fullerton.

The true Shepherd.

I was wandering and weary,
    When my Saviour came unto me;
For the ways of sin grew dreary,
    And the world had ceased to woo me;
And I thought I heard him say,
As he came along his way,
    'O silly souls, come near me;
    My sheep should never fear me;
    I am the Shepherd true.'

At first I would not hearken,
    And put off till the morrow;
But life began to darken,
    And I was sick with sorrow;
And I thought I heard him say,
As he came along his way,
    'O silly souls, come near me,' etc.

At last I stopped to listen,
    His voice could not deceive me;
I saw his kind eyes glisten,
    So anxious to relieve me:

And I thought I heard him say,
  As he came along his way,
    'O silly souls, come near me,' etc.

He took me on his shoulder,
  And tenderly he kissed me ;
He bade my love be bolder,
  And said how he had missed me ;
And I am sure I heard him say,
  As he went along his way,
    'O silly souls, come near me,' etc.

I thought his love would weaken,
  As more and more he knew me ;
But it burneth like a beacon,
  And its light and heat go through me ;
And I ever hear him say,
  As he goes along his way,
    'O silly souls, come near me,' etc.

Let us do, then, dearest brothers,
  What will best and longest please us :
Follow not the ways of others,
  But trust ourselves to Jesus :
We shall ever hear him say,
As he goes along his way,
  'O silly souls, come near me ;
    My sheep should never fear me ;
    I am the Shepherd true.'
           F. W. Faber.

Haven of Rest.

Sweet Jesus, thou a haven art
  From life's tempestuous sea ;
All find a refuge in thy heart,
  Who turn in love to thee.

Thy name falls sweet on exiles' ear,
  'Tis music from above ;

It stays the mourner's anxious fear,
   And telleth nought but love.

The broken heart with healing balm
   Thy changeless love doth fill:
Thou sayest 'Peace,' the winds are calm,
   And every wave is still.

Oh, hope and joy of life's lone way,
   May thy sweet peace arise,
Which turns the night to blissful day,
   And earth to paradise.

Sweet Jesus, when death's night shall fall,
   By thine own love so blessed,
May longing exiles hear thee call
   The weary to their rest.
F. Stanfield.

Sinner's cry to Jesus.

Jesu, meek and lowly,
Saviour, pure and holy,
On thy love relying,
Come I to thee flying.
   Prince of life and power,
My salvation's tower,
On the cross I view thee
Calling sinners to thee.
   There behold me gazing
At the sight amazing;
Bending low before thee,
Helpless I adore thee.
   See the red wounds streaming,
With Christ's life-blood gleaming,
Blood for sinners flowing,
Pardon free bestowing.
   Fountain rich in blessing,
Christ's fond love expressing,

Thou my aching sadness
Turnest into gladness.
　Lord, in mercy guide me,
　Be thou e'er beside me ;
　In thy ways direct me ;
　'Neath thy wings protect me.
　　　　　　　　H. Collins.

The Sacred Heart.

What wouldst thou have, O soul,
　Thou weary soul ?
Lo, I have sought for rest
On the earth's heaving breast,
　From pole to pole.
Sleep—I have been with her,
　But she gave dreams ;
Death—nay, the rest he gives
　Rest only seems.
Fair nature knows it not—
　The grass is growing ;
The blue air knows it not—
　The winds are blowing ;
Not in the changing sky,
　The stormy sea—
Yet, somewhere in God's wide world,
　Rest there must be.
Within thy Saviour's heart
　Place all thy care,
And learn, O weary soul,
　Thy rest is there.
What wouldst thou, trembling soul ?
　Strength for the strife ;
Strength for this fiery war
　That we call life.
Fears gather thickly round ;
　Shadowy foes,

Like unto armèd men,
  Around me close.
What am I, frail and poor,
  When griefs arise?
No help from the weak earth,
  Or the cold skies.
Lo, I can find no guards,
  No weapons borrow;
Shrinking, alone I stand,
  With mighty sorrow.
Courage, thou trembling soul,
  Grief thou must bear;
Yet thou canst find a strength
  Will match despair:
Within thy Saviour's heart—
  Seek for it there.

What wouldst thou have, sad soul,
  Oppressed with grief?
Comfort I seek in vain,
  Nor find relief.
Nature, all pitiless,
  Smiles on my pain;
I ask my fellow-men,
  They give disdain.
I asked the bubbling streams,
  But they flowed on;
I asked the wise and good,
  But they gave none.
Though I have asked the stars,
  Coldly they shine,
They are too bright to know
  Grief such as mine.
I asked for comfort still,
  And I found tears,
And I have sought in vain
  Long weary years.

Listen, thou mournful soul,
  Thy pain shall cease ;
Deep in his sacred heart
  Dwells joy and peace.
Yes, in that heart divine,
  The angels bright
Find, through eternal years,
  Still new delight.
From thence his constancy
  The martyr drew,
And there the virgin band
  Their refuge knew.
There, racked by pain without
  And dread within,
How many souls have found
  Heaven's bliss begin.
Then leave thy vain attempts
  To seek for peace ;
The world can never give
  One soul release :
But in thy Saviour's heart
  Securely dwell,
No pain can harm thee, hid
  In that sweet cell.
Then fly, O coward soul,
  Delay no more ;
What words can speak the joy
  For thee in store ?
What smiles of earth can tell
  Of peace like thine ?
Silence and tears are best
  For things divine.

Adelaide A. Procter.

Jesus our Rest.

Night falls apace ; the shades grow long
  Athwart the dewy lawn ;

Blithe birds pipe out their even-song,
    Flowers close till welcome dawn.

Behind the hill-tops, sinking low,
    Passed the great sun away;
Now paler spreads fair saffron-glow
    Amid the deepening grey.

All seek repose when night is nigh—
    The tender doves their nest,
The lambs, safe folded, sleeping lie,
    The babe on mother's breast.

So seek we, Lord, in thee to rest,
    Who lengthenest our days;
Meet offerings bring—of prayer our best,
    And sweetest songs of praise.

Care fills our lives—our cares on thee
    We cast from day to day;
Thy voice sounds gently, 'Come to me
    Who bore your sins away.'

Weak are our footsteps—thine the power
    To raise us when we fall;
Full oft we stray in evil hour;
    Do thou our souls recall.

What if we lose thee? whence our hope?
    Who else can save or cheer?
Dread were our doom unhelped to grope
    In blank despair and fear.

But thou art ours—true strength and stay;
    At morn our bread of life;
Until the closing of life's day,
    Our peace 'mid toil and strife.

Be with us, Jesus, at the end,
    When death-shades round us close;

Light in our gloom in pity send,
    And grant a sweet repose.
E. Louisa Lee.

Latus Salvatoris.

There is an everlasting home,
    Where contrite souls may hide,
Where death and danger dare not come—
    The Saviour's side.

It was a cleft of matchless love
    Opened when he had died;
When mercy hailed in worlds above
    That wounded side.

Hail, Rock of Ages, pierced for me,
    The grave of all my pride;
Hope, peace and heaven are all in thee,
    Thy sheltering side.

There issued forth a double flood,
    The sin-atoning tide,
In streams of water and of blood
    From that dear side.

There is the only fount of bliss,
    In joy and sorrow tried;
No refuge for the heart like this—
    A Saviour's side.

Thither the Church, through all her days
    Points as a faithful guide;
And celebrates with ceaseless praise
    That spear-pierced side.

There is the golden gate of heaven,
    An entrance for the Bride,
Where the sweet crown of life is given
    Through Jesus' side.
M. Bridges.

The riven Heart.

For this the wound, for this thy heart is riven,
   Where from our weary thoughts we find a home;
Within thy heart our hearts have sought their heaven,
   We come, O Lord, we come.

Our king, our brother and our friend who loves us,
   Receive our prayers into this holy shrine;
'Till every wish and will and thought that moves us,
   Be thine, O Lord, be thine.

The fleshly wound, thy soul's deep wound revealing,
   Opens the passage to our reverent gaze;
Shall we not love a God such love revealing?
   We love, adore and praise.

Bound as we are in life's oppressive fetters,
   With feeble voice our souls to thee have cried,
Whose body has been stamped with bleeding letters,
   In hands and feet and side.

O Jesu, beautiful beyond all beauty,
   Cleanse us in this bright stream that floweth still;
Here let us dwell, and work with loving duty
   Thy will, O Lord, thy will.

Lady C. Petre.

Jesus is God.

Jesus is God; the solid earth,
   The ocean broad and bright,
The countless stars, like golden dust
   That strew the skies at night,
The wheeling storm, the dreadful fire,
   The pleasant wholesome air,
The summer's sun, the winter's frost,
   His own creations were.

Jesus is God; the glorious bands
   Of golden angels sing

The Sacred Humanity.

Songs of adoring praise to him,
  Their maker and their king :
He was true God in Bethlehem's crib,
  On Calvary's cross true God,
He who in heaven eternal reigned,
  In time on earth abode.

Jesus is God ; alas, they say
  On earth the numbers grow
Who his divinity blaspheme
  To their unfailing woe :
And yet, what is the single end
  Of this life's mortal span,
Except to glorify the God
  Who for our sakes was Man ?

Jesus is God ; let sorrow come
  And pain and every ill ;
All are worth while—for all are means
  His glory to fulfil ;
Worth while a thousand years of life
  To speak one little word,
If by our Credo we might own
  The Godhead of our Lord.

Jesus is God ; oh, could I now
  But compass land and sea,
To teach and tell this single truth,
  How happy should I be :
Oh, had I but an angel's voice,
  I would proclaim so loud,
' Jesus, the good, the beautiful,
  Is everlasting God.'
F. W. Faber.

Dreams of Time.

I arise from dreams of time,
  And the shadows of this life,

And the tombs and places waste
   Of an earth of sin and strife :
I arise from dreams of time,
   And an angel guides my feet
Where, on yon altar dim,
   Thy sacred heart doth beat.

The lone lamp quivers clear,
   And a wondrous silence reigns ;
Only with low voice and mild
   The Holy One complains :
'Lo, I have waited here ;
   And while thou heed'st not me,
The heart of Mary's Son
   Beats ever on for thee.

'In the womb of Maiden meek,
   In the cradle, on the tree,
Heart of undying love,
   It lived, beat, broke for thee :
Now round me thunders speak,
   Yet, as then, behold me now—
Man of the wounded hands,
   God of the bleeding brow.'

O voice to the inward ear ;
   O voice of complaining love ;
O thou who art awful God
   To realms below and above—
Yet waitest and pleadest here,
   And wilt not from us part—
O veiled and wondrous Lord ;
   Oh, love of the sacred heart.
R. Monteith.

On the Sacred Heart of Jesus.
I dwell a captive in this heart,
   On fire with love divine ;

'Tis here I live alone in peace,
  And constant joy is mine.
It is the heart of God's own Son
  In his humanity,
Who, all enamoured of my soul,
  Here burns with love of me.

Here, like the dove within the ark,
  Securely I repose;
Since now the Lord is my defence,
  I fear no earthly foes.
Now I have found this happy home,
  God's love alone I prize;
All else is torment to my heart,
  The world I now despise.

What though I suffer, still in love
  I ever true will be;
My love of God shall deeper grow
  When crosses fall on me.
Then he who longs with me to seek
  Repose within this nest,
All love that is not love for God
  Must banish from his breast.

Ye haughty lovers of the world,
  Full of self-love, depart;
Away, away; no place is found
  For you within this heart.
Each vile and earthly chain impedes
  The soul's true heaven-ward flight;
All, all the heart belongs to God,
  Love claims his sovereign right.

From every bond of earth, dear Lord,
  Thy grace has set me free;
My soul, delivered from the snare,
  Enjoys true liberty.

I cannot love thee as I ought—
  This pains me, this alone ;
For all my love must have an end—
  Thy goodness, Lord, has none.
One thought brings comfort to my heart,
  I love a Good so great,
That though I love him all I can,
  More love he merits yet.
Nought more can I desire than this,
  To see his face in heaven ;
And this I hope, since he on earth
  His heart in pledge has given.
From St. Alphonsus.

Jesu, my Lord, I thee adore.

Jesu, my Lord, my God, my all,
Hear me, blest Saviour, when I call ;
Hear me, and from thy dwelling-place
Pour down the riches of thy grace :
  Jesu, my Lord, I thee adore ;
  Oh, make me love thee more and more.

Jesu, too late I thee have sought ;
How can I love thee as I ought ?
And how extol thy matchless fame,
The glorious beauty of thy name ?
  Jesu, my Lord, I thee adore ;
  Oh, make me love thee more and more.

Jesu, what didst thou find in me,
That thou hast dealt so lovingly ?
How great the joy that thou hast brought,
So far exceeding hope or thought ;
  Jesu, my Lord, I thee adore ;
  Oh, make me love thee more and more.

Jesu, of thee shall be my song ;
To thee my heart and soul belong ;

The Sacred Humanity.

All that I have or am is thine,
And thou, blest Saviour, thou art mine :
 Jesu, my Lord, I thee adore ;
 Oh, make me love thee more and more.
H. Collins.

Our Home.

O sacred Heart,
 Our home lies deep in thee ;
On earth thou art an exile's rest,
In heaven the glory of the blest,
 O sacred Heart.

O sacred Heart,
 Thou fount of contrite tears ;
Where'er those living waters flow,
New life to sinners they bestow,
 O sacred Heart.

O sacred Heart,
 Bless our dear fatherland ;
May England's sons to truth e'er stand,
With faith's bright banner still in hand,
 O sacred Heart.

O sacred Heart,
 Our trust is all in thee ;
For though earth's night be dark and drear,
Thou breathest rest where thou art near,
 O sacred Heart.

O sacred Heart,
 When shades of death shall fall,
Receive us 'neath thy gentle care,
And save us from the tempter's snare,
 O sacred Heart.

O sacred Heart,
 Lead exiled children home,

Where we may ever rest near thee,
In peace and joy eternally,
O sacred Heart.

F. Stanfield.

Come to Jesus.

Souls of men, why will ye scatter
  Like a crowd of frightened sheep?
Foolish hearts, why will ye wander
  From a love so true and deep?

Was there ever kindest shepherd
  Half so gentle, half so sweet
As the Saviour, who would have us
  Come and gather at his feet?

There's a wideness in God's mercy,
  Like the wideness of the sea:
There's a kindness in his justice,
  Which is more than liberty.

There is no place where earth's sorrows
  Are more felt than up in heaven:
There is no place where earth's failings
  Have such kindly judgment given.

There is welcome for the sinner,
  And more graces for the good;
There is mercy with the Saviour;
  There is healing in his blood.

For the love of God is broader
  Than the measures of man's mind;
And the heart of the Eternal
  Is most wonderfully kind.

There is plentiful redemption
  In the blood that has been shed;
There is joy for all the members
  In the sorrow of the Head.

The Sacred Humanity.

If our love were but more simple,
    We should take him at his word ;
And our lives would be all sunshine
    In the sweetness of our Lord.
                              F. W. Faber.

Piercing of the Sacred Heart.

Love, thou dost all excell ;
From that dear heart's most deep recess
The last, last drop flowed out, to bless
    The earth whereon it fell.

Oh, charity immense ;
And we, within that wounded side,
As in a sacred home may hide
    Our joys, our penitence.

'Tis there that I would meet
Those who to me most gladness bring,
Round whom my heart's affections cling
    In tenderness most sweet.

No being on this earth
In our warm love should claim a part,
Save in and through the sacred heart,
    Which gives to love its worth.

There also would I greet
Those who perchance despise me here ;
Those who have caused a pang, a tear ;
    Then peace would be complete.

Calm refuge of the soul ;
Oh, that we might thy shelter win
From the dread weariness of sin,
    Whose waves so wildly roll.

There we might ever dwell ;
It is not, Lord, thy love that fails ;
But when the evil one assails,
    Alas, we strive not well.

Yet, pardon us once more :
Let us for ever hide in thee;
So shall life's pain and misery
And weariness be o'er.
Lady C. Petre.

Two Messages.
A message from the sacred Heart :
What may its message be ?
' My child, my child, give me thy heart—
My heart has bled for thee.'
This is the message Jesus sends
To my poor heart to-day,
And eager from his throne he bends
To hear what I shall say.

A message to the sacred Heart;
Oh, bear it back with speed :
' Come, Jesus, reign within my heart—
Thy heart is all I need.'
Thus, Lord, I'll pray until I share
That home whose joy thou art :
No message, dearest Jesus, there—
For heart will speak to heart.
M. Russell.

Cento from Little Office of the Sacred Heart.
O heaven's glorious King,
Who dost thy starry throne
And its triumphant bliss postpone,
To be our offering.

Jesus, our heart's delight,
This faithful flock inspire
Of thy great heart to sing the fire,
And love with praise requite.

O heart, love's victim slain,
O heaven's lasting joy,

The Sacred Humanity.

To whom distressèd mortals fly,
   Nor fly for help in vain.
Formed of pure Virgin-blood,
Pregnant with love divine,
Thou heaven's palace dost outshine,
   A mansion fit for God.
Love did this refuge win;
Love lanced our Saviour's side;
Fond love displayed the passage wide,
   And bid us welcome in.
Oh, wondrous power of love,
God gives himself to eat;
His blood is drink, his flesh is meat,
   And he who reigns above,
Dread sovereign of the skies,
Regales his mortal guest—
Himself the donor and the feast,
   Though hid from mortal eyes.
Thy Father's only One,
Chaste spouse of lovers pure,
Who canst no rival-love endure,
   Possess our hearts alone.

Anonymous, 1765.

We come to thee, sweet Saviour.

We come to thee, sweet Saviour,
   Just because we need thee so:
None need thee more than we do;
   Nor are half so vile or low.
O bountiful salvation; O life eternal won;
O plentiful redemption; O blood of Mary's Son.

We come to thee, sweet Saviour,
   None will have us, Lord, but thee;
And we want none but Jesus,
   And his grace that makes us free.
      O bountiful salvation; etc.

Annus Sanctus.

We come to thee, sweet Saviour,
   With our broken faith again :
We know thou wilt forgive us,
   Nor upbraid us, nor complain.
      O bountiful salvation ; etc.

We come to thee, sweet Saviour,
   For to whom, Lord, can we go?
The words of life eternal
   From thy lips for ever flow.
      O bountiful salvation ; etc.

We come to thee, sweet Saviour,
   We have tried thee oft before ;
But now we come more wholly,
   With the heart to love thee more.
      O bountiful salvation ; etc.

We come to thee, sweet Saviour,
   And thou wilt not ask us why ;
We cannot live without thee,
   And still less without thee die.
O bountiful salvation ; O life eternal won ;
O plentiful redemption ; O blood of Mary's Son.
                              F. W. Faber.

Rest in the Sacred Heart.

O sacred Heart, all blissful light of heaven,
   Rapture of angels, beaming ever bright,
Ravishing joys in rich and radiant splendour,
   Flow from thy glory in torrents of delight.

O sacred Heart, O hope of sinner's sorrow,
   Rest of the weary, careworn and depressed ;
Sweetly lead home earth's lone estrangèd exiles,
   Where 'neath thy love we may lie down and rest.

O sacred Heart, thy light is softly rising
   O'er the dark night of England's cheerless gloom ;
Bright dawns the day of faith's undying glory,
   Sweetly thou seekest a loved but long-lost home.

The Sacred Humanity.

O sacred Heart, as strain of softest rapture,
  Sweet falls the music of that voice so blest:
'Come unto me all ye who mourn and labour;
  Come heavy laden, and I will give you rest.'
O sacred Heart, when shades of death are falling,
  Gather thy children 'neath the wings of love—
Hush us to rest in thine own gentle mercy—
  Bear troubled spirits to brighter realms above.
O sacred Heart, what bliss, what thrilling rapture
  E'er to rest near thee on thine own bright shore;
Ever to gaze upon thy beaming splendour,
  Never to part—to weep, to mourn no more.

F. Stanfield.

The Soul to her Beloved.

Jesu, end of my desires,
Unto whom my heart aspires,
Solace, sweetness, fount divine,
Loved by all this love of mine,
Take me in thine heart to rest;
Take me, Jesu, sweetest, best.

Come, I open thee the door;
Come, O Lord, I ask no more;
Ah, delay not, for I pine
To inclose thy heart in mine:
Here is thy repose and rest,
Come to it, O sweet soul-guest.

Wherefore wilt thou further go?
Wherefore stand outside me so?
Soul of my soul, come, abide
In my hard heart's flinty side:
Come herein; I give it thee,
Ever, ever thine to be.

Come, for ever shall it serve
Thy dear will with every nerve,

Till thou lift me to the height
Radiant with celestial light,
Where my grateful voice shall raise
Hymns to thee of endless praise.

J. C. Earle.

Confido et Conquiesco.

Fret not, poor soul, while doubt and fear
    Disturb thy breast;
The pitying angels, who can see
How vain thy wild regret must be,
    Say, 'Trust and rest.'

Plan not, nor scheme—but calmly wait;
    His choice is best:
While blind and erring is thy sight,
His wisdom sees and judges right;
    So trust and rest.

Strive not, nor struggle; thy poor might
    Can never wrest
The meanest thing to serve thy will;
All power is his alone : be still,
    And trust and rest.

Desire not; self-love is strong
    Within thy breast;
And yet, he loves thee better still,
So let him do his loving will—
    And trust and rest.

What dost thou fear? His wisdom reigns
    Supreme confessed :
His power is infinite; his love
Thy deepest, fondest dreams above—
    So trust and rest.

Adelaide A. Procter.

Index of First Lines.

Part II.

MODERN, ORIGINAL AND OTHER HYMNS.

NO.		PAGE
108.	A FIRE from heaven all-trembling came,	111
126.	A Message from the sacred Heart,	132
51.	A Stranger in the pale moonlight,	63
93.	All hail, dear Conqueror, all hail,	96
48.	All hail, ye wounds of Christ,	59
17.	Alleluia, Lord most holy,	24
2.	Ancient of days, thy throne on high,	4
19.	At hour of silent midnight,	26
82.	BEFORE the closing of the day,	88
85.	Before the closing of the day,	89
84.	Before the day's last moments fly,	89
40.	Behold and bless the solemn day,	52
55.	Bow down, my soul, for he hath bowed his head,	66
86.	Bringing life and peace and gladness,	90
35.	By the crib wherein reposing,	45
5.	CLOUDS of heaven, shower the Just One,	8
43.	Come, let us tell of him whose woes,	54
6.	Crown him with many crowns,	9
16.	DEAR Little One, how sweet thou art,	23
31.	Dear Saviour, when thy chosen three,	41
4.	Dread and strange the trumpet's tone,	7
68.	Drear is the night-fall,	79
13.	Dry your tears, ye silent mourners,	19
76.	ETERNAL source of light's clear stream,	85
107.	Eternal Spirit God supreme,	111

NO.		PAGE
71.	FINDING no place of rest,	81
118.	For this the wound, for this thy heart is riven,	124
103.	Fountain of love, thyself true God,	106
131.	Fret not, poor soul, while doubt and fear,	136
45.	Go forth, ye children of our God,	56
99.	God of life and light and motion,	102
106.	God the Father, whose relation,	110
56.	HAIL, Jesus, hail, who for my sake,	67
57.	Hail, Jesus, hail; who while they slay,	68
87.	Hail, mighty King, in risen strength victorious,	91
25.	Hail, to the ever precious Name,	34
54.	Hard is the painful wood, his bed of death,	65
10.	Hark, hark, my soul, angelic songs are swelling,	16
105.	Have mercy on us, God most high,	109
72.	Hear thy children, gentle Jesus,	82
73.	Hear thy children, gentlest Mother,	82
109.	Holy Ghost, come down upon thy children,	112
29.	Hushed is the starry night,	38
120.	I ARISE from dreams of time,	125
34.	I caused those infant tears to flow,	44
121.	I dwell a captive in this heart,	126
14.	I gaze out on the moon-lit earth,	20
112.	I was wandering and weary,	116
15.	In a silence deep at midnight,	21
69.	In that cold cave with spices sweet,	80
98.	In the brightness of the sunshine,	101
67.	In the light of all light excelling,	78
37.	In the Lord's atoning grief,	49
130.	JESU, end of my desires,	135
114.	Jesu, meek and lowly,	128
121.	Jesu, my Lord, my God, my all,	128
119.	Jesus is God; the solid earth,	124
33.	Jesus is the sweetest name,	43
64.	Jesus, O my Lord and God,	73
91.	Jesus, thy love was pleased to all,	95
26.	KING of Israel, Word incarnate,	35
61.	LAUD we Jesus, who did ease us,	71
89.	Lift up, ye princes of the sky,	93

Index of First Lines. 139

NO.		PAGE
94.	Lo, on Mount Olivet's fair height,	97
125.	Love, thou dost all excell,	131
75.	MAKER, by whose unuttered Word,	84
77.	Maker of light, most holy king,	85
92.	Mother of God, and Mother mine,	96
46.	My Jesus, say, what wretch has dared,	57
116.	NIGHT falls apace ; the shades grow long,	121
50.	Now are the days of humblest prayer,	62
80.	Now lowly sinks the fiery sun,	87
78.	O BLEST Creator of the light,	86
97.	O Christ, our glorious king,	100
74.	O Christ, thou brightness of the day,	83
59.	O Christians, ever bear in mind,	70
111.	O Heart of Jesus, heart of God,	115
110.	O Heart of Jesus, purest heart,	114
127.	O heaven's glorious King,	132
27.	O Jesus, Jesus, dearest Lord,	36
100.	O mighty Mother, why that light?	102
58.	O ruthless scourges, with what pain you tear,	69
129.	O sacred Heart, all-blissful light of heaven,	134
123.	O sacred Heart, our home lies deep in thee,	129
1.	O Wisdom that proceedest from,	3
36.	Oh, come and mourn with me awhile,	48
65.	Oh, come to the merciful Saviour that calls you,	75
23.	Oh, for the light of that fair star,	31
7.	Oh, how great shall be the fear,	11
28.	Oh, it is good for me to dwell in sweetness,	37
101.	Oh, may the Paraclete Divine his grace to us impart,	104
18.	Once to Bethlehem's lowly shepherds,	25
52.	POUR forth the wine-floods rich and dark,	64
11.	Primeval night had repossest,	18
90.	RISE, glorious Conqueror, rise,	94
3.	Rise, O Lord, in all thy glory,	5
24.	SLEEP, my Child, the Mother singeth,	33
124.	Souls of men, why will ye scatter,	130
66.	Starry hosts are gleaming,	77
20.	Stars of glory, shine more brightly,	27
47.	Steep is the hill and weary is the road,	58
113.	Sweet Jesus, thou a haven art,	117

Index of First Lines.

NO.		PAGE
70.	Sweet Saviour, bless us ere we go,	81
79.	THE blazing sun is well-nigh gone,	86
21.	The moon that now is shining,	28
38.	The olive-garden of Gethsemani,	49
39.	The purple shroud is stretched upon our altar,	50
96.	The Saviour is arisen,	99
102.	The wind rang out from depths of woods,	106
8.	The winepress, the winepress,	12
83.	Thee, God, before the close of light,	88
32.	There in the narrow manger, cold and bleak,	42
117.	There is an everlasting home,	123
22.	They leave the land of gems and gold,	31
44.	Thou, O my Jesus, thou wast pleased,	55
104.	Thou Paraclete, whom Jesus sent to me,	107
53.	Thousands have felt thy healing power,	65
30.	Three ancient men in Bethlehem's cave,	40
42.	To Christ, whose cross repaired our loss,	53
128.	WE come to thee, sweet Saviour,	133
12.	Welcome, that star in Judah's sky,	19
49.	What, O my people, have I done to thee?	61
41.	What tongue shall give thee thanks, in fitting strains repeat?	52
115.	What wouldst thou have, O soul?	119
60.	When Christ let fall that sanguine shower,	70
81.	While now the flaming sun declines,	88
62.	Who untiedst when thou diedst,	72
88.	Why is thy face so lit with smiles?	92
9.	Woe is the day of ire,	13
95.	Woeful Mary, cease from sighing,	98
63.	YE priestly hands, which on the cruel cross,	72

APPENDIX.

EARLIER VERSIONS.

Appendix.

PRIMER, 1604.

Advent.

Conditor alme siderum.

O BRIGHT Creator of the stars,
Of faithful men the lasting light,
Hear, Christ, Redeemer of us all,
The prayers of each plaining wight.
 Who grieving that, by force of death,
Destruction did the world betide,
From languishing thou didst it free,
The guilty's cure thou didst provide.
 When eventide of the world drew on,
As bridegrooms from their chambers go,
Thy Virgin Mother's worthy womb
In seemly wise thou partest fro.
 Unto whose mighty strength and power
The knees do bow and bend of all,
Both in the heaven and in the earth,
As ready bound unto thy call.
 O holy Lord, we thee beseech,
When of the world thou shalt be judge,
To save us then, and from the dart
Of our false foe to send refuge.
 Praise, honour, power and glory eke,
To God, the Father and the Son
And to the holy Comforter,
From age to age be ever done.

Christmas.

Christe, Redemptor omnium.

O Christ, Redeemer of us all,
And of the Father only Son,
Thy birth alone unspeakably
Before beginning was begun.

Appendix.

PRIMER, 1619.

Advent.
Conditor alme siderum.

BENIGN Creator of the stars,
Eternal light of faithful eyes,
Christ, whose redemption none debars,
Do not our humble prayers despise.
   Who for the state of mankind grieved,
That it by death destroyed should be,
Hast the diseased world relieved,
And given the guilty remedy.
   When the evening of the world drew near,
Thou as a bridegroom deigndst to come
Out of thy wedding chamber dear,
Thy Virgin Mother's purest womb.
   To the strong force of whose high reign,
All knees are bowed with gesture low;
Creatures, which earth or heaven contain,
With reverence their subjection show.
   O holy Lord, we thee desire,
Whom we expect to judge all faults,
Preserve us as the times require,
From our deceitful foe's assaults.
   Praise, honour, strength and glory great
To God, the Father and the Son,
And to the holy Paraclete,
Whilst time lasts and when time is done.

Christmas.
Christe, Redemptor omnium.

Christ, whose redemption all doth free,
Son of the Father, who alone,
Before the world began to be,
Didst spring from him by means unknown.

The Father's light and brightness both,
The lasting hope thou art of all ;
Attend unto thy servants' plaints
Throughout the earth on thee that call.
    Be mindful, author of our health,
That thou sometime didst take on thee,
Of a pure Virgin being born,
The form of our humanity.
    And so this day doth witness well,
By yearly course as it doth pass,
That only from thy Father's seat,
This world to save thy coming was.
    This day the heaven, the earth and sea,
This day within them all that live,
As cause that thou to us art come,
With songs rejoice and praises give.
    And we which thy most holy blood
Did freely to redemption bring,
In honour of thy day of birth,
A new song unto thee do sing.
    Glory be unto thee, O Lord,
The which the Blessed Virgin bore,
With the Father and Holy Ghost,
From this time forth for evermore.

Epiphany.
Hostis Herodes impie.

That Christ is come why dost thou dread,
O Herod, thou ungodly foe?
He doth not earthly kingdoms reave
That heavenly kingdoms doth bestow.
    The sages three did follow on,
The star their guide that they did see,
By light whereof true light they sought,
Confessing God by presents three.
    The Lamb of bliss hath touched now
The running streams so clearly dight ;
The sins he not on us imposed,
By washing he defaced quite.
    A new and mighty power it was,
In vessels water waxed red ;
And wine commanded to be filled,
From former kind the water fled.

Primer, 1619.

Thou his clear brightness, thou his light,
Thou everlasting hope of all,
Observe the prayers which in thy sight
Thy servants in the world let fall.
  O dearest Saviour, bear in mind,
That of our body, thou a Child
Did whilome take the natural kind,
Born of the Virgin undefiled.
  Thus much this present day makes known,
Passing the circuit of the year,
That thou from thy high Father's throne,
The world's sole safety didst appear.
  The highest heaven, the earth and seas,
And all that is within them found,
Because he sent thee us to ease,
With mirthful songs his praise resound.
  We also, who redeemed are
With thy pure blood from sinful state,
For this thy birthday will prepare
New hymns, this feast to celebrate.
  Glory, O Lord, be given to thee,
Whom the unspotted Virgin bore;
And glory to the Father be,
And Holy Ghost for evermore.

Epiphany.
Hostis Herodes impie.

O Herod, wicked enemy,
Why should Christ's coming thee afright?
He takes no mortal sovereignty,
Who can to heavenly realms invite.
  The sages went, even as their sight
Could note the star to go before,
They strive to find the light by light,
And him as God with gifts adore.
  The baptism of the river clear
Was hallowed by the heavenly Lamb;
He washing us, away did bear
Our sins, as without sin he came.
  He shows new power in actions strange,
The pitchers' waters ruddy grow;
That element doth nature change
When forth in wine he bids it flow.

Glory be unto thee, O Lord,
Which didst appear this present day,
With the Father and Holy Ghost,
Both now and to endure for aye.

Lent.
Audi, benigne Conditor.

O thou Creator most benign,
Unto the prayers bend thine ears,
Which in this fast of forty days
We unto thee pour forth with tears.
   O kindly searcher of the hearts,
Thou knowst the weakness of our strength;
Yield unto those that turn to thee
Thy grace of pardon at the length.
   We sinned have exceedingly,
Yet pardon those their faults confess;
And for the glory of thy name,
Unto the sick vouchsafe redress.
   As outwardly the body pines,
By inward abstinence provide,
The sober mind be so restrained,
That there no blots of sin abide.
   Grant that, O blessed Trinity,
Vouchsafe one only Unity,
The duties of this fasting may
Unto thy servants fruitful be.

Passion-tide.
Vexilla regis prodeunt.

The banners of the king come forth,
The mystery of the cross displayed,
Whereon in flesh, as on a tree,
He hanged was that flesh hath made.
   And when with sharp and piercing spear
Thereon his body wounded was,
Then that he might us wash from sin,
From him did blood and water pass.
   What faithful David spake in verse,
The same was now fulfilled plain,
How God, amidst the race of men,
Should on a tree possess his reign.

Glory, O Lord, be given to thee,
Who has appeared upon this day,
And glory to the Father be
And to the Holy Ghost for aye.

Lent.
Audi, benigne Conditor.

O merciful Creator, hear
Our prayers to thee devoutly bent,
Which we pour forth with many a tear
In this most holy fast of Lent.
   Thou mildest searcher of each heart,
Who knowst the weakness of our strength,
To us forgiving grace impart,
Since we return to thee at length.
   Much have we sinned to our shame;
But spare us who our sins confess;
And for the glory of thy name,
To our sick souls afford redress.
   Grant that the flesh may so be pined,
By means of outward abstinence,
As that the sober watchful mind
May fast from spots of all offence.
   Grant this, O blessed Trinity;
Pure Unity, to this incline;
That the effects of fast may be
A fruitful recompense for thine.

Passion-tide.
Vexilla regis prodeunt.

Now forth the kingly banners go,
Now shines the cross' mystery;
He on this gibbet suffers woe
In flesh, who caused all flesh to be.
   Here also he received a wound
By sharpness of a cruel spear,
Whence blood and watery streams abound,
That he from crime might wash us clear.
   And now those things fulfilled be,
Which David sang in faithful strains;
Saying, that on the holy tree
God over all the nations reigns.

O thou right fair and comely tree,
Whose worthy chosen stock was such
As kingly purple did adorn,
And did so holy members touch.
 Blest be the tree upon whose boughs
This world's value did depend;
His body made the price so just;
To free from hell it did extend.
 All hail, O cross, our special hope
Now at this present passion time;
Uprightness in the good increase,
And quit the guilty of their crime.
 O God, the supreme Trinity,
Let thee each ghost with praise adore,
Whom by thy cross' sign thou savst,
Direct and govern ever more.

Easter.
Ad cœnam Agni providi.

At supper of the Lamb prepared,
And with white vestures pure and chaste,
To Christ our prince let us sing praise,
The Red Seas being overpast.
 Whose corpse most holy did remain,
In torture on the cross distrest,
By tasting of his blood so red,
Our life alone in God doth rest.
 Protected on the paschal eve
From that same angel which destroys,
And we from Pharao freed are
Of thraldom that the most annoys.
 Our paschal Christ is now become
The Lamb he was and sacrificed;
His flesh the bread both sweet and pure,
That for the offering hath sufficed.
 O worthy sacrifice and true,
Which didst the force of hell restrain,
And captive people didst redeem,
And yield rewards of life again.
 Forth of his tomb when Christ arose,
As conqueror from hell he came,
To bands he did the tyrant bring,
And heaven's open passage frame.

Tree with clear light and beauty deckt,
Which drest with royal purple is,
Whose worthy stock God did select,
Such holy limbs to touch and kiss.
   Blest, on whose arms he hung that paid
The ransom which the world revived,
The balance which his body weighed,
And hell of all his prey deprived.
   Hail cross, sole hope of our release
Now in this doleful passion time;
Justice in godly souls increase,
And free the guilty from their crime.
   Be thou, O God, high Trinity,
By every spirit glorified,
Those, whom the cross' mystery
Hath saved, do thou for ever guide.

Easter.

Ad cænam Agni providi.

Now, at the supper of the Lamb,
Watchful and clad in garments white,
Let us, who through the Red Sea came,
To Christ our Lord sweet hymns indite.
   Whose holy body for our food
Was on the cross' altar broiled,
By tasting of whose rosy blood
We lead to God a life unsoiled.

Now Christ our pasch is offered,
The Lamb that immolated dies;
His flesh the pure unleavened bread,
Is made a perfect sacrifice.
   O host right worthily esteemed,
Which the infernal bars down throws,
Which hath the imprisoned souls redeemed,
And the rewards of life bestows.

We pray thee, author of us all,
During this joyful Eastertide,
Thou wilt vouchsafe from brunt of death
Thy people's safety to provide.
   All glory be to thee, O Lord,
Which from the death didst rise again,
With the Father and Holy Ghost,
That world without end may remain.

Ascension.
Jesu, nostra redemptio.

O our redemption, Jesu Christ,
Our love and our desire always;
O. God, that every thing didst make,
And Man became in later days.
   What clemency subdued thee so,
That thou wouldst take our sins on thee;
For us to suffer cruel death,
Thereby from death to set us free?
   And piercing through the gates of hell,
Thine to redeem that were distrest,
As conqueror with triumph great,
On thy Father's right hand to rest.
   Let pity of itself thee urge,
That thou our evils do subdue,
And sparing us with filled desire,
Of thy sweet face to take the view.
   Our joy therefore vouchsafe to be,
Which art the hire that we attend,
Let all our glory rest in thee,
And that it never have an end.

Whit Sunday.
Veni, creator Spiritus.

Come, Holy Ghost, that us hath made,
Thy servants' minds vouchsafe to see,
And fill the hearts with heavenly grace,
Which have created been by thee.
   Thou that the Comforter art high,
The gift of God excelling all,
The well of life, the fire and love,
The unction which we ghostly call.

We pray thee who hast framed all,
Now in this joyful paschal time,
Defend thy people lest they fall
Into some deadly harm or crime.
    Glory, O Lord, be given to thee,
Whom from the dead thyself could raise ;
And glory to the Father be
And Holy Ghost, beyond all days.

Ascension.
Jesu, nostra redemptio.

O Jesu, who our souls dost save,
On whom our love and hopes depend,
God, from whom all things being have,
Man, when the world drew to an end.
    What clemency thee vanquished so,
Upon thee our foul crimes to take ;
And cruel death to undergo,
That thou from death us free mightst make?
    Thou diving to the depths of hell,
And thence thy captives having gained,
Dost at thy Father's right hand dwell,
Thy noble triumph thus obtained.
    Let thine own goodness so thee bend,
That thou our sins mayst put to flight ;
Spare us, and as our wishes tend,
Oh, satisfy us with thy sight.
    Mayst thou our joyful pleasure be,
Who shalt be our expected gain ;
And let our glory be in thee,
While any ages shall remain.

Whit Sunday.
Veni, creator Spiritus.

Creator Holy Ghost, descend,
Visit our minds with thy bright flame,
And thy celestial grace extend,
To fill the hearts which thou didst frame.
    Who Paraclete art said to be,
Gift, which the highest God bestows,
Fountain of life, fire, charity,
Ointment, whence ghostly blessing flows.

Thou art in gifts full sevenfold,
The finger eke of God's right hand ;
·Thou art thy Father's promised plight,
By thee to speak we understand.
　Our senses with thy light enflame,
Thy love into our hearts distil,
Restore our bodies' strength decayed,
By virtue that endureth still.
　Right far from us repel our foe,
Us with thy present peace endue ;
So that thyself become our guide,
Each noisome thing we may eschew.
　The Father let us know by thee,
The Son vouchsafe we likewise know,
And thee the Spirit from them both,
And that our faith be ever so.
　To God the Father glory be,
And to the Son that rose again,
As also to the Comforter,
All endless ages to remain.

Trinity Sunday.
O Lux beata Trinitas.

O blessed Light, O Trinity,
O Unity that is the chief,
Since now the fiery sun retires,
Thy light let be our hearts' relief.
　To thee at morn in verse of praise,
To thee at evening let us pray ;
Our humble glorifying thee,
Vouchsafe it may thee praise for aye.
　Glory to God the Father be,
And so unto his only Son,
And glory to the Holy Ghost,
Both now and evermore be done.

Corpus Christi.
Pange lingua gloriosi corporis.

Of Christ, his body glorious,
Sing my tongue the mystery ;
And also of his precious blood,
Which the world's price to be,

Thy sevenfold grace thou down dost send,
Of God's right hand thou finger art;
Thou by the Father promised,
Unto our mouths dost speech impart.
 In our dull senses kindle light,
Infuse thy love into our hearts,
Confirming with perpetual might
The infirmites of fleshly parts.
 Far from our dwelling drive our foe,
And quickly peace unto us bring;
Be thou our guide before to go,
That we may shun each hurtful thing.
 Be pleased to instruct our mind,
To know the Father and the Son;
Thee Spirit, who them both doth bind,
Let us believe while ages run.
 To God the Father glory great,
And to the Son who from the dead
Arose, and to the Paraclete,
Beyond all time imagined.

Trinity Sunday.
O Lux beata Trinitas.

O Trinity, O blessed Light,
O Unity most principal,
The fiery sun now leaves our sight,
Cause in our hearts thy beams to fall.
 Let us with songs of praise divine
At morn and evening thee implore,
And let our glory bowed to thine
Thee glorify for evermore.
 To God the Father glory great,
And glory to his only Son,
And to the holy Paraclete,
Both now and still whilst ages run.

Corpus Christi.
Pange lingua gloriosi corporis.

Sing thou my tongue with accent clear
The glorious body's mystery,
And of those drops of blood so dear,
By which he set the lost world free,

The king of nations did shed forth,
Fruit of noble womb was he.
  On us bestowed and for us born
Of a Maid untouched indeed,
Conversant upon the earth,
Sowing of his word the seed,
And of his time of being here,
Strangely he the end decreed.
  The night he with his brethren sate,
And his supper last did make,
In full observance of the law,
Law assigned meats did take,
Himself food to the apostles twelve,
With his hands he did betake.
  The Word now being flesh become,
So very bread flesh by the word,
And wine the blood of Christ is made,
Though our sense it not afford,
But this in heart sincere to fix
Faith sufficeth to accord.
  Wherefore a sacrament so great
Humbly prostrate we adore,
And unto rites begun of late,
Laws must yield that were before,
And where our sense is seen to fail,
There must faith supply restore.
  Unto the Father and the Son,
Joy and praise ascribed be,
And saving health, honour and power,
As also benedicite ;
And to him that from both proceeds,
Praises like acknowledge we.

Transfiguration.
Quicunque Christum quæritis.

Whoso you be that Christ do seek,
Your eyes aloft lift up and see,
Where well you may the sign perceive
Of glory that must lasting be.
  A sight we see of clearness great,
The which no limits may include;
High, lofty and without all end,
More old than heaven and chaos rude.

Whom the most noble womb did bear,
To whom all nations subject be.
  He given for us, born for our sakes,
A pure Maid for his Mother chose;
He in the world his dwelling makes,
And here his seed of doctrine sows;
His stay, when he the earth forsakes,
He doth with wondrous order close.
  At his last supper, made by night,
He with his brethren takes his seat,
And having kept the ancient rite,
Using the law's prescribed meat,
His twelve disciples doth invite,
From his own hands, himself to eat.
  The Word made flesh to words imparts
Such strength, that bread his flesh is made;
He wine into his blood converts,
And if our sense here fail and fade,
To satisfy religious hearts,
Faith only can the truth persuade.
  Then to this sacrament so high,
Low reverence let us now direct;
Old rites must yield in dignity
To this, with such great graces deckt;
And faith with all, those wants supply
Wherein the senses feel defect.
  To the Father and the Son we bring
Praises, and joyful songs we frame;
Their honour, health and strength we sing,
And ever bless their holy name;
And he who from them both doth spring
Must have like praise and equal fame.

Transfiguration.

Quicunque Christum quæritis.

All you that seek Christ, let your sight
Up to the height directed be,
For there you may the sign most bright
Of everlasting glory see.
  A radiant light we there behold,
Endless, unbounded, lofty, high;
Than heaven, or that rude heap more old,
Wherein the world confused did lie.

Lo, this of Gentiles is the king,
And of the Jews the king indeed,
First promised to Abraham
And ever after to his seed.
 By words and signs him prophets show,
His Father doth him witness bear,
And in him bids us to believe,
And to his words incline our ear.
 All glory be to thee, O Lord,
Which didst appear as on this day,
With the Father and Holy Ghost,
To last for ever and for aye.

Primer, 1619.

The Gentiles this great prince embrace,
The Jews obey this king's command,
Promised to Abraham and his race
A blessing, while the world shall stand.
　By mouths of prophets free from lies,
Who seal the witness which they bear,
His Father bidding, testifies
That we should him believe and hear.
　Glory, O Lord, be given to thee,
Who hast appeared upon this day;
And glory to the Father be,
And to the Holy Ghost for aye.

Appendix.

PRIMER, 1685.

Advent.
Creator alme siderum.

BRIGHT Builder of the heavenly poles,
Eternal light of faithful souls,
Jesu, Redeemer of mankind,
Our humble prayers vouchsafe to mind.

Who, lest the fraud of hell's black king
Should all men to destruction bring,
Didst, by a strong impulse of love,
The fainting world's physician prove.

Who, from a sacred Virgin's womb,
Didst an unspotted victim come
Unto the cross, to cleanse the sin
The wretched world was plunged in.

The sound of whose high power and name
No sooner any voice can frame,
But all in heaven, and those that be
In hell, bow down with trembling knee.

Thee Christ, who at the latter day
Shalt be our judge, we humbly pray,
Such arms of heavenly grace to send,
As from our foes may us defend.

Be glory given and honour done,
To God the Father and the Son
And to the Holy Ghost on high,
From age to age eternally.

Christmas.
Jesu, Redemptor omnium.

Jesu, the ransomer of man,
Who, ere created light began,
Didst from the sovereign Father spring,
His heavenly glory equalling.

Appendix.

PRIMER, 1706.

Advent.

Creator alme siderum.

CREATOR of the stars above,
The light by which thy faithful move,
The righteous cause, and humble vows
Of those whom you redeemed, espouse,
    Who, lest the specious wiles of hell
Should o'er the yielding world prevail,
Compelled by love's enforced decree
Do make yourself its remedy.
    Your earthly sufferings now begin
To save the world involved in sin;
And from the Virgin's sacred womb
Continue to the cross and tomb.
    The voice no sooner sounds the fame
Of the almighty Jesus' name,
But heaven and hell at once agree
And jointly bend their trembling knee.
    Vouchsafe, O sovereign judge, we pray,
That at the last accounting day,
Our foe may not prevail, or we
Give up the souls were made for thee.
    May each succeeding age proclaim
Thy glory and eternal fame;
And sing with the celestial host
The Father, Son and Holy Ghost.

Christmas.

Jesu, Redemptor omnium.

O Christ, the world's redemption,
Co-partner of your Father's throne,
Whose equal unbeginning light
With lustre filled primeval night.

Thou light and splendour of God's mind,
The eternal hope of humankind,
Regard the prayers, which from our sphere
Thy servants pour into thine ear.
   Divine Creator, bear in mind
That thou of our corporeal kind
The form assumedst heretofore,
When thee a sacred Virgin bore.
   This present day does witness bear,
Sliding in the circle of the year,
That thou the world's relief alone
Descendedst from thy Father's throne.
   Thee the bright stars, the seas, the land,
Thee all things under heaven contained,
In a new canticle do bless,
As author of our sweet redress.
   And we, who have been washed o'er
With streams of thy most sacred gore,
The tribute of an hymn do pay
In honour of thy natal day.
   To Jesus, from a Virgin sprung,
Be glory given and praises sung;
The like to God the Father be,
And Holy Ghost eternally.

Epiphany.
Crudelis Herodes, Deum.

Most cruel Herod, whence does spring
Thy fear, lest Christ should come as king?
He seizes not on realms below,
Who realms celestial does bestow.
   The sages followed the bright
Preceding star they had in sight;
By light to find our light they sought;
They God confess, by gifts they brought.
   The heavenly Lamb, though spotless, took
The baptism of a crystal brook;
By washing us he cleansed the blot
Of sin, which he contracted not.
   A novel kind of power he shows,
Ruddy the pitchers' water grows,
Which bid by him to send forth wine,
The water changed its origin.

Reflection of your Father's rays,
The hope and end of all our ways,
With gracious ear our vows attend,
Whilst round the world our prayers ascend.
  Remember you, O gracious Lord,
The eternal God's co-equal Word,
In Virgin's womb a creature made,
Our nature wore for nature's aid.
  Witness this joyful noon of night,
When you alone, our endless light,
Descended from your Father's throne,
Brought down the world's redemption.
  For this glad earth erects her head,
The waters purl and wash their bed,
The joyful spheres in music roll,
Heaven and earth your birth extol.
  Whilst these contrive new ways to sing,
New life restored, the new born king;
We ransomed, most of all rejoice
With double hymns of heart and voice.
  May age to age for ever sing
The Virgin's Son and angels' king;
And praise with the celestial host
The Father, Son and Holy Ghost.

Epiphany.
Crudelis Herodes, Deum.

Why, Herod, dost thou fear in vain,
That Christ should take thy place and reign?
He seeks not here an earthly throne
Who comes to make all heaven our own.
  Behold, a star descends to-day,
And leads the sages on their way;
To carry their mysterious load
By light, to light's own fountain, God.
  To-day the Lamb descends, and laves
His heavenly fleece in Jordan's waves;
To wash with a celestial dew
The stains of sin he never knew.
  And since the hardened Jews mistook
Both Bethlem's star and Jordan's brook,
The waters to reproach their sin
At Cana blush, and turn to wine.

To thee be glory, Christ, who hast
Thy beams upon the Gentiles cast;
The like unto the Father be,
And Holy Ghost eternally.

Lent.
Audi, benigne Conditor.

Benign Creator, lend thine ears
To prayers accompanied with tears,
To celebrate this sacred fast,
For forty days ordained to last.
 Clear searcher of all hearts, 'tis known
To thee how weak our strength is grown;
The favour of remission deign
To such as turn to thee again.
 We have offended in excess,
Yet pardon who their faults confess;
For thy name's glory do not stick
To give a cordial to the sick.
 Grant that our flesh by abstinence
May so be tamed, that from offence
Our souls may fast; nor e'er let in
The flood that's apt to nourish sin.
 O blessed Trinity, afford,
O single Unity, accord,
The duties of this fast to be
Fruitful to those rely on thee.

Passion-tide.
Vexilla regis prodeunt.

Abroad the regal banners fly,
Now shines the cross' mystery;
Upon it life did death endure,
And yet by death did life procure.
 Who, wounded with a direful spear,
Did, purposely to wash us clear
From stain of sin, pour out a flood
Of precious water mixed with blood.
 Fully accomplished are the things
David in faithful metre sings,
Where he to nations does attest,
God on a tree his reign possest.

Glory to thee, O Christ, whose rays,
Illustrated the Gentiles' ways;
With equal praises still repeat
The Father and the Paraclete.

Lent.
Audi, benigne Conditor.

Hear, O thou bounteous Maker, hear,
Our humble vows with gracious ear;
Turn not thy saving face away,
Whilst on this solemn fast we pray.
 Great searcher of our hearts, to thee
We here deplore our misery;
Behold, we to thy mercies fly,
Do thou thy healing grace apply.
 Great are our sins, O Lord, but thou
Canst pardon more than we can do;
May our defects, like shadows, raise
The beauty and the life of grace.
 May fasts extinguish in our will
The fuel and desire of ill,
That thus our souls, from fetters free,
May only thirst and follow thee.
 Grant, O most sacred Trinity,
One undivided Unity,
That abstinence may here improve
Our claim to reign with thee above.

Passion-tide.
Vexilla regis prodeunt.

Behold the royal ensigns fly,
The cross' shining mystery,
Where life itself gave up its breath,
And Christ by dying conquered death.
 The audacious steel let out a flood
Of water mixed with saving blood;
Whilst man's redemption, with the tide,
Came rushing from the Saviour's side.
 What David's faithful number told,
Succeeding nations thus unfold;
That God should rule from main to main,
And wood, not steel, assert his reign.

O lovely and refulgent tree,
Adorned with purpled majesty,
Called from a worthy stock to bear
Those limbs which sanctified were.

Blest tree, whose happy branches bore
The wealth that did the world restore;
The beam that did that body weigh
Which raised up hell's expected prey.

Hail cross, of hopes the most sublime,
Now in this mournful passiontime;
Improve religious souls in grace,
The sins of criminals efface.

Blest Trinity, salvation's spring,
May every soul thy praises sing;
To those thou grantest conquest by
The holy cross, rewards apply.

Easter.
Ad regias Agni dapes.

At the Lamb's regal banquet, where
We must in candid robes appear,
After the Red Sea past, let's sing
A hymn of praise to Christ our king.

Whose charity divinely good,
Makes tender of his sacred blood,
While love doth sacrifice, as priest,
The body whereon souls do feast.

The striking angel dreads the gore
He sprinkled finds about the door;
The yielding sea divides his waves,
The foes there meet their liquid graves.

Now Christ our pasch we rightly name,
Our paschal victim is the same;
Who is to souls that purged be,
Pure azyme of sincerity.

O heavenly sacrifice, by whom
The depths of hell are overcome,
And death's strong bonds dissolved, for which
Life's crown his temples doth enrich.

Christ, victor o'er infernal foes,
His conquered trophies does expose,
And having heaven unlocked, enslaves
The king that rules hell's darksome caves.

Hail, beauteous tree, whose branches wore
The purple of his royal gore ;
Preferred to bear those arms, from whence
Spring all our blessing and defence.
    On thee, as in the world's great scales,
The ransom of the world prevails ;
Our sin, though great, his pains outweigh,
And rescue hell's expected prey.
    All hail, O happy mournful tree,
Our hope with Christ is nailed on thee ;
Grant to the just increase of grace,
And mediate, for the sinner, peace.
    Blest Trinity, to thee we sing,
From whom, above, all graces spring ;
Thy crowns above on us bestow
Who conquer by the cross below.

Easter.
Ad regias Agni dapes.

From purple seas and land of toil
We come to feed on Egypt's spoil ;
May whitest robes our souls prepare
To meet the Christian passover.
    Christ's love the priestly function played,
The victim on the altar laid ;
His blood, inflamed with love for man,
At every saving channel ran.
    The wasting angel passes o'er
The posts distained with sacred gore ;
The yielding sea divides its waves,
Egyptians float in liquid graves.
    Now Christ becomes our heavenly fare,
Our sacrifice and passover ;
By him, the pure unleavened bread,
The pure and faithful minds are fed.
    O true celestial sacrifice,
By whom hell's slaves from death arise ;
By thee death's adamantine laws
Submit, and life regains its cause.
    Hence dost thou, crowned with laurels, rise
And leadst thy triumph through the skies ;
Loaded with spoils each axle reels,
And hell and death attend the wheels.

That, Jesu, thou to souls mayst be
A paschal joy eternally,
Free from the horrid death of sin
Us, who regenerate have been.
   Be God the Father glorified,
With Christ his Son, who for us died
And rose again ; so likewise be
The Holy Ghost eternally.

Ascension.
Salutis humanæ Sator.

Jesu, who man's Redeemer art,
The solace of each godly heart,
The ransomed world's great architect,
Chaste light of souls which thee affect.
   What mercy conquered thee, my God,
That thou wouldst bear our sinful load?
And innocent, wouldst death endure,
That us from death thou mightst secure?
   Thou breakst through hell, where captives pent
Thou freest from their imprisonment;
And with a noble triumph graced,
Art on the Father's right hand placed.
   Thee let commiseration press,
To give our damages redress;
And by fruition of thy sight,
To enrich us with a blessed light.
   Thou, guide to heaven and path to rest,
Be thou the scope of every breast;
Be thou the comfort of our tears,
Our sweet reward above the spheres.

Whit Sunday.
Veni, creator Spiritus.

Come, Creator, Spirit divine,
Visit now the souls of thine,
Fill with grace distilled from heaven,
Hearts to which thou life hast given.
   Whom the Comforter we call,
Gift of God transcending all,
Living spring, fire, fervent love,
Ghostly unction from above.

From death of sin, O Jesus, free
Them that are born again to thee;
Be thou alone our chosen guest,
And everlasting paschal feast.
 May endless worlds the glories tell
Of Christ, who vanquished death and hell;
And one eternal praise repeat
The Father and the Paraclete.

Ascension.
Salutis humanæ Sator.

O Christ, the Saviour of mankind,
The light and comfort of the mind,
Creator of this earthly frame,
Thy lovers' chaste endearing flame.
 What strange excess of clemency
Prevailed so far with guiltless thee,
That thou the sinners load shouldst bear
And die, to pay his forfeiture?
 Thou laidst the dead's black dungeon ope,
To loose their chains and crown their hope;
And now resumst thy conquering throne,
Reared on the spoils and trophies won.
 With equal clemency repair
The failings of our exile here;
That we with joy may end our race,
And see thy glory face to face.
 Thou, Lord, the truth, the life and way,
Preserve us, lest our hearts should stray;
And grant our eyes one day to see
The sweet reward of life in thee.

Whit Sunday.
Veni, creator Spiritus.

Creator Spirit, by whose aid
The world's foundations first were laid,
Come, visit every pious mind;
Come, pour thy joys on human kind,
From sin and sorrow set us free,
And make thy temples worthy thee.
 O Source of uncreated light,
The Father's promised Paraclete,

Sevenfold grace thou dost impart,
And God's right hand finger art;
Thou the Father's promise, which
Tongues with language doth enrich.
 Kindle light in every sense,
Love into our hearts dispense,
Strengthen what in flesh is frail,
With a virtue cannot fail.
 Drive away our mortal foe,
Peace upon us soon bestow,
As a guide before us shine,
That all vice we may decline.
 By thee may it so be done,
That we Father know and Son;
And in thee believe that dost
Flow from both, the Holy Ghost.
 Glorious may the Father reign,
And the Son, who rose again;
So the holy Paraclete,
During ages infinite.

Trinity Sunday.

Jam sol recedit igneus.

Now doth the fiery sun retire;
Eternal Unity most bright
And blessed Trinity, inspire
Our hearts with a celestial light.
 Thee, in the morn and close of day,
We praise in verse, with chaste desires;
Vouchsafe that we thy suppliants may
Praise thee among the heavenly quires.

Thrice holy fount, thrice holy fire,
Our hearts with heavenly love inspire;
Come, and thy sacred unction bring
To sanctify us while we sing.
 Plenteous of grace, descend from high,
Rich in thy sevenfold energy;
Thou strength of his almighty hand,
Whose power does heaven and earth command,
Proceeding Spirit, our defence,
Who dost the gifts of tongues dispense
And crown thy gift with eloquence,
 Refine and purge our earthly parts,
But oh, inflame and fire our hearts;
Our frailties help, our vice control,
Submit the senses to the soul;
And when rebellious they are grown,
Then lay thy hand and hold them down.
 Chase from our minds the infernal foe,
And peace, the fruit of love, bestow;
And lest our feet should step astray,
Protect and guide us in the way.
 Make us eternal truths receive,
And practise all that we believe:
Give us thyself, that we may see
The Father and the Son by thee.
 Immortal honour, endless fame
Attend the Almighty Father's name;
The Saviour Son be glorified,
Who for lost man's redemption died;
And equal adoration be,
Eternal Paraclete, to thee.

Trinity Sunday.

Jam sol recedit igneus.

The fiery sun now rolls away,
And hastens to the close of day;
Thy brightest beams, O Lord, impart,
And rise in our benighted heart.
 To us the praises of thy name
Are morning song and evening theme;
So may we sing ourselves to rest
Amidst the music of the blest.

To God the Father and the Son
And to the Holy Ghost in heaven,
As hitherto it hath been done,
Let glory evermore be given.

Corpus Christi.
Pange lingua gloriosi corporis.

Sing, O my tongue, devoutly sing,
The glorious body's mystery;
And of that precious blood the king
Of nations poured forth, to free
The world from a disastrous doom,
O blessed fruit of noblest womb.
 On us bestowed, for us by birth
He from a Virgin did proceed,
And being conversant on earth,
Till he had sown the gospel's seed,
The time of his prolonged stay
He closed in an admired way.
 He, on the final supper night
Among his brethren taking seat,
And well observing the ancient rite,
Touching the law's prescribed meat,
Gave to the twelve, his chosen band,
Himself for food, with his proper hand.
 The incarnate Word, by words he said,
Turned into flesh substantial bread;
And wine the blood of Christ was made,
Though sense found nothing altered;
This to confirm in hearts sincere,
There needs no more, if faith be there.
 To this great sacrament, therefore,
Let's give the prostrate worship due;
And may the ancient rite no more
Take place, but yield it to the new;
Let faith in Jesus Christ supply
The senses' insufficiency.
 To Father and the Son let's bring
Triumphant praises; let's aspire
Their honour, power and bliss to sing,
While benedictions fill the choir:
To him that from them both is sprung,
Let equal praise come from our tongue.

Primer, 1706.

To God, the Father and the Son
And Holy Spirit, Three in One,
Be endless glory, as before
The world began, so evermore.

Corpus Christi.
Pange lingua gloriosi corporis.

Sing, O my tongue, adore and praise
The depth of God's mysterious ways;
How Christ, the Gentiles' king, bestowed
His flesh, concealed in human food;
And left mankind the blood, that paid
The ransom of the souls he made.

Born from above and born for man,
From Virgin's womb his life began;
He lived on earth and preached to sow
The seeds of heavenly truth below;
Then sealed his mission from above,
With strange effects of power and love.

'Twas on that evening, when the last
And most mysterious supper past,
When Christ with his disciples sat
To close the law with legal meat,
And with his hands himself bestowed,
The Christian's food and Lamb of God.

The Word made flesh, for love of man,
With words of bread made flesh again;
Turned wine to blood unseen by sense,
By virtue of omnipotence;
And here the faithful rest secure,
Whilst God can vouch and faith ensure.

To this mysterious table now
Our knees, our hearts and sense we bow;
Let ancient rites resign their place
To nobler elements of grace;
And faith for all defects supply,
Whilst sense is lost in mystery.

To God the Father, born of none,
To Christ his co-eternal Son,
And Holy Ghost, whose equal rays
From both proceed, one equal praise;
One honour, jubilee and fame
For ever bless thy glorious name.

Transfiguration.
Quicunque Christum quæritis.

1685. All that seek Christ, your eyes erect,
On Thabor's mount your sight reflect;
For there you may behold a sign
Of glory, which shall ever shine.
    We there a radiant object see
Which cannot circumscribed be,
Endless, sublime, existing e'er
Or heaven, or chaos framed were.
    This is the king whose sovereign sway
The Gentiles and the Jews obey;
Promised to Abraham and his race
A grant which time shall not deface.
    Him do the prophets' mouths display
Who seal the truth of what they say;
His Father too doth witness give,
Bidding us hear him and believe.
    May none thy glory, Christ, conceal,
Who dost thyself to babes reveal;
The like unto the Father be,
And Holy Ghost eternally.

1706. O all who seek with Christ to rise,
To Thabor's mount erect your eyes;
And see how Christ in glorious rays
The majesty of God displays.
    Behold a sun more old than night,
A blaze of uncreated light,
So high, so deep and vast of space
It knows no bounds of time or place.
    'Tis he, the king, whose sovereign sway
The Jews and Gentiles both obey,
The promised ruler heaven decreed
For Abraham and his endless seed.
    In him the law and prophets join;
His truths they both attest and sign;
Him God, from his paternal throne,
Commands the world to hear and own.
    Glory to Christ, whose light displays
To little ones his saving ways;
Whilst endless hymns of praise repeat
The Father and the Paraclete.

Other Hymns.

PRIMER, 1685.

Veni, sancte Spiritus.

COME into us, Holy Ghost ;
From thy bright celestial coast,
Send us a resplendent beam.
　Come, thou father of the poor,
Come, thou willing gift-bestower,
Come, thou heart-reviving gleam.
　Thou, of comforters the best,
Thou, the soul's delightful guest,
A refreshing sweet relief.
　Thou, in toil a resting seat,
Temper in excessive heat,
Solace to a soul in grief.
　O thou blessedest of lights,
Those that love to observe thy rites,
With thyself their bosoms fill.
　While thou art absent nothing can
Be regardable in man,
Nothing can he act but ill.
　What is sordid mundify,
Water what is over-dry,
What is wounded render sound.
　Pliant make what's hard to yield,
Cherish what with cold is chilled,
Govern what is vagabond.
　In the faithful that confide
In thy mercies, cause reside
All the train of seven-fold grace.
　Give what virtue's merit is,
Give the accomplishment of bliss,
Joys of an eternal race.

M M

PRIMER, 1706.
Veni, sancte Spiritus.

Shine, heavenly Dove, descend and dwell
Within our breasts' benighted cell,
And thence the shades of sin expel.
  Descend, thou father of the poor ;
Of gifts thou unexhausted store,
Thy heavenly light our hearts implore.
  Thou only comfort of our breast,
The happy soul's delightful guest,
And sweet refreshment of the blest.
  In thee when tired we find repose ;
In heat a breeze that gently blows ;
And comfort in excess of woes.
  O sweetest flame, thy beams impart,
And penetrate our inmost heart,
With light and warmth in every part.
  In man, without thy sovereign light,
But dreams and fictions haunt his sight,
And nought remains but sin and night.
  Wash every stain of sin away ;
With grace our scorching fires allay ;
And heal our mass of wounded clay.
  Our stubborn hearts with mildness bend,
Where love decays thy warmth extend,
And show lost sheep their journey's end.
  Make all thy seven-fold fountains flow
On those that trust in thee below,
And in those streams thyself bestow ;
  Thyself, the crown of all our pain,
Our happy end and everlasting gain.

PRIMERS, 1685 AND 1684 AND EVENING OFFICE, 1725.
Jesu, dulcis memoria.

Jesu, the only thought of thee
Fills with delight my memory ;
But when thou dost thy presence show,
Heaven seems into my breast to flow.
  No theme so sweet nor voice can be,
Nor to the ear such harmony ;
No heart can thoughts so charming frame
As Jesus his most precious name.

Jesu, our hope when sins we grieve,
Thy mercies all our wants relieve,
If good to those that seek thy grace,
What art thou when they see thy face?
 Jesu, in whom we comfort find,
Fountain of life, light of our mind;
Thou dost our hearts with true joys feed,
Our utmost wish thy gifts exceed.
 No eloquence of tongue can teach,
Nor art of pen this secret reach,
Only the experienced soul does prove,
What sweets they taste who Jesus love.
 Him then I'll seek, retired apart,
Shutting the world out of my heart;
And 'midst my business, him I'll strive
With fresh pursuit still to retrieve.
 Early with Magdalen I'll come
A pilgrim to my Saviour's tomb;
Wailing my sins in mournful cries,
I'll seek him with my mental eyes.
 My tears shall on his grave distil,
And faithful sighs the garden fill;
Prostrate before him on my face,
His sacred feet I'll fast embrace.
 Jesu, in thy blest steps I'll tread,
Striving to follow where they lead;
Nor shall my soul give o'er to mourn,
'Till to thy favour it return.
 O Jesu, most admired king,
Who didst triumph o'er death's sharp sting;
Thy mystic sweetness first excites,
Then satisfies all appetites.
 Thy quickening visits life bestow,
Thy lights true good so clearly show
That they who once have relisht thee,
Know all the world's mere vanity.
 Come then, dear Lord, possess our hearts,
Inflame our love with thy chaste darts,
All clouds of error drive away,
And change our night to thy bright day.
 To thee our hearts and voices sing,
To thee our vows and prayers we bring,
That when we end this life's short race,
In heaven with thee we may have place.

www.ingramcontent.com/pod-product-compliance
Lightning Source LLC
Chambersburg PA
CBHW051852300426
44117CB00006B/364